T0182865

Lecture Notes in Computer Science 10109

Commenced Publication in 1973
Founding and Former Series Editors:
Gerhard Goos, Juris Hartmanis, and Jan van Leeuwen

More information about this series at http://www.springer.com/series/7409

Padmanabhan Krishnan · P. Radha Krishna
Laxmi Parida (Eds.)

Distributed Computing and Internet Technology

13th International Conference, ICDCIT 2017
Bhubaneswar, India, January 13–16, 2017
Proceedings

 Springer

Editors
Padmanabhan Krishnan
Oracle Labs
Brisbane, QLD
Australia

Laxmi Parida
IBM Thomas J. Watson Research Center
Yorktown Heights, NY
USA

P. Radha Krishna
Infosys Limited
Hyderabad
India

ISSN 0302-9743   ISSN 1611-3349   (electronic)
Lecture Notes in Computer Science
ISBN 978-3-319-50471-1   ISBN 978-3-319-50472-8   (eBook)
DOI 10.1007/978-3-319-50472-8

Library of Congress Control Number: 2016958999

LNCS Sublibrary: SL3 – Information Systems and Applications, incl. Internet/Web, and HCI

This Springer imprint is published by Springer Nature
The registered company is Springer International Publishing AG
The registered company address is: Gewerbestrasse 11, 6330 Cham, Switzerland

Preface

It is our pleasure to welcome you to the proceedings 13th International Conference on Distributed Computing and Internet Technology, ICDCIT 2017, held in Bhubaneswar, India, during January 13–16, 2017. The conference was sponsored by the Kalinga Institute of Industrial Technology (KIIT) University and hosted on their campus. The ICDCIT conference series focuses on foundations and applications of distributed computing, and Internet technologies. The conference enables academics, researchers including students, practitioners, and developers to present their research findings and also to have an exchange of ideas on various relevant topics. Since the inception of the ICDCIT series, the conference proceedings have been published by Springer as *Lecture Notes in Computer Science*, and the 2017 volume is number 10109 in the series.

The call for papers attracted 118 abstracts and 90 full submissions. The full versions were reviewed by members of the Program Committee (PC) and other reviewers. On average each paper received three reviews. After receiving the reviews, the PC had an electronic discussion to finalize the acceptance of the submissions. After a robust discussion that took into account technical merit, presentation style, and relevance to the conference, a total of 25 papers (less than 28%) were accepted. Of these 17 were accepted as full papers and eight as poster papers. Subsequently five of the poster papers were withdrawn.

We wish to thank all the authors for their contributions, and also thank all the 28 PC members and 14 external reviewers for their diligent reviews, which enabled us to have a quality program.

The program also included invited lecturers by Dr. Jorge Cuellar (Siemens, Germany), Prof. Kamalakar Karlapalem (IIIT-Hyderabad, India), Prof. Rajat Moona (C-DAC, India), Prof. Partha Majumder (ISI, NIBG, India), Prof. S. Sudarshan (IIT-Bombay, India), and Prof. Lenore Zuck (UIC, USA). We are very thankful to all the invited speakers for taking time out of their busy schedule and sharing their expertise.

We record our special thanks to KIIT for their generous support and express our gratitude to Dr. Achyuta Samanta (Founder of KIIT University) for his patronage and to the vice-chancellor and administration of the university for providing us with the infrastructure and logistical arrangements. We thankfully acknowledge the support KIIT provides in hosting ICDCIT conferences since the inception of the series.

We are very grateful to the Advisory Committee members for their guidance on all matters pertaining to the conference. We also greatly appreciate the invaluable support and tireless efforts of the organizing chair, finance chair, publicity chair, registration chair, session management chair, the publications chair, and all members of various committees who made a great contribution to the conference's success. We would like to thank Arup Acharya in particular, for his help in communicating all matters related to registration and submissions. We would also like to thank the chairs of the satellite events, the student symposium, and the industry symposium. Hrushikesha Mohanty, N. Raja, and D.N. Dwivedy deserve special mention for their unwavering support, guidance, and timely advice.

It is our pleasure to acknowledge EasyChair for enabling efficient and smooth handling of all activities starting from paper submissions to preparation of the proceedings. We sincerely thank Alfred Hofmann and Anna Kramer from Springer for their cooperation and constant support throughout the publication process of this LNCS volume. We wish to specifically acknowledge the financial support received from Springer, which enabled us to give special awards.

Finally, we thank all the participants without whom there would have been no conference. We hope you found the conference to be valuable for your own professional development.

January 2017   Padmanabhan Krishnan
                                                                        P. Radha Krishna
                                                                           Laxmi Parida

Organization

Program Committee

Nikolaj Bjorner	Microsoft Research, USA
Hung Dang Van	UET, Vietnam National University, Hanoi, Vietnam
Manik Lal Das	DA-IICT, India
Jens Dietrich	Massey University, New Zealand
Guenter Fahrnberger	University of Hagen, Germany
Marc Frincu	University of Southern California, USA
Francois Gauthier	Oracle, Australia
Vikram Goyal	IIIT-Delhi, India
Kishore Kothapalli	International Institute of Information Technology, Hyderabad, India
Laura Kovacs	Vienna University of Technology, Austria
Paddy Krishnan	Oracle, Australia
Pradeep Kumar	IIM Lucknow, India
Markus Lumpe	Swinburne University of Technology, Australia
Hrushikesha Mohanty	University of Hyderabad, India
Animesh Mukherjee	Indian Institute of Technology, Kharagpur, India
Krishnendu Mukhopadhyaya	Indian Statistical Institute, India
Dmitry Namiot	Moscow State University, Russia
Raja Natarajan	TIFR, India
Manas Ranjan Patra	Berhampur University, India
Dana Petcu	West University of Timisoara, Romania
Tatjana Petrov	IST, Austria
Radha Krishna Pisipati	Infosys, India
Sanjiva Prasad	Indian Institute of Technology Delhi, India
Vikram Pudi	IIIT-Hyderabad, India
Smruti Sarangi	IIT-Delhi, India
Nagesh Sristy	IDRBT, India
Phil Stocks	Bond University, Australia
Giri Tayi	SUNY at Albany, USA
Mahesh Tripunitara	University of Waterloo, Canada
Ennan Zhai	Yale University, USA

Additional Reviewers

Atluri, Vani Vathsala
Das, Gautam K.
H.N., Lakshmi
Jana, Abhik
Lal, Rajendra Prasad

Mandal, Partha Sarathi
Mukhopadhyaya, Srabani
Negi, Atul
Patro, Jasabanta
Sarkar, Soumya

Sau, Buddhadeb
Sikdar, Sandipan
Truong, Hoang
Vo, Hieu

Invited Presentations

Privacy-Enhanced Authorization in IoT

Jorge Cuéllar

Principal Research Scientist, Siemens AG
jorge.cuellar@siemens.com

Abstract. It is well known that in Internet of Things applications, at home, mobility scenarios, health and sport, etc., the sensor data will be high in volume and quality, and that, even when the data does not to contain personal identificators, inferences can be drawn that result in the identification of users and personal information is generated. This creates a need to protect the privacy of IoT data, as has been concluded in the 36th International Conference of Data Protection & Privacy Commissioners. On the other hand, an easier, flexible, exchange of information is sought, allowing plug-and-play of devices and applications.

The two goals are in conflict with each other. We expect that user-centric policies will be required in constrained devices, and that devices will have to reason about those policies and credentials, authentication and authorization protocols. In the presentation we discuss some ideas how this complex issue can be approached.

From Distributed Database to Cloud Database:
A Design Perspective

Kamalakar Karlapalem

Centre for Data Engineering, IIIT-Hyderabad, India
kamal@iiit.ac.in

Abstract. From early 1980s until middle 1990s, over fifteen years, a lot of work done on designing distributed databases for a given set of queries. There were two problems that were addressed (i) fragmentation: reducing irrelevant data accessed by a query, and (ii) allocation: reducing the amount of data transferred between sites for executing a query. Many algorithms were designed and evaluated for fragmentation and allocation. In particular, queries change over time, methodology, algorithms, and policies for when and how to redesign a distributed database was proposed.

In the last decade, with the advent of modern database systems supported by columnar stores and Hadoop like cloud database systems, the users have been following ad-hoc or pre-determined database design methodologies. In this work, we present backgrounds of distributed database design and cloud database systems, and propose possible solutions for cloud database design based on fragmentation and allocation solutions.

ESign: Digital Signature Combined with Power of Online Authentication

Rajat Moona

Centre for Development of Advanced Computing (C-DAC), Chennai, India
moona@cdac.in

Abstract. Digital signatures provide a non-repudiation mechanism for documents or messages. The digital signature are used to validate the integrity of the documents or messages to protect them against tampering as well as to establish the authenticity and to provide genuineness. In order to establish the non-repudiation, digital signature mechanism is backed up by a complex certifying authority (CA) mechanism to certify the individual signers so that their public key can be used with trust on the CA to verify the digital signatures. This mechanism however requires the issuance of digital signature certificates, verification of the individual's credentials and the legal support for digital signatures. Often the verification of the credentials involve physical means for the verification, as is usually demanded by law.

India provides a unique proposition of Aadhaar, where the residents of the country are provided a unique online-verifiable identity after credential verifications, registration of fingerprint and iris biometric. Aadhaar provides a service of authentication as well as "know-your-customer" through online authorization by the identified individual. These services are provided by Aadhaar through a network of Aadhaar-authorized agencies.

Esign integrates the powerful Aadhaar authentication service with certification authority services and provides one-time use certificates along with digital signatures on the documents provided by an individual. This mechanism therefore provide an instant method of obtaining a variety of e-governance services which are tenable under the applicable laws and provide non-repudiation.

In this talk, we discuss the mechanism of ESign, its powerful features and domains where such technology can be effectively used. We also discuss implementation and issues related to the implementation and techniques to overcome them.

Genomic Excitement and Quantitative Challenges

Partha P. Majumder

Indian Statistical Institute and National Institute of Biomedical Genomics,
Kalyani, India
ppml@nibmg.ac.in

Abstract. Recent advances in statistical genetics theory and genomic technologies have created a revolution in evolutionary and disease-related inferences. Estimation of the extent of genomic diversity and structures of human populations, reconstruction of their origins, and tracing trails of human migration have become possible in exquisite detail and precision. In this talk, I shall provide a synthesis of the findings of our studies on these aspects conducted during the last decade. The search of genes that drive cancer is important and is now a global endeavor. This search comprises massively-parallel DNA sequencing during which very large data sets are generated. The statistical challenge that one is confronted with is to manage, curate and find patterns in these data that are of statistical significance and biological relevance. In this talk, I shall also provide some relevant results of our analysis of oral cancer genomes and the implications of these findings for precision medicine.

Holistic Optimization of Data Access from Imperative Programs

S. Sudarshan

Subrao Nilekani Chair Professor Indian Institute of Technology, Bombay, India
sudarsha@cse.iitb.ac.in

Abstract. In this talk we address the problem of optimizing performance of data access from imperative programs. Database optimizers today focus on queries expressed declaratively. However, one of the major causes of performance problems in applications today is inefficiency of data access from imperative code. This inefficiency is addressed neither by database query optimizers, nor by compilers researchers, even though it is a real problem faced by many users of enterprise applications.

In the DBridge project at IIT Bombay, over the past 8 years we have been working on rewriting imperative programs to optimize data access. In this talk we first provide an overview of our results on rewriting application programs to automatically perform batching and prefetching of data access requests. While these techniques are well known and can be done manually, manual rewriting of applications to implement these optimizations is error prone. We describe how we use static analysis of imperative code along with a set of rules for transforming imperative code, akin to algebraic transformation rules used in database query optimizers, to optimize imperative code. Our approach makes it possible to prove correctness of the transformations regardless of the complexity of the code. We then move on to more recent results, which allow parts of imperative code to be rewritten into SQL, which can provide even large performance gains when applicable, especially for legacy ERP code.

Our techniques have been implemented using the SOOT program analysis framework. Our experiments on several real world applications demonstrate the applicability and significant performance gains due to our techniques.

Describes joint work with K. Venkatesh Emani, Karthik Ramachandra, Ravindra Guravannavar, Subhro Bhattacharya and Mahendra Chavan, published at VLDB 2008, ICDE 2011, SIGMOD 2012, ICDE 2014, IEEE TKDE 2015, and SIGMOD 2016.

Ethics in Computer Science Research circa the 21st Century

Lenore Zuck

Department of Computer Science, University of Illinois at Chicago,
60607-7053, Chicago, IL, Italy
lenore@cs.uic.edu

Abstract. Traditionally ethics is a branch of philosophy while computer science is a branch of the techne. The two seem to have nothing in common. But when software, with its inherent biases, is underlying much of what we do, the lines between the two have been blurred. The Russell-Einstein manifesto is perhaps the first to warn about the ethical impact of the techne. Unfortunately, it has been largely forgotten. For example, the core of much of the dystopian literature (1984, Fahrenheit 451, The Minority Report, to name a few) is government surveillance and its adverse impact on humanity. The surveillance we are under nowadays, aided by "big" data mining, is much more comprehensive than that envisioned by the authors of this literature. Unlike the society described by such dystopian literature, current societal tendencies are to welcome such surveillance for the material conveniences they provide.

The talk will discuss some of the ethical aspects of the work of software developers, from privacy to the impact of cryptography to democracies. Examples will be given from diverse areas such as medical data and autonomous (lethal or not) robots, with emphasis on data sharing and transfers across jurisdictions and borders.

Contents

Virtual Machines

Access Control

Security and Privacy

Poster Papers

Mobile Computing

A Distributed Approach Based on Hierarchical Scalar Leader Selection for Enhanced Event Coverage in Wireless Multimedia Sensor Networks

Sushree Bibhuprada B. Priyadarshini and Suvasini Panigrahi[✉]

Veer Surendra Sai University of Technology, Burla, Sambalpur, Odisha, India
bimalabibhuprada@gmail.com,
spanigrahi_cse@vssut.ac

Abstract. This research addresses a novel distributed algorithm based on determination of scalar leaders for camera sensor activation so as to attain enhanced coverage of the geographic event region under consideration. The selection of scalar leaders is accomplished so that the leaders are organized in a hierarchical pattern with each of the child placed at least at a distance of twice of depth of field of camera nodes. Such distance is chosen so as to avert the possible overlapping among the field of views of cameras. Further, the chosen leaders perform as the agent of scalars that impart the concerned event information to their respective cameras. Experiments have been carried out to test the veracity of our proposed scheme. The least camera actuation, enhanced coverage ratio, least redundancy ratio, lowered energy as well as power expenditure attained from the investigation justify the efficacy of the proposed scheme.

Keywords: Scalar leader · Field of view · Event grade · Activation list

1 Introduction

In recent years, with the precocious technological proliferation, the adoration of sensors is basically because of their divergent panorama of applications; resulting in manifold challenges most of which still sojourns as unexplored fields of investigation. The prominent ultimatum in these networks is to realize an effective enhanced coverage of the region under speculation, while minimizing the amount of redundant data transmission. This redundant data transmission takes place due to overlapping of *Field of Views (FOVs)* of camera nodes such that the scalar sensors lying at these common super-imposed overlapping zones apprise the same information with respect to the prevailing event to their corresponding cameras [1]. Since same data is communicated multiple times, this leads to unnecessary energy and power expenditure. Therefore, the amount of redundant data transmission should be minimized. This can be accomplished by actuating only lowered number of cameras. However, the ultimate aim is that the actuation of cameras should be done such that the amount of event area coverage will be maximized along with minimization of redundant data transmission.

© Springer International Publishing AG 2017
P. Krishnan et al. (Eds.): ICDCIT 2017, LNCS 10109, pp. 3–14, 2017.
DOI: 10.1007/978-3-319-50472-8_1

In this paper, we have presented a newfangled distributed approach called "*Hierarchical Scalar Leader Selection for Enhanced Event Coverage (HSLS-EC)*" that selects scalar leaders among the scalars in a hierarchical fashion such that the selected child node of a given parent node is placed relatively at a distance of twice of depth of field of the cameras. Each node in the hierarchy can have a maximum of two children. The scalar leaders operate as the representative of the scalars that convey the event information to their respective cameras. The main contributions of the *HSLS-EC* approach lies in the following aspects:

- The *HSLS-EC* method involves the selection of scalar leaders for camera actuation to cover the geographic region effectually.
- The scalar leader selection is accomplished so that the cameras actuated due to the selected scalar leaders can cover more distinct portions of the occurring event zone. This results in actuation of lower number of cameras with minimum amount of overlapping among the *FOVs* of activated cameras, emerging in reduced amount of redundant data transmission.
- Furthermore, the amount of energy and power expenditure for camera actuation is minimized in the proposed approach due to actuation of least number of cameras.

The rest of the paper is organized as follows: Sect. 2 discusses the related work done in the field. Section 3 elaborates the proposed approach along with the detailed methodology involved in the proposition. Section 4 presents the results obtained from experimental study. Finally, in Sect. 5, we conclude the paper with directions for future research.

2 Related Work

There are several threads of work found in literature in the field of redundant data minimization and region coverage. One of the pioneering work by Andrew and Newell [1] proposes a distributed scheme called "*Distributed Collaborative Camera Actuation based on Scalar Count (DCA-SC)*" [1], in which the camera nodes collaboratively decide which among them are to be activated, based on descending order of their scalar count values. Further, another work namely, *Distributed Collaborative Camera Actuation scheme based on Sensing region Management (DCCA-SM)* as presented in [2], actuates the cameras based on the remaining energy carried by them. This paper is based on dividing the entire sensing field into a number of sensing regions. In each of the sensing regions, a scalar cluster head is chosen among the scalar nodes which inform its corresponding camera about the event occurrence. A *Non-Heuristic (N-H)* approach given in [3] activates the cameras those cover the exact event region and keeps the cameras that are activated due to sensing of event outside the event region in turned off state. Hence, the amount of redundant data communication occurring due to the undesired camera actuation is minimized. An alternate work discussed in [4] suggests the idea of cover-set that helps in tracking all the targets in a disposed monitored zone.

Moreover, in this paper an impressive coverage algorithm is propounded that is capable of generating both disjoint cover sets as well as non-disjoint cover sets. Disjoint cover sets are the cover sets with no common sensors where as non-disjoint cover sets signify the cover sets with common sensors. Wang et al. [5] adduced the notion of directional coverage where individual targets are associated with discriminated priorities. In addition, a minimum subset of directional sensors can track all the concerned targets satisfying their recommended priorities. Likewise, a different methodology on path coverage is introduced in [6], where the network coverage of two-dimensional area is analyzed for random deployment of sensors. Further, in this paper, the properties of a two-dimensional Poisson sensor network have been considered to track a path in the field. The work in [7] emphasizes on multiple directional cover sets problem. Moreover, Girault advanced an algorithm which proceeds in two passes for redundant data removal [8]. At first, a global data-flow analysis is performed which computes the set of different variables, known at the beginning of the state for each state of automaton. Afterwards, a local elimination is applied that removes redundant messages locally in each state of the automaton. Similarly, a data similarity based redundant data elimination technique has been elaborated in [9]. Furthermore, an optimal deployment strategy for sensor nodes has been described in [10].

Despite the fact that various methods have been devised as discussed above, still none of them cover the event regions effectively because while actuating the camera sensors; always there is a tradeoff between the number of cameras actuated and the portions of event region covered. Such situation prevails as for covering greater portions of event zone, more number of cameras is to be actuated, which results in greater overlapping among the *FOVs*. Hence, it becomes imperative to actuate only the required number of cameras that affords enhanced coverage of corresponding event region along with minimized redundant data transmission.

3 Proposed Approach

In this article, we have devised a novel approach called *Hierarchical Scalar Leader Selection for Enhanced Event Coverage* (*HSLS-EC*) which activates minimum number of cameras that are desired to provide appreciatively greater coverage of the prevailing event zone while lowering the redundant data transmission at the same time. This is realized through the selection of scalar leaders (*SLs*) for camera activation in a hierarchical manner as portrayed in Fig. 1. The choice of *SLs* in this pattern contributes their effective spacing such that the cameras activated due to them have least overlapping among their depth of fields (*DOFs*), thus, reducing the redundancy in data transmission. The methodology involved in the proposed approach can be summarized by the following steps:

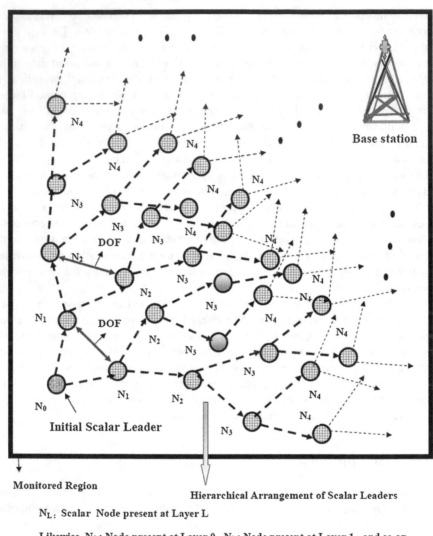

Fig. 1. Hierarchical organization of scalar leaders in proposed HSLS-EC approach

Step 1: Deployment of Sensors

- Initially, all the cameras and scalars are randomly sprinkled in the region to be tracked. Cameras and scalars broadcast *Camera Sensor Information Message (CSIM) and Scalar Sensor Information Message (SSIM)* respectively. *CSIM* and

SSIM are the messages broadcasted by camera and scalar sensors respectively, which contain the *id* and location information of the concerned sensors.

- A list called *ACTIVATION LIST* (*AL*) is maintained that retains the *ids* of activated cameras, which is empty at the beginning. Further, the *ids* of all the cameras are maintained in a list called *MYWAITING LIST* (*MWL*).

- After receipt of the *CSIM* and *SSIM messages*, the sensors compute the *Euclidian distance* between each other. If the *Euclidian distance* between a camera and a scalar is less than the depth of field (*DOF*) of the camera, then it can be inferred that the scalar lies within the *FOV* as well as *DOF* of the concerned camera.

Step 2: Hierarchical Selection of Scalar Leaders (SLs)

- At first, a scalar that is placed at farthest distance from the base station is chosen as the initial scalar leader as shown in Fig. 1. From the initial scalar leader, the subsequent *SLs* are selected hierarchically such that each of the child nodes is placed at least at a distance of twice of the *DOF* of a camera node. The twice the *DOF* signifies the entire diameter through which a camera senses the event. This distance is chosen so as to avert the possible overlapping among the field of views of cameras. Further, the chosen *SLs* operate as the agent of scalars that impart the prevailing event information to their respective cameras.

- As soon as the two leaders are selected, the subsequent scalar leader's selection commences. From the already selected *SLs*, new *SLs* are chosen following the same distance criteria (2 × *DOF* of Camera). This procedure is continued till no more leaders can further be selected i.e. no more scalar is available to become the next scalar leader. The condition is that always the children of the same parent should maintain a distance of at least 2 × *DOF* of camera from each other. However, for the children belonging to different parent nodes can have distance less than or equal to 2 × DOF but greater than or equal to *DOF*. This criterion is chosen so as to select appreciatively sufficient number of scalars for effective event tracking.

- During selection of child nodes they are placed hierarchically such that N_L represents node present at level *L*. Likewise, N_0 represents the scalars present at level 0, N_1 represents the scalars present at level 1, N_2 represents the scalars present at level 2 and so on. The nodes present at the same level can have 0, 1, or 2 children. Generally, the nodes have two children. However, when selection of two children is not possible for given parent considering the distance constraint then that node can have 0 child or 1 child based on the situation. Moreover, the leaf nodes are the *SLs* present at the end of the hierarchy which have no children.

Step 3: Event Occurrence and Detection

- When any event prevails in the monitored region, it is detected by those *SLs* only that operate as the representative of the scalars for event information tracking. The *SLs* then report this information to their concerned cameras by broadcasting *MyDetect Message* (*MDM*), containing the *ids* and location information of the concerned *SLs*.

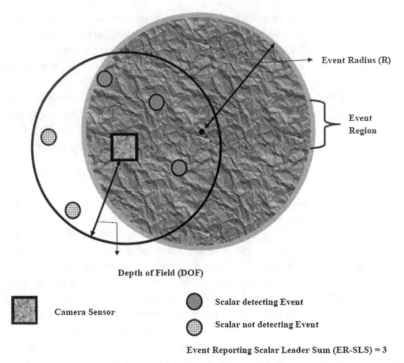

Fig. 2. ER-SLS calculation for camera sensor during event occurrence

- Thereafter, the cameras update their E*vent Reporting Scalar Leader List* (*ERSLL*), which is maintained by each camera comprising of the event detecting *SL ids*.

Step 4: Camera Collaboration and Activation

- In this step, all the cameras estimate the sum of event reporting scalar leaders present within their *FOV*s called *Event Reporting Scalar Leader Sum* (*ER-SLS*) value as portrayed in Fig. 2. The calculation of *ER-SLS* value is made as follows:
  - Set *count* = 0.
  - For any camera i and any scalar leader j, find the *Euclidian distance* ($Edist_{i,\,j}$) between them for each of the sensors.
  - If $Edist_{i,\,j} < DOF$ of camera, then *count* = *count* +1;
  - For every camera i, perform this calculation for each of the scalar leaders j. Update the *count* value each time, if their respective $Edist_{i,\,j} < DOF$ of camera
  - The updated *count* value gives *ER-SLS* value of camera i.

- After calculating the *ER-SLS* values, the cameras include their *ids* to either *multi leader camera list* (*MLCL*) or *single leader camera list* (*SLCL*) based on their *ER-SLS* values. *MLCL* and *SLCL* are the lists containing the *ids* of cameras in ascending order having *ER-SLS* ≥ 2 and *ER-SLS* $= 1$ respectively. The *ids* of cameras in *MLCL* and *SLCL* are maintained in the same order as that of *MWL*.
- The camera whose *id* comes first in *MLCL* is activated first and its *id* is added to *AL* and is deleted from *MWL*. As soon as a camera is activated, it broadcasts a *Update Scalar Leader* (*USL*) message to rest of the cameras. *USL* contains the *ids* of *SLs* present within the *FOVs* of activated cameras, which are determined based on the calculated *Euclidian distance* between the *SL* and the activated camera.
- After receipt of *USL* message, the *Update Message id List* (*UM-IL*) is updated that contains the *ids* of *SLs* present in the concerned *USL* message. Later on, the immediately next camera in the *MLCL* (say, *j*) matches the *ids* of *SLs* maintained in its *ERSLL* with the *ids* of *SLs* contained in *USL* message, broadcasted by activated camera sensor. The following situation then occurs:

If (both the leader ids maintained by USL message and those maintained in ERSLL list match completely)

Then {No need to activate the camera j}

Else

If (scalar leader ids maintained by both do not match completely)

Then {Camera j has to be actuated}

Similarly, rest of the cameras, maintained sequentially in *MLCL* list can take decision to actuate based on matching their *SL ids* maintained in their *ERSLL* list with the *SL* ids maintained in *USL* message based on the above two cases. As soon as a camera is activated its *id* is added to *AL* and is discarded from *MWL*. After, the desired cameras present in *MLCL* list are activated, then the *ids* of scalars present in *USL* messages of all the activated cameras, maintained in *UM-IL* for *MLCL* list are matched with the *SL ids* maintained in *ERSLL* list of cameras present in *SLCL* list. If the scalar *ids* maintained in *ERSLL* of camera (s) present in *SLCL* list matches completely with *SL ids* maintained in updated *UM-IL*, then no need to activate the concerned camera (s). If in any case a mismatch is found, then that camera of *SLCL* will be activated. The activated camera of *SLCL* list now broadcasts *USL* message. This process continues till all the cameras make decision either to be activated or to be kept in off state. Subsequently, *AL* gets updated. The number of cameras present in *AL* represents the total number of activated cameras i.e. the *Event Grade*. The entire process involved in the proposed method is depicted in the form of a flow chart as shown in Fig. 3.

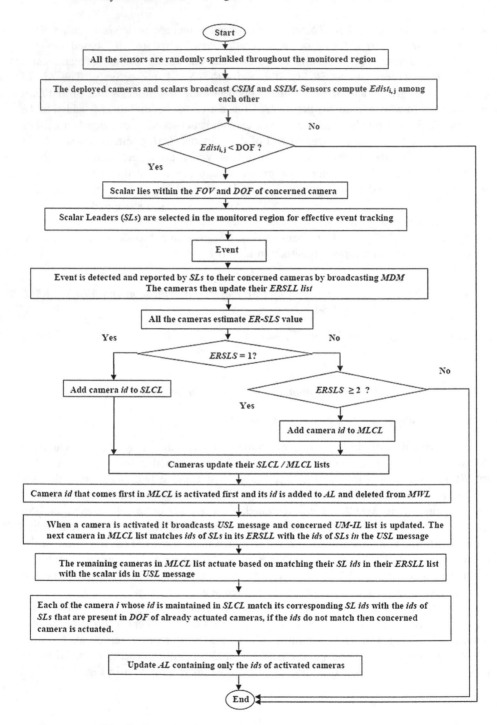

Fig. 3. Steps involved in the proposed HSLS-EC approach

4   Experimental Results

The proposed algorithm *HSLS-EC* has been implemented in *C* ++. The performance analysis of *HSLS-EC* is accomplished by comparing it with three other recent approaches, namely, *DCA-SC* [1], *DCCA-SM* [2] and *N-H* [3] for justifying its superiority over the other methods.

4.1   Assumptions

The sensors are assumed to be randomly deployed. In this work, we have considered the same *DOF* value for all the cameras for simplicity and ease of implementation. We have varied the number of cameras and observed its impact on the number of cameras activated in case of our proposed *HSLS-EC* approach and other three approaches [1–3] based on the following parameters:

- *Number of cameras activated*: It represents the number of cameras that finally undergo activation. Less is the number of cameras activated; lower is the amount of redundant data transmission.
- *Coverage Ratio*: It is defined as "the ratio of area of event covered by activated cameras to the total area of the occurring event" [1]. More value of coverage ratio ensures better coverage of the prevailing event region.
- *Redundancy Ratio*: It is defined as the ratio of total portions of overlapping regions of *FOVs* of activated cameras covering the occurring event region to the total unique portions of the event region that is covered by the activated camera sensors. Reduced value of redundancy ratio indicates lower amount of redundant data transmission.
- *Energy and Power Consumption for Camera Activation*: The energy and power consumed by the activated cameras signify the amount of energy and power expenditure during the actuation of cameras. Lower number of camera actuation leads to lesser energy and power consumption.

4.2   Performance Evaluation

We have observed the variation of the number of cameras deployed against various performance metrics - number of cameras activated, coverage ratio, redundancy ratio, energy and power consumption for camera activation for all the approaches. Figure 4 shows that with increase in number of cameras, the number of cameras actuated increases progressively in all the approaches. This is due to the fact that with increase in number of deployed cameras, the number of cameras covering the event region increases. Further, the number of cameras activated in our proposed *HSLS-EC* approach is found to be the minimum.

Similarly, it is evident from Fig. 5 that with rise in number of cameras the coverage ratio increases gradually for all the approaches and is found to be the maximum in case of the proposed method ensuring improved coverage over other methods [1–3]. As the number of actuated cameras is the minimum in *HSLS-EC*, hence, the amount of energy and power expenditure is the lowest as evident from Fig. 6(a) and (b). However, the value of redundancy ratio goes up with rise in the number of deployed cameras for all the approaches as portrayed in Fig. 7 and is the minimum in our proposal. This is due to the fact that only the chosen *SLs* communicate regarding the occurring event to the camera sensors in our proposed method unlike reporting by all the scalars.

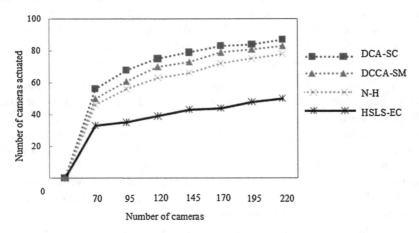

Fig. 4. Effect of varying number of cameras on number of cameras actuated

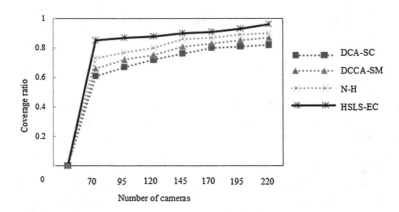

Fig. 5. Effect of varying number of cameras on coverage ratio

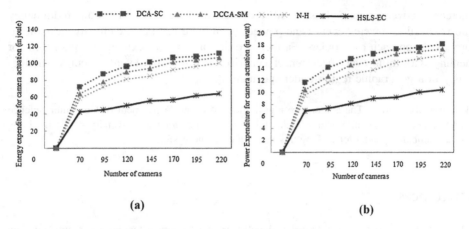

Fig. 6. Effect of varying number of cameras on (a) Energy consumption for camera activation (joule). (b) Power consumption for camera activation (watt)

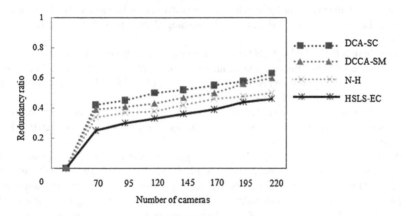

Fig. 7. Effect of varying number of cameras on redundancy ratio

5   Conclusions

This article presents a novel approach called *Hierarchical Scalar Leader Selection for Enhanced Event Coverage* that involves the selection of scalar leaders aimed at achieving desired camera actuation along with effective geographic event region coverage. This is accomplished by choosing the scalar leaders hierarchically at a distance of at least twice of *DOF* so as to minimize the amount of overlapping among the *FOVs* of the activated cameras. Furthermore, instead of all the scalars, only the selected scalar leaders those come under the purview of occurring event, communicate the event information to their concerned cameras. Experiments were conducted to evaluate the performance of our proposed approach as compared to three other recent approaches proffered in the literature. The results obtained from the investigation in terms of increased coverage ratio, least number of activated cameras, minimum redundancy ratio as well as lowered energy and power expenditure justifies the effectiveness of our proposed approach over others. Further, we are planning to extend our algorithm for dealing with multi-event occurrence scenario when multiple events occur simultaneously in a geographic region under speculation.

Acknowledgements. The authors are highly grateful to the Department of Computer Science and Engineering and Information Technology, Veer Surendra Sai University of Technology, Burla, Sambalpur, India for making this investigation successful.

References

1. Newell, A., Akkaya, K.: Distributed collaborative camera actuation for redundant data elimination in wireless multimedia sensor networks. Ad Hoc Netw. **9**(4), 514–527 (2011). Elsevier
2. Luo, W., Lu, Q., Xiao, J.: Distributed collaborative camera actuation scheme based on sensing-region management for wireless multimedia sensor networks. Int. J. Distrib. Sens. Netw. **2012**, Article ID: 486163, Hindawi Publishing Corporation (2012). doi:10.1155/2012/486163
3. Priyadarshini, S.B.B., Panigrahi, S.: A non-heuristic approach for minimizing the energy and power consumption in wireless multimedia sensor networks. In: International Conference on Computational Intelligence and Networks (CINE), pp. 104–109. IEEE, Bhubaneswar, 12–13 January 2015, doi:10.1109/CINE.2015.29
4. Zorbas, D., Glynos, D., Kotzanikolaou, P., Douligeris, C.: Solving coverage problems in wireless sensor networks using cover sets. Ad Hoc Netw. **8**(4), 400–415 (2010). Elsevier Science publishers
5. Wang, J., Niu, C., Shen, R.: Priority-based target coverage in directional sensor networks using a genetic algorithm. Comput. Math Appl. **57**(11–12), 1915–1922 (2009). Elsevier
6. Sundhar Ram, S., Manjunath, D., Iyer, S.K., Yogeshwaran, D.: On the path coverage properties of random sensor networks. IEEE Trans. Mob. Comput. **6**(5), 494–506 (2007)
7. Cai, Y., Lou, W., Li, M., Li, X.-Y.: Target-oriented scheduling in directional sensor networks. In: 26th IEEE International Conference on Computer Communications (IEEE INFOCOM 2007), pp. 1550–1558, Barcelona, 6–12 May 2007
8. Girault, A.: Elimination of redundant messages with a two-pass static analysis algorithm. Parallel Comput. **28**, 433–453 (2002)
9. Ghaddar, A., Razafindralambo, T., Tawbi, S., et al.: Algorithm for data similarity measurements to reduce data redundancy in wireless sensor networks. In: 2010 IEEE International Symposium on a World of Wireless, Mobile and Multimedia Networks (WoWMoM), Montreal, QC, pp. 1–6, Canada, 14–17 June 2010 (2010). ISBN:978-1-4244-7264-2
10. Toumpis, S., Tassiulas, L.: Optimal deployment of large wireless sensor networks. IEEE Trans. Inf. Theory **52**(7), 2935–2953 (2006)

Gathering Multiple Robots in a Ring and an Infinite Grid

Durjoy Dutta, Tandrima Dey, and Sruti Gan Chaudhuri[(✉)]

Department of Information Technology, Jadavpur University, Kolkata, India
srutiganc@it.jusl.ac.in

Abstract. Gathering can be coined as one of the primary interaction parameters in systems of autonomous mobile agents or sensors, known as robots. These robots are identical and placed in the nodes of an unlabeled graph. They operate in wait-look-compute-move cycles. In one cycle, first the sensors of the robots are activated independent of each other (wait). Then a robot takes a snapshot of the current configuration (look), makes a decision to stay idle or to move to one of its adjacent nodes (compute), and in the latter case makes an instantaneous move to this neighbor (move). Then the robot again goes back to its initial phase (wait). Cycles are performed asynchronously for each robot. The robots are oblivious, i.e., they do not use any computed data from the previous cycle. The robots do not agree on a common coordinate system. They cannot differentiate between a node having single robot and a node having multiple robots, i.e., multiplicity of a node. The robots are not able to see all the nodes of the graph. They do not know the total number of robots in the system. In this paper, we have developed two algorithms to gather these robots at a single node (not known beforehand) of a Ring Graph and an infinite Grid, in finite time. To the best of our knowledge, this is one of the first reported results on gathering multiple robots under limited visibility in an infinite grid and a ring.

Keywords: Gathering · Limited visibility · Ring · Infinite grid · Asynchronous · Oblivious · Mobile robots

1 Introduction

The swarm robots are a system of multiple autonomous identical mobile robots work in collaboration to execute a given task. Though large in numbers, the cost of this system of robots is comparatively lower than a traditional big robot. Operated by simple hardware and software, these robots are easy to deploy and maintain even in very harsh environment. These robots are used to locate objects in a hazardous environment, which naturally takes disaster hit areas into consideration [10]. The robots can even work together to build a complex 3D structure [10]. Other applications include mining in hazardous areas, agricultural tasks like foraging [10]. A large number of robots can act as an autonomous army. The U.S. Navy has created a swarm of boats which can track an enemy boat, surround it and then destroy it [11]. A fundamental job of a system of

© Springer International Publishing AG 2017
P. Krishnan et al. (Eds.): ICDCIT 2017, LNCS 10109, pp. 15–26, 2017.
DOI: 10.1007/978-3-319-50472-8_2

swarm robots is to move and coordinate their activities for executing some given task, e.g., forming a said pattern or meeting at a location which is the scope of this paper.

1.1 Framework

In the system of swarm robots [2,6] considered in this paper, the robots are distributed in nature. They move and compute of their own independent of other robots. Each robot is capable of sensing or observing (look) its immediate surroundings, performing computations on the sensed data to determine a destination to move to (compute), and moving towards the computed destination (move); its behavior is an endless cycle of sensing, computing, moving and being inactive. However, it can not be inactive for an infinite time. Since the robots are autonomous, there is no centralized mechanism to control them. The robots do not have any common coordinate system. They are asynchronous [6], in the sense that, the amount of time spent in observation, computation, movement and inactivity is finite but not bounded or predictable or same for all the robots. The robots are anonymous, identical in nature and exhibit the same deterministic algorithm which takes the observed positions of the robots within the visibility radius as input and returns a destination point towards which the executing robot moves. After moving to this computed destination, another fresh cycle is initiated and the computed data of the past cycle is removed.

The robots are deployed randomly on the nodes of a graph [1,2]. The movements of the robots are instantaneous, they are always perceived over nodes and not over the links. The robots are memoryless (oblivious) which means they do not have the capacity to remember their previous calculations or observations or leave any mark at the visited nodes. The robots cannot communicate or send messages to each other. Having limited visibility [2,5], the robots cannot observe the entire spatial universe but a part of it which may not contain the positions of all other robots at that time. Thus the robots are not aware of the total number of robots in the system. The robots also can not differentiate between a node having single robot and a node having multiple robots (multiplicity).

The robots are initially randomly placed in the nodes of an anonymous graph. Our objective is to give a deterministic and distributed movement strategy for the robots in order to collect them at a single node without letting the robots to detect multiplicity of nodes. In this paper we have considered an infinite grid graph (where the number of nodes and edges of the graph is not restricted) and a ring graph and proposed two algorithms for gathering of the robots for these two types of graphs.

1.2 Related Works

Gathering in Ring: There have been a large number of researches [2,3,7–9] going on for gathering robots in a ring. D'Angelo et al. [2] have proposed an algorithm to gather asynchronous oblivious robots in a ring with the help of *global weak multiplicity*[1] detection capability. D'Angelo et al. [3] have also presented an algorithm to gather six robots on anonymous symmetric rings where *global strong multiplicity*[2] detection capability is used. Kamei et al. [7] have proposed an algorithm to gather asynchronous mobile robots from symmetric configurations without global multiplicity detection capability. However, the authors put forward a gathering protocol for an odd number of robots in a ring-shaped network that allows symmetric but not periodic configurations as initial configurations, using only local weak multiplicity detection capability, where a robot can identify the existence of other robots in its own node. Izumi et al. [5] have proposed an algorithm to gather mobile robots using local weak multiplicity detection capability. Klasing et al. [9] have presented an algorithm to gather asynchronous oblivious robots in a ring, taking advantage of symmetries and global weak multiplicity detection capability. The algorithm provides procedures for gathering all configurations on the ring with more than 18 robots for which gathering is feasible. Various cases of gathering in ring are listed under the section of open problems. So far the only successful results reported are by using multiplicity detection capability. Even multiplicity detection capability does not solve all the cases in ring topology e.g., sp4 problem [9]: presence of 4 robots in a 5-node ring where each node is occupied by one robot initially, rendezvous problem [2]: gathering two robots in a ring.

Our Contribution (I): All the proposed results for successful gathering in a ring are based on the multiplicity detection capabilities of the robots. In this paper we have investigated an approach to get rid of this assumption. Moreover, we also restrict the robots in terms of their visibility range. The robots can not see the complete ring at a glance. Instead a robot can capture $\lceil \frac{N}{2} \rceil$ nodes (where N is the number of nodes of the ring) at its both sides and combines the results to get a complete ring. It is true that if we club two $\lceil \frac{N}{2} \rceil$ strings then it becomes full visibility, however, $\lceil \frac{N}{2} \rceil$ strategy can be implemented using less powerful cameras of robots in practical sense and also it can reduce the number of computations on collected data by the robots. We also consider that the robots agree on orientation of the ring. Without this assumption it is not possible to solve 2-node problem where only two nodes of a ring is occupied by the robots and all other nodes are free. The robots are strictly asynchronous, i.e., there exists always a robot which is not in the same phase of cycle with the others. Taking advantages of $\lceil \frac{N}{2} \rceil$ visibility, orientation of the ring and asynchrony of the robots, our algorithm is able to gather the robots in all configurations and any number of robots >1 and without any extra assumption. It also successfully works for sp4 problem [9] and the rendezvous problem [8]. Section 2 presents an algorithm for gathering in ring and its proof of correctness.

Gathering in Grid: A complete characterization of gathering in finite grid have been reported by D'Angelo et al. [1]. For finite grid there exists some special

---

[1] The robots can identify the node with multiple robots but can not count the number of robots.

[2] The robots can count the number of robots in a node.

vertices like corner vertices which play an important role to fix the gathering node. However, even with full visibility and multiplicity detection capabilities of the robots, gathering is still not possible in some specific configurations in finite grid. In case of infinite grid computing a gathering node is much more challenging, since there is no boundary. Di Stefano et al. [4] have presented a full characterization for optimal gathering in infinite grid where the robots are able to observe all other robots in the system.

Our Contribution (II): All the reported results on gathering in grid consider that the robots can see all other robots. In this paper we have proposed an algorithm where the robots can see up to a certain radius, 2 node hop distance around itself for this paper. The robots do not know the total number of robots. They also can not detect the multiplicity of the nodes. The infinite grid is embedded in a Cartesian plane. The robots agree on common direction and orientation of the coordinate axes. The algorithm works for any scheduling of the cycle of the robots. Section 3 presents an algorithm for gathering in grid and its proof of correctness.

2   Gathering in Ring

We consider a set of autonomous mobile robots endowed with visibility sensors and motion actuators but that are otherwise unable to communicate. The robots initially randomly deployed in the nodes of a ring graph. The robots exhibit the characteristics of being anonymous, oblivious, silent, asynchronous, and having $\lceil \frac{N}{2} \rceil$ visibility in both sides (N is the number of nodes of the ring). The ring graph is disoriented in nature and the robots reside in the nodes. Neither the nodes nor the edges or the links between the nodes have any label. The robots can be only perceived in the nodes and not over the edges or the links. The robots have to gather at a single node that is unknown beforehand, and to remain there thereafter. Though the ring and the robots are anonymous, for describing the algorithm we have assigned the names n_1, n_2 and so on to the nodes and r_1, r_2 and so on to the robots.

2.1   Algorithm Description

The robots study the occupancy rate on both sides of a robot and then decide on the direction in which the robot should take the next hop. The algorithm is as follows: -

- Step 1: - A robot generates two strings of length $\lceil \frac{N}{2} \rceil$ from its both directions. If the robot finds a node to be occupied then it puts a 1 against that node in the string or if the robot finds a node to be unoccupied then it puts a 0 against that node in the string. For example, in Fig. 1 the strings generated by r_1 are $\{0, 1, 1, 1\}$ in clockwise direction and $\{1, 0, 0, 1\}$ in anticlockwise direction.
- Step 2: - The robot checks the occupancy rate on both sides i.e. the number of nodes occupied by other robots on each side. The robot may do so simply by counting the number of 1s and 0s in the strings.

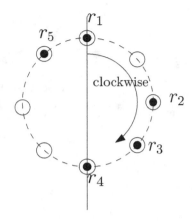

Fig. 1. An example of occupancy rate study

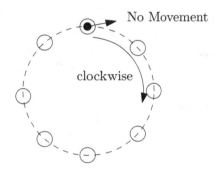

Fig. 2. Case 3.1.

- Step 3: - This is the most important step since in this step the robot makes a decision on its movement. The cases are listed as follows: -
    - Case 3.1: - If the occupancy rate is nil on both sides then the robot does not make any movement (Fig. 2).
    - Case 3.2: - If the occupancy rate is equal on both sides then the robot makes one hop movement to the side with closer neighboring occupied nodes (Fig. 3(a)) or any of the sides if there is a tie (Fig. 3(b)).
    - Case 3.3: - If the occupancy rate is more on the counter-clockwise direction but the clockwise string is nil then the robot does not make any movement (Fig. 4(a)) else it makes one hop movement to the counter-clockwise direction (Fig. 4(b)).
    - Case 3.4: - If the occupancy rate is more on the clockwise direction then the robot makes one hop movement to the clockwise direction (Fig. 5).

2-Node Problem: The main concern which may act as a thorn on the path of gathering is the 2-node problem, where two nodes in the ring are occupied by

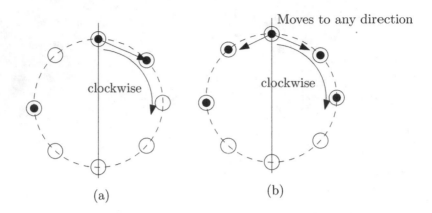

Fig. 3. Case 3.2.

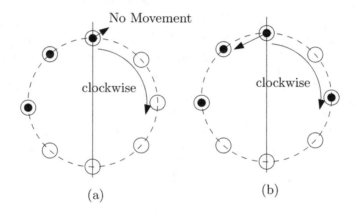

Fig. 4. Case 3.3.

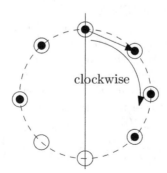

Fig. 5. Case 3.4.

the robots. In fact the inclusion of the property of chirality in the algorithm is just to tackle the 2-node problem otherwise $\lceil \frac{N}{2} \rceil$ visibility range alone would be enough for the gathering to complete. So we put a special condition in case 3.3 under step 3 to counter the 2-node instability. If a robots finds more occupied nodes on the counter-clockwise direction but the clockwise string is nil then the robot does not make any movement else it makes one hop movement to the counter-clockwise direction. This is done to check the increment in the number of nodes between two gathering points or rather in 2-node problem as shown in Fig. 6.

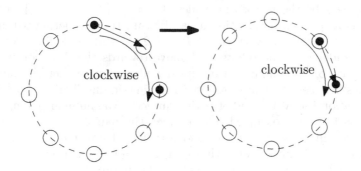

Fig. 6. An example of 2-node problem

2.2   Correctness

The algorithm has been studied extensively in strictly asynchronous model where there exists always a robot which is out of phase of the others. The correctness of the algorithm is proved by the following facts.

- The robot movements are always towards a congested area of the ring and maintain this congestion.
- The robots keep executing the cycles of movement till it finds both half sides of it having only empty nodes.
- The agreement in orientation helps the robots to get into non-repeated configurations by putting restrictions in their movements.

Following lemmas are presented to support these facts.

Lemma 1. *All robots will gather at a single node.*

Proof. According to the algorithm, a robot continues to move until and unless it finds the occupancy rate in both the strings to be nil. This may only happen when all the robots have gathered on a single node.

   This lemma also stands true for 2-node problem where the gathering forms at two nodes but the ultimate task is to gather all the robots at a single node.   □

Lemma 2. *The algorithm guarantees progress, i.e., there will be no deadlock.*

Proof. According to the algorithm, a robot does not make a movement only in a situation where each robot finds both its strings to be nil, i.e., gathering is achieved. In all other situation the robots necessarily make one hop movement to any side in all the cycles as per step 3. Hence, there will be no deadlock.   □

Lemma 3. *Gathering takes place in finite time.*

Proof. For contradiction, let us assume that the gathering takes place in infinite time. Let $t = \{t_1, t_2, \ldots, t_T\}$ be the set of time intervals. Let $n = \{n_1, n_2, \ldots, n_N\}$ be the set of ring nodes. Let $r = \{r_1, r_2, \ldots, r_R\}$ be the set of robots. So as per our assumption it can be said that gathering will not take place even in t_T time intervals where, $T = 1, 2, \ldots$ But according to the algorithm, the tendency of the robots is to move towards the direction where the occupancy rate or the number of occupied nodes is more. Let the number of empty nodes between the pair of robots at the maximum distance be $N1$. After the first iteration i.e., at the end of t_1 time interval, the number of empty nodes (distance) on the more occupied side between the pair of robots at the maximum distance will be maximum $N1 - 1$ or less. This distance is decreasing as the robots move. This implies that within t_T time intervals, gathering is achieved where, T is finite. Here we get contradiction. Therefore, the algorithm confirms gathering in finite time.   □

3   Gathering in an Infinite Grid

Given an infinite grid G. We assume that the infinite grid is embedded in a Cartesian plane. A set of robots R is deployed in various nodes of G. The robots in R have to gather at a single node in G. This gathering node is not given in advance. The robots agree on directions of coordinate axes. Any robot can observe its 360 degree surrounding up to 2 node hop distance. For example in Fig. 7, r_i can not see any robot outside the dotted circle. A *visibility graph* (G_R) is defined as: *The robot positions are considered as the nodes of G_R; If two robots r_i and r_j are visible to each other, there exists an edge between r_i and r_j in G_R.*

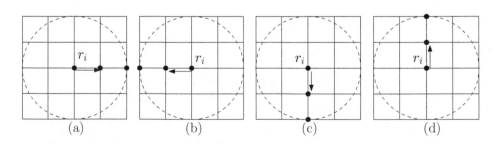

(a)   (b)   (c)   (d)

Fig. 7. Case 1.

3.1   Algorithm Description

The proposed algorithm for gathering is based on following two assumptions.

- Initially G_R is connected.
- Initially G_R is acyclic.

The robots keep these assumptions invariant throughout the algorithm. According to the algorithm different movement strategies for the robots are described as below.

- Case 1: If a robot r_i in R finds robots in two consecutive nodes at its east or west or south or north (any one side), it moves one hop to that side (Fig. 7).
- Case 2: If a robot r_i in R finds robot only in its adjacent node at east or south (any one side), it moves to that node (Fig. 8(a), (c)).
- Case 3: If a robot r_i in R finds robot in its east or west or south or north (any one side) which is not adjacent to r_i, it moves one hop to that side (Fig. 9).
- Case 4:
  - a: If a robot r_i in R finds robot only in its south-east or east-north (any one side), it moves one hop to east side (Fig. 10(a), (b)).
  - b: If a robot r_i in R finds robot only in its north-west or west-south (any one side), it moves one hop to west side (Fig. 10(c), (d)).
- Case 5: For all other cases r_i does not move.

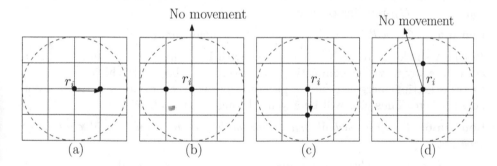

Fig. 8. Case 2.

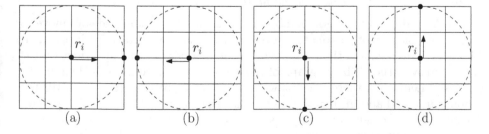

Fig. 9. Case 3.

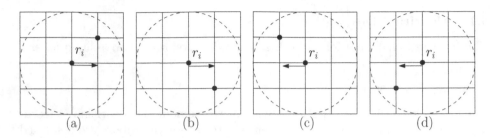

Fig. 10. Case 4.

3.2   Correctness

The correctness of the algorithm is followed from the following facts:

- The assumptions on connectivity and acyclic features of G_R remain as invariant till the robots gather.
- There exists always a robot in G_R eligible for movements till the robots gather.
- The number of nodes in G_R is strictly decreasing by the robot's movements. Finally the number of nodes in G_R becomes *one*, i.e., the robots gather.

Following lemmas are presented to prove these facts.

Lemma 4. *G_R will be connected throughout the algorithm.*

Proof. A robot is selected for movement only if it has degree one. It always moves towards a node occupied with other robots. Thus it does not loose any connectivity. G_R remains connected. □

Lemma 5. *G_R will be acyclic throughout the algorithm.*

Proof. A single degree robot is merging with its immediate neighbor. It does not create any new edge connection. Moreover, the robot with which the moving robot is getting merged is not a part of any cycle. So cycle formation is not possible here. Thus, G_R will be acyclic throughout the algorithm. □

Lemma 6. *The proposed algorithm for gathering in infinite grid guarantees progress.*

Proof. Since G_R is always cycle free, there exists a robot of degree one which moves, unless the robots are already gathered. Hence, progress is assured.

Lemma 7. *The robots gather using finite number of movements.*

Proof. According to the algorithm by case 1, 2, and 4 the robots always move to a node occupied by other robots. Case 3 changes the configuration to case 2. (i) Thus, the movements of the robots reduce the number of robot positions on the grid. Moreover, the visibility graph of the robots remains connected (Lemma 4). (ii) From Lemma 6, there exists always a robot eligible for movement till the robots gather. (i) and (ii) together imply that the number of nodes in G_R strictly decreases by movements of the robots. Thus the number of nodes in G_R becomes *one* in a finite number of movements of the robots, i.e., the robots gather using finite number of movements. □

4   Conclusion

In this paper we have proposed two algorithms, one for gathering robots in a ring and another for gathering robots in an infinite grid. Both the cases open up new scopes for continuation:

- It would be interesting to explore if orientation can be removed to solve gathering in ring in general or clubbed with any other minimal number of additional characteristics. Effort can be made to restrict the vision of the robots as much as possible, e.g., one hop visibility range. Developing optimal gathering algorithm by minimizing the number of movements, is another open direction.
- In the case of grid, the proposed algorithm works under axes agreement. The continuation of this work will be to remove this assumption if possible or to prove that without axes agreement gathering is not possible without any other assumptions. Removing the assumption on cyclic visibility graph may be another immediate future work.

References

1. D'Angelo, G., Di Stefano, G., Klasing, R., Navarra, A.: Gathering of robots on anonymous grids and trees without multiplicity detection. Theoret. Comput. Sci. **610**, 158–168 (2016). Part B
2. D'Angelo, G., Stefano, G., Navarra, A.: How to gather asynchronous oblivious robots on anonymous rings. In: Aguilera, M.K. (ed.) DISC 2012. LNCS, vol. 7611, pp. 326–340. Springer, Heidelberg (2012). doi:10.1007/978-3-642-33651-5_23
3. D'Angelo, G., Stefano, G., Navarra, A.: Gathering of six robots on anonymous symmetric rings. In: Kosowski, A., Yamashita, M. (eds.) SIROCCO 2011. LNCS, vol. 6796, pp. 174–185. Springer, Heidelberg (2011). doi:10.1007/978-3-642-22212-2_16
4. Di Stefano, G., Navarra, A.: Optimal gathering on infinite grids. In: Felber, P., Garg, V. (eds.) SSS 2014. LNCS, vol. 8756, pp. 211–225. Springer, Heidelberg (2014). doi:10.1007/978-3-319-11764-5_15
5. Izumi, T., Izumi, T., Kamei, S., Ooshita, F.: Mobile robots gathering algorithm with local weak multiplicity in rings. In: Patt-Shamir, B., Ekim, T. (eds.) SIROCCO 2010. LNCS, vol. 6058, pp. 101–113. Springer, Heidelberg (2010). doi:10.1007/978-3-642-13284-1_9
6. Kamei, S., Lamani, A., Ooshita, F., Tixeuil, S.: Asynchronous mobile robot gathering from symmetric configurations without global multiplicity detection. In: Kosowski, A., Yamashita, M. (eds.) SIROCCO 2011. LNCS, vol. 6796, pp. 150–161. Springer, Heidelberg (2011). doi:10.1007/978-3-642-22212-2_14. Proceedings of the 37th International Symposium on Mathematical Foundations of Computer Science (MFCS), vol. 7464, pp. 542–553. Springer, Heidelberg (2012)
7. Klasing, R., Kosowski, A., Navarra, A.: Taking advantage of symmetries: gathering of many asynchronous oblivious robots on a ring. Theoret. Comput. Sci. **411**, 3235–3246 (2010)
8. Klasing, R., Markou, E., Pelc, A.: Gathering asynchronous oblivious mobile robots in a ring. Theoret. Comput. Sci. **390**, 27–39 (2008)

9. Koren, M., Klasing, R., Markou, E., Pelc, A.: Gathering asynchronous oblivious mobile robots in a ring. Theoret. Comput. Sci. **390**(1), 27–39 (2008)
10. Michael, N., Fink, J., Kumar, V.: Cooperative manipulation and transportation with aerial robots. Auton. Robots **30**(1), 73–86 (2011)
11. Steinberg, M.: Intelligent autonomy for unmanned naval systems. In: In Defense and Security Symposium, p. 623013. International Society for Optics and Photonics (2006)

WiFi-Related Energy Consumption Analysis of Mobile Devices in a Walkable Area by Abstract Interpretation

Enrico Eugenio and Agostino Cortesi[✉]

DAIS, Ca' Foscari University, Venezia, Italy
cortesi@unive.it

Abstract. The huge increase in the usage of mobile devices has led to the need of sophisticated optimization techniques in order to minimize energy wastage. In this paper we analyze energy consumption of mobile devices during the exchange of data, while walking in a WiFi network area, in order to study the dynamic of the power absorption. This analysis can be used in particular to develop suitable optimizations in case of poor signal. The analysis is obtained as an instance of the Abstract Interpretation framework for semantics-based software verification, and the results are validated by a preliminary real-case experimental evaluation.

1 Introduction

With the prominent growth of smartphone and mobile devices, more and more apps use a constant data stream in order to let real-time systems (Call & Video-call, as Skype, Facebook Massenger, Whatsapp...) keep a certain quality of service. When using these services it is recommended (when possible) to use a WiFi connection instead of LTE technology, because of the greater stability, the less energy consumption, and to prevent data overuse with respect to current phone plans. *Is it always necessary to keep active a WiFi connection?* The performance in terms of connection speed and energy consumption gradually degrades as the user walks away from the center of the cell of the nearest access point. When the connection lower bound is reached, in order to get an acceptable QoS, an expensive, and often useless, aggressive use of battery resources takes place. As the battery lifetime is a very important limitation in mobile devices, is becomes crucial to understand how to optimize the management of WiFi data exchange. Display, hardware and network connections are considered the most power-hungry components in small devices, followed by third-part advertisements displayed in most free applications [18].

At the state of art, various analyses have been proposed on the use of different modules, integrated into modern mobile devices. The analyses developed so far can be clustered in the following groups:

- Network connection analyses, focusing on the use of energy caused by the transmission of data via WiFi by the internet based applications [19,20] and

© Springer International Publishing AG 2017
P. Krishnan et al. (Eds.): ICDCIT 2017, LNCS 10109, pp. 27–39, 2017.
DOI: 10.1007/978-3-319-50472-8_3

aimed at tuning the performance and consequent consumption among the new LTE networks and 3G networks / WiFi [14];

- WiFi module analyses, studying the use of WiFi sensors (e.g. managing situations in which the user is moving) for a set of applications that make use of real time stream (e.g. Videochat) [16];
- Benchmarking of the modules that can adversely affect energy consumption (CPU, WiFi, bluetooth, GPS, accelerometers, cameras, antenna, displays) [4].

We introduce a novel approach, based on a combination of static and dynamic techniques in order to estimate and manage energy consumption, by instantiating the Abstract Interpretation framework [12] for semantics-based software analysis. The object of the analysis is the power consumption, which defines the total amount of energy expenditure of each component, in a specific system. It is interesting to identify those instructions that involve energy expenditure. In this way, we can under-approximate the power consumption of a single module. The Android framework, together with the Linux kernel, provide basic features to the applications and the services; the Android framework encapsulates components, to make programming easier, but this makes it difficult to know how much energy consumes each module. Focusing on the energy consumption of the Wifi module, we can see from Fig. 1 the profiling of the power consumption of the module involved. As previously mentioned, an empirical measure of a single module may not be precise, but by concentrating on the state 'Idle - Run', we can see frequent power spikes. These power peaks of different intensity are directly related to the WiFi signal strength. The components that affect the rise of the energy absorbed during the exchange of the data are many and of various nature [5]: channel width, limited bandwidth, channel noise and channel capacity.

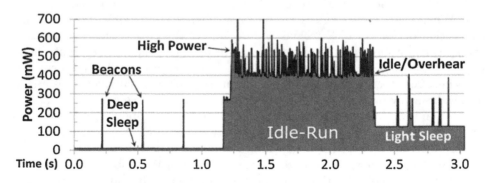

Fig. 1. Power consumption of the WiFi module over time per each state [17]

In power consumption, a key issue is the occurrence of weak wireless signal strength, which forces the module to compensate by increasing its transmission and reception power, with a significantly increase of energy drain of apps that perform network activities. A weak wireless signal strength can be seen as a possible root cause for unusual battery drain spikes. Moreover, as observed in [13], a wireless channel can be noisy, and this noise can affect the capacity of the channel and consequently affects the achievable network performance. Furthermore, an estimated signal strength equal to or less than $-80\,\text{dBm}$ (poor signal strength) gives negative effects not only on the speed of data transfer but also on energy consumption. The distance between communicating endpoints will affect a given radio performance in term of throughput, due to higher latencies which depends to channel noise and this implies more retransmissions for reliable communication. So the channel capacity can change due to the distance between the base station and the device, and this effect contributes to the higher power consumption of WiFi networks.

In this context the results we present in this work are the following:

1. we formalize an energy consumption analysis in the Abstract Interpretation framework, which is parameterized with respect to a (dynamic) device environment,
2. we show the effectiveness of the analysis on the Telegram application,
3. we validate the results of the analysis with empirical experiments, by computing the power consumption related to wifi connection activity in a walkable area.

The rest of the paper is structured as follows: Sect. 2 formalizes the analysis, focusing on the semantics of the application and on the formal analysis of the power consumption. In Sect. 3 a mathematical software is used to simulate an ideal environment, to be used by the analysis. Section 4 shows the results of the empirical validation of our analysis. Section 5 concludes.

2   Abstraction

Abstract interpretation is a general semantic-based technique of static analysis. The key idea is to formalize an abstract execution of the program on a domain that captures a property of interest. The result of the analysis is an over-approximation of the concrete semantics of the program, which is sound with respect to the property to be analyzed [12]. Roughly speaking, abstract interpretation consists to run the program in an simpler domain, called *abstract domain* that contains only the information which is necessary to be able to answer the question of interest. The advantage of this approach is that the precision of the analysis can be tuned by combining a suitable choice of abstract representation of the concrete values managed by the program [7,11], and that the convergence of the analysis is ensured by means of widening operators [6]. There are interesting examples of the effectiveness of such approach on different application contexts [10,15,21] and more recently for the analysis of mobile apps [2,3,8]. We refer here to an extension of Abstract Interpretation to system analysis, as presented in [9].

The environment we consider is $\Phi = \Sigma \times \mathcal{E}$ where:

- Σ is the set of all possible application internal memory environments
- $\mathcal{E}$ is the set of all possible external environments (by the device side)

Let $\langle \sigma, \varepsilon \rangle = \phi \in \Phi$, we define a *state* as the pair $\langle q, \phi \rangle$, where $q \in Q$ is a program point, and the set of all *states* by $\texttt{States} = \Phi \times Q$. A trace semantics of an Android application can be expressed by a set of functions on $\texttt{States}$. For instance, the function $\texttt{read\_sign}$ which returns the value of the wifi signal, reading it from the external environment ε, is:

$$\frac{SysDev.getSign = s, s \in [0, 100]}{< \texttt{read\_sign}, < \sigma, \varepsilon >> \to < \sigma, \varepsilon[sign \to s] >}$$

where SysDev represents the state of the device.

The semantics can be described as a transition system of set of states. A transition relation $\tau : \texttt{States} \to \texttt{States}$ is a pair $\tau = \langle s_i, s_{i+1} \rangle$, denoting the transition between a state s_i and its (possible) successor s_{i+1}. We denote by T the set of all possible transitions. A series of transitions is called **trace**, and we denote by $\texttt{States}^*$ the set of *finite partial execution traces*.

$$\texttt{States}^* = \{s_1 \to s_2 \to ... \to s_n \mid n \geq 1 \wedge \forall i \in [0, n-1] : \langle s_i, s_{i+1} \rangle \in T\}$$

We can define the complete lattice of partial execution traces as:

$$\langle \wp(\texttt{States}^*), \subseteq, \emptyset, \texttt{States}^*, \cap, \cup \rangle$$

The concrete domain of execution of mobile apps can be modeled by $\langle \wp(\texttt{States}^*), \subseteq \rangle$ [9,12]. Sets of traces can be represented by suitable abstract elements, which capture properties of interest of them, while disregarding other execution properties. The relationship between the concrete and an abstract domain A is formalized through a pair of adjoint functions α and γ. The function $\alpha : \wp(\texttt{States}^*) \to A$ is called the abstraction function, and $\alpha(\texttt{S})$ represents the best approximation in A of the set of traces $\texttt{S} \in \wp(\texttt{States}^*)$. The function $\gamma : A \to \wp(\texttt{States}^*)$ is called the concretization function and it returns the set of traces that are captured by an abstract property $a \in A$.

The abstraction and concretization functions must satisfy the following property:

$$\alpha(\texttt{S}) \sqsubseteq a \Leftrightarrow \texttt{S} \subseteq \gamma(a) \tag{1}$$

so α and γ form a Galois connection between abstract and concrete domain:

$$\langle \wp(\texttt{States}^*), \subseteq \rangle \xrightleftharpoons[\alpha]{\gamma} \langle A, \sqsubseteq \rangle.$$

Let $\mathbb{S}^\sharp[P]$ be the (computable) abstract semantics of the application P on the domain A. By the Abstract Interpretation framework properties, once local operations are provided on the abstract domain A that safely overapproximate the corresponding concrete statements, $\mathbb{S}^\sharp$ is sound with respect to the concrete semantics on traces $\texttt{S}$, i.e.

$$\gamma(\mathbb{S}^\sharp[P]\alpha(\texttt{S})) \sqsupseteq \mathbb{S}[P]\texttt{S}$$

Therefore, by (1) and by the fact that α and γ are monotone adjoint functions, we get

$$\alpha(\mathbb{S}[P]\texttt{S}) \sqsubseteq \mathbb{S}^\sharp[P]\alpha(\texttt{S}). \tag{2}$$

As shown in [9], if we verify that a property $p^{\sharp}$ is satisfied by $\mathbb{S}^{\sharp}[\![P]\!]\alpha(\mathbb{S})$, i.e. $\mathbb{S}^{\sharp}[\![P]\!]\alpha(\mathbb{S}) \sqsubseteq p^{\sharp}$, this yields to $\alpha(\mathbb{S}[\![P]\!]\mathbb{S}) \sqsubseteq p^{\sharp}$. Then, combining (1) and (2), by the monotonicity of γ and the transitivity of the ordering relation, we get that p is also true in all concrete executions $\mathbb{S}[\![P]\!]\mathbb{S}$. This mean that P respects the property p.

2.1 Power Consumption Analysis

We can express the analysis of energy consumption in the theoretical scenario just depicted, by following the guidelines expressed in [9]. The trend of the energy consumption is proportional to the distance between the mobile device and the access point; this is translated as the level of the signal received from the smartphone.

Definition 1. *Let P be a program, and let strength $\in [\wp(\boldsymbol{States}^*) \to \mathbb{N}]$ be the intensity of the Wifi signal, and $\langle \wp(\boldsymbol{States}^*), \subseteq \rangle \xleftrightarrow[\alpha]{\gamma} \langle \mathbb{N}, \sqsubseteq \rangle$ be a Galois connection defined by:*

$$\alpha = \lambda\tau.\,min(\{strenght(\tau) \,|\, \tau \in T\}) \tag{3}$$

$$\gamma = \lambda n.\,\{\tau \in \wp(\boldsymbol{States}^*) \,|\, strenght \leq n\}, \tag{4}$$

we can say that the system respects the power efficiency requirement threshold t if

$$\alpha(\mathbb{S}[\![P]\!]\mathcal{S}) \leq t.$$

By applying the analysis, we aim to find a lower bound to signal read during the execution of a system. As said before, this can be used to automatically verify signal strength requirements. Then, in order to make the program efficient we have to define a threshold level beyond which the sending data is too power-hungry.

2.2 Application of the Analysis

First, we have to analyze how an application sends a message. As an interesting case study, we analyze Telegram[1], a cross-platform instant messaging application. Telegram was chosen because it is a wide spread app, it is released under an open source license, and the software was created with the intent to be fully customizable. To perform the analysis, we have shrunk the original code to adapt it to our needs: in order to simplify the analysis of the code, our version of the application allows to send text messages only. By adapting the results of [13] to our study, we discover that the energy consumption of the data transfer does not follow a linear trend compared to the level of the signal strength. So, from 0 dBm to -40 dBm, we define the absorption of current constant at 165 mA. With

---

[1] https://telegram.org/.

a signal level lower than -40 dBm the consumption will be quadratic. At this point we have to understand how long the transmission of the data is in the wireless channel, in order to determine the electric charge so that it can be directly subtracted to the value of the battery charge. Thanks to the data provided by [1] we are able to interpolate a cubic function from -90 dBm to -50 dBm and a linear one from -50 dBm to 0 dBm, that allows us to approximate the transfer rate compared to the wifi signal strength. We define three thresholds of signal strength:

- **Good:** higher than $-60\,dBm$
- **Fair:** between $-60\,dBm$ and $-80\,dBm$
- **Poor:** lower than $-80\,dBm$

For the sake of clarity, the java code of the **Send_Message** procedure (see the Algorithm 1 below) has been faithfully converted to pseudocode, maintaining consistency with the original one and respecting the semantics previously defined; moreover, additional instrumental statements were added to help us conduct our analysis. By analyzing a simulated execution, it follows that, given a 10kBytes message, the **IF** statement is *true*, and the **WHILE** loop run for 3 iterations. Using a 20 Mbps connection, we define three different scenarios, receiving an intensity of signal equal to -40 dBm, -65 dBm and -85 dBm. In this way we obtain, three electric charge consumptions (EC) every time 4096 bytes are sent.

- $Throughput_{-40\,dBm} = 16.42 Mbps$ and $EC_{-40\,dBm} = 3.3\,\mu Ah$
- $Throughput_{-65\,dBm} = 10.17 Mbps$ and $EC_{-65\,dBm} = 5.5\,\mu Ah$
- $Throughput_{-85\,dBm} = 8.7 Mbps$ and $EC_{-85\,dBm} = 8\,\mu Ah$

The states of the optimized program are **States** $= \{2, 3, 4, 5, 6, 7, 8, 9, 10, 11\} \times \Sigma$, and the transitions are:

$$\tau'_0 = \{< 1, \phi > \rightarrow < 2, \phi >\}$$
$$\tau'_1 = \{< 2, \phi > \rightarrow < 3, < \sigma, \varepsilon[batt \rightarrow b] >>\}$$
$$\tau'_2 = \{< 3, \phi > \rightarrow < 4, \phi >\}$$
$$\tau'_3 = \{< 4, \phi > \rightarrow < 5, \sigma[dim \rightarrow d], \varepsilon >\}$$
$$\tau'_4 = \{< 5, \phi > \rightarrow < 6, \phi >\}$$
$$\tau'_5 = \{< 6, \phi > \rightarrow < 7, \phi >\}$$
$$\tau'_6 = \{< 7, \phi > \rightarrow < 8, < \sigma, \varepsilon[sign \rightarrow s] >>\}$$
$$\tau'_7 = \{< 8, \phi > \rightarrow < 9, \phi >\}$$
$$\tau'_8 = \{< 9, \phi > \rightarrow < 10, < \sigma, \varepsilon[batt \rightarrow b] >>\}$$
$$\tau'_9 = \{< 10, \phi > \rightarrow < 11, \phi >\}$$
$$\tau'_{10} = \{< 11, \phi > \rightarrow < 6, \sigma[dim \rightarrow dim - 4096], \varepsilon >\}$$
$$\tau'_{11} = \{< 3, \phi > \rightarrow < \bot, \phi >\}$$
$$\tau'_{12} = \{< 6, \phi > \rightarrow < \bot, \phi >\}$$
$$\tau'_{13} = \{< 7, \phi > \rightarrow < 6, < \sigma, \varepsilon[sign \rightarrow s] >>\}$$

Algorithm 1. Optimized algorithm

```
1: procedure SEND_MESSAGE(text)
2:     read_batt
3:     if read_dim > 0 then
4:         count = read_dim / 4096
5:         a = 0
6:         while a <= count do
7:             if read_sign > Threshold then
8:                 sendMessage(text[a])
9:                 read_batt
10:                a = a + 1
11:            write_app(dim, read_dim − 4096)
```

Now, we define Env_i as the set of environments at program point i and $Env_\perp$ is the environment at the end of the procedure. On the left side of the table below there is the definition of the environments; on the other side, the graph of the evolution of the system.

$Env'_1 : \perp$

$Env'_2 : Env'_1 \sqcup \varepsilon[batt \to b]$

$Env'_3 : Env'_2 \sqcup (\sigma[dim \to d] \sqcap (0, \infty])$

$Env'_4 : Env'_3$

$Env'_5 : Env'_4$

$Env'_6 : Env'_5 \sqcup Env'_{11}$

$Env'_7 : Env'_6 \sqcup (\varepsilon[sign \to s] \sqcap (Threshold, \infty])$

$Env'_8 : Env'_7$

$Env'_9 : Env'_8 \sqcup \varepsilon[batt \to b]$

$Env'_{10} : Env'_9$

$Env'_{11} : Env'_{10} \sqcup \sigma[dim \to dim - 4096] \sqcap (\varepsilon[sign] \sqcap [-\infty, Threshold])$

$Env'_\perp : Env'_6 \sqcap (Env'_3 \sqcap (\sigma[dim \to d] \sqcap [-\infty, 0]))$

Env'_1
$\downarrow \tau'_0$
Env'_2
$\downarrow \tau'_1$
$Env'_3 \longrightarrow \tau'_{11}$
$\downarrow \tau'_2$
$Env'_6 \xrightarrow{\tau'_{12}} Env'_\perp$
$\tau'_{13} \Uparrow \downarrow \tau'_5$
Env'_7
$\downarrow \tau'_6$
Env'_9
$\downarrow \tau'_8$
Env'_{11}

τ'_{10}

The threshold is a fundamental parameter in our analysis, in fact a too low threshold level would allow the sending of data in case of low signal level, thus increasing the battery power consumption and making the optimization useless. On the other hand, a too high threshold level would require a high signal level in order to send data, reducing the user experience in areas where the signal is weak. To highlight the effectiveness of the algorithm, the study is conducted with a user that sends data while passes from a state of **fair** signal ($-65\,$dBm), to a **poor** signal ($-85\,$dBm), then returns to a state of **good** signal to complete the sending. In order to do this, the threshold is set to $-75\,$dBm.

Once defined the behavior of the system and set up the threshold, as abstract property, we will simulate the scenario of execution of the algorithm, to send data in walkable area covered by wifi network. In the following sections we will define two models: a theoretical one, which simulates an ideal environmental scenario, and an empirical one, which uses the data collected from the device via an App developed ad-hoc for our purposes. The final aim will be to compare the two models in order to verify whether there is a correlation between the intensity of the WiFi signal and the energy consumption, and to be able to quantify the effective energy saving data from the analysis of the code of the previous section and holding the analysis in a combined static/dynamic way.

3   Theoretical Simulation of a WiFi Scenario

First of all, we need to define how the WiFi signal strength degenerates as the device moves away from the Access Point. In network theory, the ratio between signal strength and distance from transmitter is governed by the FSLP law (free-space path loss). Once defined the model of the Access Point in the free space, assuming we know the route of a device in space, we can define the spatial trajectories. These trajectories define the path, inside of which the signal received by the device is varying. To simulate this process, we use the random walk method, which is a Markov process that formalizes the idea of taking a series of steps in pseudo-random directions. Using the MatLab software, we implement a model that simulates the evolution in the space. We build a virtual square area, with side of 100 meters; in the central point (coordinates [50,50]) there is an ideal Access Point, simulated using the previously defined model with a power equal to -10 dBm and frequency of 2.5 GHz. Assuming that the user travels 120 steps from 1 m each, starting from the point with coordinate [0,50] (the simulator does not allow to go beyond this limits) and every step is sent a 4096 byte packet. Based on of this result, we repeat the analysis applying a threshold and sweeping this from -90 dBm to -50 dBm (with step 1 dBm), iterating 100 times every value. Then, we interpolate the curve which describes the trend of the power consumption in the theoretical model (see Fig. 5), leading to an energy saving of approximately 72% during a random walk over the same case without threshold, with a maximum error of about 5%.

4   Empirical Evaluation

Let us look at the real energy savings using a physical device. We used a OnePlus One smartphone, a latest generation device that uses the Cyanogen OS 13.0 operating system, based on Android 6.0.1. The approach used in this empirical analysis is not the same as the theoretical method, in fact, we can not detect the energy absorbed from a single sending because of precision limitations of the methods made available by Android for this type of analysis, and also because of the poor accuracy of the sensors of the same device. The technique used is to send a series of packets, with variable size, by saving for each sending the signal strength, the current consumed at that instant and the average frequency of 4 Core of the device in the moment of sending.

A first analysis was done by sending packets from 512 KB, 1024 KB, 1536 KB, 2048 KB, each one repeating sending 25 times. The packages were chosen after a first analysis that showed how a package smaller than 512 KB and bigger 2048 KB would lead to a greater dispersion of data collected and did not highlight a markedly trend. This procedure was performed in two scenarios. In the first case the device is located very close to the access point, with a fixed signal intensity of about -10 dBm; in the second one the device is far from it, with a signal strength of about -80 dBm.

We choose a package size by 1024 kb, as this is the average size with less dispersion. We repeat the data retrieve procedure, this time keeping the packet size to 1024 kB and increasing the number of iterations to 100. We repeat the procedure for 4 different signal intensities: approximately -80 dBm, approximately -65 dBm, approximately -45 dBm and approximately -10 dBm. We analyze these packages to see if there is a correlation between current consumption and frequency of CPU. From the Fig. 2 we can see that there is no obvious trend: it highlights the fact that we are not able to isolate the various components of the device so as to minimize the measurement error.

Then, we analyze the relationship between signal strength and current consumption for each CPU frequency. We notice an obvious trend, which underlines the increasing of current delivered as the received signal decreases. Therefore, we are going to take the plot that has more occurrences of the same frequency and analyze it. The outliers (the power peaks), that are below the 15% and more than 85% of the estimators distributed around a normal curve were also removed; the final result is plotted in Fig. 3.

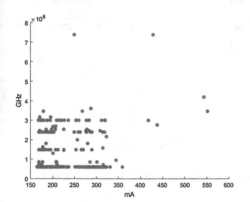

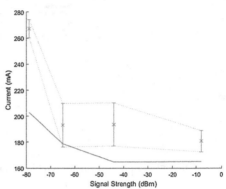

Fig. 2. Correlation between current consumption and CPU frequency (Color figure online)

Fig. 3. Refined data with standard deviation and theoretical curve (Color figure online)

The lower curve (in blue) represents the interpolation of the theoretical data, and the upper one (in red) represents the empirical data with their range of error. Notice that the theoretical model is similar to the curve of the data, and there is an additional constant given by the factors external to our analysis (ex. Screen).

4.1   Comparing Analysis and Empirical Evaluation Results

Once we have the two curves we can fit them between −90 and −10 dBm, From the Fig. 5 we can see a similarity between the theoretical and empirical curve. They are not entirely equal because, as pointed out, the real data above are affected by measurement errors which we were not able to eliminate. We can say that the results obtained, despite being affected by a great error component, allows us to highlight the trend which makes real sense of our research. Although we could not quantify the amount of energy expended by the device under low wifi signal level conditions, we still found a strong correlation between lower received signal level and increase in current consumption.

4.2   Further Tests

New tests were done to give more robustness to the research, using two Galaxy Tab 2 tablet with the original Android 5.0.2 operative system, a Huawei P8 Lite and a Samsung Galaxy S Advance.

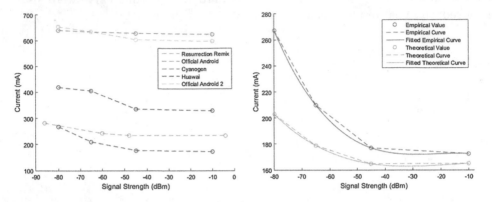

Fig. 4. Current Consumption trends of each device (Color figure online)

Fig. 5. Comparing the Theoretical and Empirical curves (Color figure online)

In Fig. 4 we compare all 5 devices to show in an explicit manner the different trends of current absorption. We notice that the results obtained from two the Galaxy Tab 2 (red and yellow curves) show a slight trend compared to the data obtained from the other devices; we highlight a high offset current values, due to the screen, which, being larger than the other (10.1 in. vs. 6 in. for the One Plus and Huawei, and ad 5 in. for the Samsung S Advance), will draw more current than the other devices. In the middle of the plot we can see the curve of the Huawei P8 Lite (black curve), this is the most power-hungry smartphone in our test, most likely due to the fact that this device is the most performant and the only one with a 4 core CPU working at 1.2 GHz. Although the Resurrection Remix ROM (green curve) is optimized to have a reduced energy consumption, in the graph it shows a higher current offset with respect to the Cyanogen OS curve. The blue curve represent the One Plus device.

5   Combined Analysis

Now we perform a simulation in a real path, using a smartphone with a battery of 3000 mAh. The device sends a packet, with size of 1024 kb, in a succession of points. We consider the following signal values: $-80, -60, -49, -30, -40,$ $-54, -67, -75$ dBm. In the previous simulation we built the curves to model the trend of the current consumption; we now use these curves to get the real current value for each signal value. Then, each current value is converted in charge capacity consumption, in a 20 Mbps connection using the data provided by [1]. This

Table 1. Charge capacity per signal strength

Signal (dBm)	Transfer rate (Mbps)	Transfer time (s)	Charge capacity (mAh)
−30	18,95	0,0540	0,2737
−40	18,60	0,0550	0,2807
−49	18,28	0,0560	0,2912
−54	17,52	0,0584	0,2912
−60	16,80	0,0609	0,3393
−67	15,25	0,0671	0,3960
−75	13,40	0,0763	0,4812
−80	12,40	0,0825	0,5643

yields to the results depicted in Table 1. By applying these values to the static analysis in our two case study algorithms, we get to an estimation of final battery level equal to 97.0598% in the case of the original algorithm, and 98.1053 % in case of the adapted algorithm, with a threshold set to −75 dBm.

6   Conclusions

In this paper we presented an approach to the analysis of energy consumption programs in a mobile environment, applied to Android OS. The Abstract Interpretation framework has been instantiated, by parameterizing the analysis on environmental data. Environmental data can be provided either by a theoretical simulation, or by real-case experimental collection. The comparison of the data provides evidence of the effectiveness of the analysis on theoretical simulation. This analysis may lead to interesting optimizations once applied dynamically, in order to decide whether the actual wifi signal strength allows to guarantee the minimum service status to the user without major power consumption, in particular for streaming video and audio applications.

References

1. Azini, A.S., Kamarudin, M.R., Jusoh, M.: RSSI and throughput performances. Telecommun. Syst. **61**(3), 569–577 (2016)
2. Barbon, G., Cortesi, A., Ferrara, P., Pistoia, M., Tripp, O.: Privacy analysis of android apps: implicit flows and quantitative analysis. In: Saeed, K., Homenda, W. (eds.) Computer Information Systems and Industrial Management. LNCS, vol. 9339, pp. 3–23. Springer, Heidelberg (2015). doi:10.1007/978-3-319-24369-6_1
3. Barbon, G., Cortesi, A., Ferrara, P., Steffinlongo, E.: DAPA: degradation-aware privacy analysis of android apps. In: Barthe, G., Markatos, E., Samarati, P. (eds.) Security and Trust Management. LNCS, vol. 9871, pp. 32–46. Springer, Heidelberg (2016). doi:10.1007/978-3-319-46598-2_3

4. Carroll, A., Heiser, G.: An analysis of power consumption in a smartphone. In: Proceedings of the 2010 USENIX Conference on USENIX Annual Technical Conference, pp. 21–21 (2010)
5. Chandra, R., Mahajan, R., Moscibroda, T., Raghavendra, R., Bahl, P.: A case for adapting channel width in wireless networks SIGCOMM. Comput. Commun. Rev. **38**, 135–146 (2008)
6. Cortesi, A.: Widening operators for abstract interpretation. In: Proceedings of 6th IEEE International Conference on Software Engineering and Formal Methods, SEFM 2008, pp. 31–40 (2008)
7. Cortesi, A., Costantini, G., Ferrara, P.: The abstract domain of trapezoid step functions. Comput. Lang. Syst. Struct. **43**, 41–68 (2015)
8. Cortesi, A., Ferrara, P., Pistoia, M., Tripp, O.: Datacentric semantics for verification of privacy policy compliance by mobile applications. In: D'Souza, D., Lal, A., Larsen, K.G. (eds.) VMCAI 2015. LNCS, vol. 8931, pp. 61–79. Springer, Heidelberg (2015). doi:10.1007/978-3-662-46081-8_4
9. Cortesi, A., Logozzo, F.: Abstract interpretation-based verification of non-functional requirements. In: Jacquet, J.-M., Picco, G.P. (eds.) COORDINATION 2005. LNCS, vol. 3454, pp. 49–62. Springer, Heidelberg (2005). doi:10.1007/11417019_4
10. Cortesi, A., Dovier, A., Quintarelli, E., Tanca, L.: Operational and abstract semantics of the query language G-Log. Theoret. Comput. Sci. **275**(1–2), 521–560 (2002)
11. Costantini, G., Ferrara, P., Cortesi, A.: A suite of abstract domains for static analysis of string values. Softw. Pract. Exper. **45**(2), 245–287 (2015)
12. Cousot, P., Cousot, R.: Abstract interpretation: a unified lattice model for static analysis of programs by construction or approximation of fixpoints. In: Conference Record of the Sixth Annual ACM SIGPLAN-SIGACT Symposium on Principles of Programming Languages, pp. 238–252 (1977)
13. Ding, N., Wagner, D., Chen, X., Pathak, A., Hu, Y.C., Rice, A.: Characterizing and modeling the impact of wireless signal strength on smartphone battery drain. ACM SIGMETRICS Perform. Eval. Rev. **41**, 29–40 (2013)
14. Huang, J., Qian, F., Gerber, A., Mao, Z., Morley, Z., Sen, S., Spatscheck, O.: A close examination of performance and power characteristics of 4G LTE networks. In: Proceedings of the 10th International Conference on Mobile Systems, Applications, and Services, pp. 225–238 (2012)
15. Halder, R., Cortesi, A.: Abstract interpretation of database query languages. Comput. Lang. Syst. Struct. **38**(2), 123–157 (2012)
16. Kim, K.H., Min, A.W., Gupta, D., Mohapatra, P., Pal Singh, J.: Improving energy efficiency of Wi-Fi sensing on smartphones. In: 2011 Proceedings of INFOCOM, pp. 2930–2938. IEEE (2011)
17. Manweiler, J., Roy Choudhury, R.: Avoiding the rush hours: WiFi energy management via traffic isolation. In: Proceedings of the 9th International Conference on Mobile Systems, Applications, and Services, pp. 253–266 (2011)
18. Pathak, A., Hu, Y.C., Zhang, M.: Bootstrapping energy debugging on smartphones: a first look at energy bugs in mobile devices. In: Proceedings of Hotnets 2011 (2011)
19. Ou, Z., Dong, S., Dong, J., Nurminen, J.K., Ylä-Jääski, A., Wang, R.: Characterize energy impact of concurrent network-intensive applications on mobile platforms. In: Proceedings of the Eighth ACM International Workshop on Mobility in the Evolving Internet Architecture, pp. 23–28 (2013)

20. Xiao, Y., Cui, Y., Savolainen, P., Siekkinen, M., Wang, A., Yang, L., Ylä-Jääski, A., Tarkoma, S.: Modeling energy consumption of data transmission over Wi-Fi. In: IEEE Transactions on Mobile Computing, pp. 1760–1773 (2014)
21. Zanioli, M., Ferrara, P., Cortesi, A.: SAILS: static analysis of information leakage ith sample. In: Proceedings of the ACM Symposium on Applied Computing, pp. 1308–1313. ACM Press (2012)

Analytics

A Collision of Beliefs: Investigating Linguistic Features for Religious Conflicts Identification on Tumblr

Swati Agarwal[1(✉)] and Ashish Sureka[2]

[1] Indraprastha Institute of Information Technology Delhi (IIITD), New Delhi, India
swatia@iiitd.ac.in
[2] ABB Corporate Research, Bangalore, India
ashish.sureka@in.abb.com

Abstract. Research shows that with the unexpected emergence of religion and faith, identifying religious conflicts within society has become an important problem for the government and law enforcement agencies. Many social science researchers and domain experts conduct manual surveys on offline and online bases for finding such conflicts. On the other hand, it is seen that people use social media websites for sharing their religious opinions, sentiments and beliefs. We create a hypothesis that social media websites are a rich source of information for mining these beliefs and automatically identifying the religious conflicts among users which overcomes the gaps of offline studies. In this paper, we address the challenge of ambiguity and multilingual scripts in social media posts and distinguish them into various religious sentiments of users. In order to evaluate our hypothesis, we conduct our study on Tumblr- the second most popular online micro-blogging service. We create a dataset of all Tumblr posts (published since 2007) consisting of several tags commonly used in religion based posts and make it publicly available for benchmarking and comparison. We investigate the efficiency of natural language based features for identifying the Tumblr posts that discuss about a religion and belong to one of the nine categories of users' sentiments. For example, disagreement, defensive, annoyed and disappointment. We manually analyze these posts and our result shows the proposed features are discriminatory and support our hypothesis. Furthermore, our results reveal that despite the subjectivity in Tumblr posts, it is technically challenging to mine the religious sentiments of bloggers.

Keywords: Intelligence and security informatics · Mining user generated data · Religious conflicts · Social computing · Text classification · Tumblr

1 Introduction

Tumblr[1] is one of the most popular online micro-blogging service that allows users to make public posts about anything. Tumblr website facilitates its bloggers

---

[1] www.tumblr.com.

P. Krishnan et al. (Eds.): ICDCIT 2017, LNCS 10109, pp. 43–57, 2017.
DOI: 10.1007/978-3-319-50472-8_4

to post seven types of multi-media content including text, image, video, audio, chat, quote and URL. It also allows bloggers to send anonymous private messages to which receiving blogger can reply privately or publicly (referred as 'ask' post in Tumblr). Tumblr is widely used and popularly known for open discussion on various television shows, movies and every day events. Bloggers use reaction gif images showing attitude and emotions (referred as 'feels') about these events [6]. However, many bloggers on Tumblr take leverage of freedom of speech and post content about a variety of sensitive topics including religion and race [2]. Bloggers post their sentiments, opinions, beliefs and reactions on various topics on religion. We observe that a lot of discussions happen and posts are created on Tumblr around the topic of religion which consists of fundamental disagreement or conflicts within society. According to the definition of freedom of speech [7] and Tumblr guidelines[2], bloggers can share their opinions on religious topics however, it does not allow them to post racist and harsh comments that can hurt religious sentiments of an individual. Based on our analysis on Tumblr website, we found that while searching for a religious keyword, 50% of the posts have different opinions about the same religion showing religious conflicts among the bloggers. Figure 1 shows concrete examples of four Tumblr posts showing different sentiments and opinion of bloggers about Islam religion. Figure 1 reveals that one user posts negative and harsh comments about Islam religion. Whereas, another user posts positive sentiments after converting his/her religion to Islam.

(a) Islam Religion (Photo and Text Posts)   (b) Christian Religion (Answer Post)

Fig. 1. Two concrete examples of different tumblr posts showing differences and conflicts among Bloggers on Islam (Multiple Posts) and Christian (Single Post) religions

Further, it is seen that many young age people are getting influenced from social media and joining religious wars [5]. Therefore, monitoring such content and identifying religious conflicts on social media websites is important for the government and law enforcement agencies. According to Tumblr statistics, a large percentage ($\sim$ 40%) of the bloggers are aged between 18 to 35 years, increasing the rate of getting influenced by the presence of such content on the website [1,4]. However, due to the dynamic nature of the website (high velocity and large volume of data), manual identification and monitoring of such content

---

[2] https://www.tumblr.com/abuse/maliciousspeech.

is overwhelmingly impractical [1]. As of July 2016, Tumblr has 307 million active blogs and 137 billion posts made in 16 different languages.

Background: We conduct a literature survey and find that over the past three decades, many social science researchers conducted offline surveys for identifying religious conflicts within society. We however observe that the automatic identification of such conflicts using computer science applications is not yet explored. Therefore, we discuss only some of the closely related articles to the study presented in this paper. Kojetin et al. [8] present the results of an offline survey conducted on three groups of people (college students, church members and seminary students). Their analysis reveal that problem of identifying conflicts religious and society context is challenging and still persists. Swinyard et al. [10] present an offline study and examine the relationship between people's happiness and their religious beliefs and experiences. Wilt et al. [11] examine the temporal correlation between anxiety and religious/spiritual beliefs of an individual. Yang et al. [12] conduct an exploratory analysis on three main-stream newspapers in Malaysia. Their study reveals the impact of low coverage of HindRAF (Hindu Rights Action Force) event on religious conflicts among citizens. In addition to social science researchers, various non-profit organizations like Pew Research Center[3] conduct public opinion polls, offline exploratory and content analysis on social media data to identify various religious trends and issues in society. Some of their recent studies include exploratory analysis of religion related terrorist activities in different countries, influence of religious beliefs & biases in politics and gender gaps in Muslim and Christian religions around the world.

Motivation and Aim: The work presented in this paper is motivated by the existing literature and a need to develop an automatic solution to mine user generated content and identify religious conflicts on social media platforms. However, automatic identification of such posts is technically challenging due to the presence of multilingual script, incorrect grammar, misspelt words, short text, acronyms and abbreviations, sarcasm based posts [9]. Further, the ambiguity and hidden intent of blogger makes posts difficult to classify even for human annotation [2]. The specific research aim of the study presented in this paper is the following:

1. To investigate the efficacy of natural language processing techniques on Tumblr dataset for identifying religious conflicts among bloggers.
2. To investigate the application of linguistic features such as topic modeling, emotional range and use of topic specific key-terms (female mentions) for mining religion specific opinions of bloggers.
3. To conduct empirical analysis on real word dataset and examine the effectiveness of proposed multi-class text classification approach.
4. Furthermore, our aim is to create an annotated dataset of Tumblr posts and make it publicly available to the research community for benchmarking.

---

[3] http://www.pewresearch.org/topics/religion-and-society/.

2   Research Contributions

In contrast to the existing work, our paper makes the following novel and technical contributions:

1. To the best of our knowledge, we present the first study on investigating linguistic features for identifying collision of religious beliefs on social media.
2. We address the challenge of presence of multimedia and multilingual content in Tumblr posts for identifying linguistic features from the content.
3. We publish the first ever database of all types of Tumblr posts posted since 2007 and associated with tags and keywords related to religious topics [3].

3   Why Tumblr?

We conduct our experiments on Tumblr micro-blogging website since Tumblr overcomes the limitations of offline surveys conducted in previous literature. As discussed above Tumblr facilitates users to make posts in 8 different multimedia formats (image, audio, text, video, url, quote, chat and ask). Unlike Twitter, despite being a micro-blogging platform, Tumblr has no character limit for captions, body content or tags of a post [1]. Due to no restriction on content length bloggers are allowed to write longer posts and can express their opinions, emotions and thoughts on a topic in open and descriptive manner which is not there in in-person or offline surveys. Tumblr facilitates blogger to send anonymous messages which further gives them a leverage to express their opinions without revealing their identity. Furthermore, Tumblr provides a community space to bloggers sharing similar interest without caring about the real identity or credibility of the blogger.

4   Experimental Setup

Experimental Dataset Collection: Fig. 2 shows the high level architecture for the experimental setup. In order to collect our dataset, we create a list of tags that are commonly used in religious post and call them as seed tags S_{tag} (hinduism, islam, muslim, religion, isis, jihad, jews, christian, islamophobia and jews). We use Tumblr search API[4] and extract all available posts that contains any of these tags. Tumblr API allows us to extract only 20 most recent posts. Therefore, we use an iterative process and extract the posts created before the timestamp of 20th post in search results. We extract all eight types of posts for these tags published since 2007. Using Tumblr Search API, we were able to extract a total of 107, 586 posts (Religion: 7, 019, Islam: 6, 143, Muslim: 31, 113, ISIS: 28, 768, Islamophobia: 2, 927, Christian: 923, Jews: 17, 785, Judaism: 4, 515, Hinduism: 1, 826, Jihad: 6, 567). Figure 3(a) shows the statistics of total number of posts collected in each category of Tumblr posts. Figure 3(a) reveals that

---

[4] https://www.tumblr.com/docs/en/api/v2.

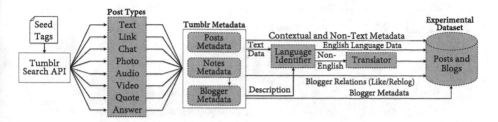

Fig. 2. A general research framework of experimental dataset collection and enhancement- primarily consisting of tumblr posts collection, metadata extraction, non-english posts translations and combining metadata of posts and bloggers

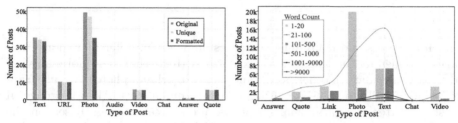

(a) Number of Posts Extracted and For-   (b) Number of Posts Consisting of Differ-
matted for Seed Tags   ent Word-Length (Varying up to 13,318)

Fig. 3. Various data statistics of number of posts for 8 types of categories available on Tumblr

maximum number of posts consisting of religious tags are either posted as photo $(49,072)$ or text $(34,902)$ posts. Similarly, URL or link types of posts $(10,062)$ are relatively higher in comparison to chat (507), audio (390) and answer/ask box $(1,077)$ categories. We extract the contextual metadata of each post and divide them into three parts: posts metadata, notes metadata and blogger metadata. We publish our experimental dataset on Mendeley Data[5] and make it publicly available to the research community for benchmarking and comparison [3].

Since, each category posts in Tumblr has different and unique attributes, we extract the type of each post and acquire related metadata accordingly. Since, the aim of this study is to build a multi-class text classifier, we keep only the textual metadata of each post. For example, caption of photo and video posts, phrases in chat posts and question-answer in an answer post. We merge all the posts collected for all 10 tags and remove all duplicate entries from our dataset. Figure 3(a) shows the statistics of number of unique posts collected in each category. Figure 3(a) reveals that there is only slight difference in originally collected posts and unique posts. This happens due to the fact that while re-blogging a post in Tumblr, users are least likely to add new tags. While Tumblr Search API extracts only the posts that contains a search term in their associated tags. Since, the aim of this study is to identify various linguistic features from textual

---

[5] https://data.mendeley.com.

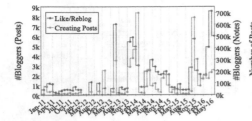

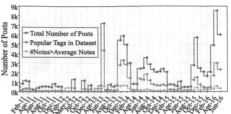

Fig. 4. Number of bloggers creating new posts and participating in community by liking and re-blogging these posts

Fig. 5. A timeline based review of number of posts extracted, consisting of popular tags and more than average notes

metadata of posts and many religious posts are made in different regional languages. We identify the language of textual post (text, chat and quote, answer) and textual metadata of other posts (audio, video, url and photo). We use Yandex language API[6] to translate all non-English content to English language. If a post is written in multilingual script, we use source language based on the maximum content written in one language. We further remove the posts that contains no text, for example, a photo post with no caption, a post consisting of only external url or only emojis. For video posts consisting of no text, we extract the title of videos by parsing the url mentioned in the post. Figure 3(a) shows the statistics of number of posts obtained in each category after cleaning the data. We however, discard the audio posts due to the very short text present in the metadata such as artist name and album name.

Fig. 3(b) shows the distributions of posts in each category based on the number of word counts. Despite being a micro-blogging website, Tumblr has no word limit for text content (posts and tags). However, it is challenging to extract the similar features for short as well as long text. Therefore, we divide our dataset into 6 categories and compute the number of posts in each category. Figure 3(b) reveals that maximum number of posts have a content of 21 to 100 word length while only 4 posts have word length more than 10000. Among which Photo and Texts have the maximum number of posts (19908 and 7206 respectively). Figure 3(b) also shows only text posts have a reasonable number of posts (1394) that have more than 500 words in the textual content.

Evolution of Religion Based Posts: We also study the evolvement of various topics and tags on Tumblr and their popularity on the website. We identify the popular tags P_{tag} (different than the seed tags) that are commonly used in religion based posts on Tumblr and compute the number of posts consisting of these tags. For example, allah, jihad, islamic state, god, faith and racism. We also extract the number of notes (likes and re-blogs) on each post in our experimental dataset. We compute the number of posts in each month having more than average number of notes (50) in our experimental dataset. Figure 5

---

[6] https://tech.yandex.com/translate/.

shows the timeline based graph of monthly distribution of total number of posts in our dataset, number of posts consisting of other popular tags and number of posts having more than 50 notes. Figure 5 reveals that the number of posts consisting of P_{tag} follows the same patterns as the number of posts consisting of S_{tag}. We observe that maximum of these tags are related to Islam religion. For example, among seed tags, muslim keyword has the maximum number of posts (35254) on our experimental dataset. While among other popular tags, Allah, Quran and Syria key-terms are associated with 9223, 6215 and 5523 posts respectively.

Community Participation: Experimental dataset reveals that Tumblr is being used as an active platform for posting content related to religion/spiritual topics. However, it is also important to analyze the involvement of bloggers posting about such topics. Figure 4 shows a timeline based graph of community participation on Tumblr posting about various topics related to religion. X-axis shows the monthly timeline since 2011. While Y-axis shows the distribution of number of bloggers participating in the community. Y axis on right of the Fig. 4 shows the number of bloggers creating new and distinct posts while Y axis on the left side of the Fig. 4 shows the number of distinct bloggers liking or re-blogging these posts. We observe that over the past six years a majority of bloggers have been actively posting religion based content on Tumblr website. While in last three years number of distinct bloggers has reached up to approximately 85K (89, 803). Figure 4 also reveals that not only the users who create new posts but also the users liking and further re-blogging these posts are also increasing rapidly. Number of distinct bloggers liking and re-blogging these posts shows the huge community participation of Tumblr bloggers. Figure 4 shows that in 2016, these numbers reach up to 0.7 million (recorded in May 2016).

5 Measuring Conflicts Within Social Media Data

5.1 Dimensions of Conflicts

We conduct a survey among 50 people (10 groups of 5 people) having different religious, spiritual and race beliefs. We ask them questions regarding their activity on social media websites and if they share religious and race based post. We showed them recent incidents related to religious conflicts and war and further ask them the type of sentiments they would like to share on social media (Facebook, Twitter and Tumblr). Based on the reviews and types of emotions of these 10 groups, we decide 9 dimensions that can lead to conflicts and disagreements among users on social media websites. Table 1 shows examples of Tumblr posts in each of these categories posted for Islam and Christian religions. However, due to the space limit, we present examples of only small posts.

Information Sharing (IS): In first category, blogger are only willing to share some information related to a religion or any incidents caused by religious activists. These users do not depict any emotions in their posts and only share such posts for awareness.

Table 1. Concrete examples of various dimensions of sentiments and emotions in Tumblr posts created for islam and christian religions

Type	Post Content
IS	**Islam:** Afghan cleric defends 'marriage' to six-year-old girl http://www.independent.co.uk/news/world/middle-east/afghanistan-child-marriage-afghan-cleric-religious-offering-a7164826.html
	Christian: Christianity, the World's Most Falsifiable Religion http://credohouse.org/blog/christianity-the-worlds-most-falsifiable-religion
Query	**Islam:** How are you so firm and comfortable with your beliefs? I am Muslim and i am struggling so much with islam. (1) How did you know islam was the right religion. (2) are religions inherently misogynist?ic. (3) how can i overcome doubt?
	Christian: Hi there! Recently your post about how atheists can be Christian normative appeared on my dash. Could you explain the part about how it's Christian normative to "treat secularized versions of Christian holidays as if they were truly secular"? What is the difference between something that's been secularized and something truly secular?
Defense	**Islam:** Can you please stop using ISIS as an excuse to hate Muslims and Islam? It's like using IDF to hate Judaism, it doesn't make any sense. Thanks
	Christian: My spirit is filled with hope and joy and light even when my circumstances tell me to fear and complain. That's God
Annoyance	**Islam:** 1.6 billion muslims in the world And when you decide to hate them all, you're playing into ISIS's and al-Qaeda's hands. They want people to think the west has an agenda against Islam. It's not working. But when they attack and you hate innocent men, women and children, you're making their work easier. Don't be stupid. Don't be a pawn in their f**king cowards' war
	Christian: Tell me one time a christian made an attack and headlines spread: radical christian terrorism. think before you shout radical islamic terrorism
Disgust	**Islam:** Honestly Muslim men who defend non Muslims who appropriate the hijab are revolting because 99% of the time they just want the girl to convert or some sh*t and when their own women are threatened, assaulted & denied opportunities for following their religion these men turn a blind eye but defend white girls with niqabs to death
	Christian: Funny to think that Christianity and other religions make it okay to be a carnist by saying humans have an immortal soul and animals do not. There seems to be some cognitive dissonance between the doctrine of love and the diet of cruelty
Insult	**Islam:** The mudslimes, including London's muslim mayor (lol), are celebrating Ramadanas I should send pics of pork meat to some them and wish them a happy HAMadan
	Christian: F**king Christians and their sanctimonious "The problem isn't [guns/homophobia/transphobia/racism], it's homes without Godbulls**t
Sarcasm	**Islam:** Theory of evolution is such whackas it's good it is not attributed to a Muslim lol
	Christian: at my school there's a rumor that i hate christians lmao its all true
Disappoint	**Islam:** If you're more concerned with people criticizing Islam and the role it plays in these attacks than the damage these extremists have caused, and continue to cause, you're part of the problem
	Christian: Jesus died for us. He takes away the sins of the world. But now, we are changing what He already fixed. We are hypocrites. We are ungrateful. Also remember that the apostles experienced martyrdom for our freedom. Shame on us!
CS	**Islam:** *Question*: You know what I hate? When muslim immigrants come into my country and try to normalise cousinf**king *Answer*: You know what I hate? When white people try to normalize that this is their country
	Christian: *Question*: that anti-circumcision thing you posted is islamophobic *Answer*: Ummm?.. no it's not? First thing, it doesn't even mention Islam. Second thing, there are many non-Muslim people who practice circumcision

Query: Based on users' answers and our observation on Tumblr website, we find that many bloggers ask questions related to various religions. These users seek for the information and do not depict any positive or negative emotion but a curiosity towards that religion.

Defensive: In defensive posts, users share positive, sensitive and justifying comments about a religion. We observe that on Tumblr users make such posts by sharing their beliefs in form of quotes. However, it is challenging to identify a defensive post if the user is comparing two religions and sometimes it can be misclassified as a promotion post due to the presence of persuasive content [2].

Counter-Statement (CS): In counter statement posts, blogger shows his/her disagreement with a religion or certain ethics. Due to the absence of tags in re-blogged posts, Tumblr API does not extract the comments added on a post. Further, notes information can extract only most recent hits on a post. Therefore, disagreement dimension of conflicts can be identified only in "answer" posts.

Sarcasm: Bloggers on social media misuse the freedom of expression by sharing funny comments about a religion and community (referred as trolls and memes). We observe that majority of sarcastic posts on Tumblr are posted in form of photos and reaction gif images.

Annoyance: These posts on Tumblr depict the frustration of the blogger towards a religion or community. these posts consists of an informal and personal writing rather than a formal structure. We observe that majority of such posts are posted after influencing from some religious incident.

Disappointment: Similar to annoyance and disagreement posts, in these posts users share their difference in opinions. However, such posts contains higher rate of sadness and less rate of anger. These posts target a community and users show their disappointment towards a religion or race for certain actions.

Insult: The nature of these posts is similar to sarcastic posts. However, the aim of these post is not to make fun or jokes but to post rude and harsh comments that can hurt the sentiments of targeted community.

Disgust: Based on our survey and observation, these posts have content similar to annoyance and disappointment posts. However, the emotional range of these posts is higher than the disappointment and lower than the annoyance posts. Majority of these posts are consists of factual content and written quoting real word incidents.

5.2   Constructing Feature Vectors

In this Section, we discuss the various linguistic features extracted from Tumblr posts. Figure 6 shows the high level framework for feature extraction from Tumblr posts and bloggers metadata, primarily consisting of three phases: topic modeling, word count based features and named entity recognizer.

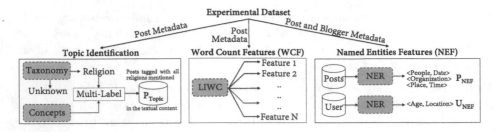

Fig. 6. A General Research Framework for Extracting Linguistic Features from Tumblr Posts- Primarily Consisting of Topic Modeling, Linguistic Word Count and Named Entity Based Features

Topic Modeling: We observe that bloggers on Tumblr use religion based tags in irrelevant and non-religious posts. Therefore, before identifying the conflicts of religious beliefs on Tumblr it is important to identify if a post belongs to a religion based topic or not [2]. We perform topic modeling on these posts and use the algorithm implemented in our previous work Agarwal and Sureka [2] to identify the topic of a post. We create a binary vector where 1 denotes a post to be a religion based post while 0 denotes an unknown post. For all the posts identified as 1, we extract the name of religion being discussed in the post. For example, an insulting or disagreement post can have more than one religion.

Table 2. Concrete examples of tumblr posts showing the presence of named entities for mapping them with real time incidents

ISIS is honoring **President Obama**. He is the founder of **ISIS**. He is the founder of **ISIS**, OK? He's the founder. He founded **ISIS**. And I would say the co-founder would be crooked **Hillary Clinton**
Donald trumpal talk: why hasn't **donald trump** been cursed to have snakes and toads fall from his mouth whenever he speaks
I honestly CANNOT BELIEVE how popular that '**Hillary** is an **advocate** for rapists' meme is when it takes literally one google search to find out that it's completely inaccurate. I CANNOT BELIEVE there are some people who have let this meme convince them to vote for a man WHO IS AN ACTUAL RAPIST #**DonaldTrump**. I AM STEAMING
7/27/2016 - Protesting the **Trump** rally in downtown **Toledo**. #ToledoTrumpsHate
If terrorism has no religion, than name a **Christian** suicide bomber. Name the last **Buddhist** bombing. A confusion shooting. Name someone who yelled ? deus vault? before opening fire on gays. Play the audio of someone saying ? **God** is good all the time, and all the time **God** is good? right before flying a plane into a tower. Any way you spin it, **Islam** is not a religion of peace. It brings with it death and violence wherever it goes. If you think **Islam** is a religion of peace, than turn on the news and open a **Quran**

Linguistic Word Count Features: Inspired by our precious work on author personality traits [2], we compute the correlations between various linguistic features using Linguistic Inquiry and Word Count (LIWC)[7]- a text analytics based tool for identifying feelings, sentiments and personality traits. We extract twelve types of LIWC categories for religion based posts and examine their correlations for different religions. In order to identify the sentiments and opinions in Tumblr posts, we compute five types of emotions *positive emotion, negative emotion, anger, anxiety and sadness*. We also compute various linguistic features for identifying the severity, factual content and personal beliefs in subjective posts- *social, family, female* mention, *obscene* or *sexual* words, *certain* (certainty of comments), *swear* and *informal* words counts. LIWC computes the relative percentage of these features for each post. For example, if a post contains a total of 200 words and 30 terms reflecting swear words and slang language in the content then the score of swear attribute will be 15%.

Named Entities Feature: As discussed in Sect. 5.1 and shown in Fig. 5, majority of religious conflicting posts are created after an incident influencing the beliefs and sentiments of users. Therefore, in order to map these conflicts with real time incidents and investigating the role of emotions and linguistic features, we extract several named entities from these posts. We use Stanford Named Entity Recognizer API[8] and extract five named entities for each post. We extract the person names, location, organization, date and time in a post to check the credibility of a post and improve the efficiency of computational linguistic features. Table 2 shows the examples of three posts created after the attack happened in Paris. Examples reveal the conflicts of sentiments and beliefs between two different communities. Further, we extract the age and location from the user profile and enhance the blogger data for making it publicly available.

6 Empirical Analysis

In this Section, we conduct an empirical analysis on our experimental dataset and examine the performance of proposed features for various religions being discussed in Tumblr posts. We discuss each feature vector in the following subsections.

6.1 Tag VS Content

As discussed in Sect. 4, our dataset contains Tumblr posts that are associated with religion specific search terms i.e. (S_{tag}). However, in our previous study Agarwal and Sureka [2], we find that not all the posts consisting of religion specific tags and key-terms are religion based posts. Therefore, we use topic modeling based features (taxonomy and concepts) for identifying the topic of a

---

[7] http://liwc.wpengine.com/.
[8] http://nlp.stanford.edu/software/CRF-NER.shtml.

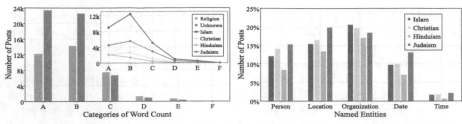

(a) Word Length Based Distribution of Religion and Unknown Posts

(b) Religion Based Distribution of Posts Consisting of Featured Named Entities

Fig. 7. Distribution of topic modeling and named entities features for tumblr posts identified as religion posts

post. Since, the performance of Alchemy Language API[9] varies for different size of text input. Therefore, we divide our dataset into 6 categories based on the word count (WC) of each post. A: 1–20, B: 21–100, C: 101–500, D: 501–1000, E: 1001–9000 and F: WC >9000. Figure 7(a) shows the WC based distribution of posts classified as topic (any religion) and unknown. In comparison to Figs. 3(b), 7(a) reveals that category A and B have the maximum number of posts in our dataset. But due to the presence of short text only 33% of the posts are classified as religion based post. While, the number of topic related posts increases as the length of a post increases. We see a similar pattern for C, D and E categories of posts. Since, the number of posts having more than 9000 terms are only four, values of topic and unknown posts are negligible. While, the statistics reveal all 4 posts to be the topic related posts.

We further identify the name of the religion being discussed in these posts. Figure 7(a) reveals that the maximum number of religion based posts in all categories are about Islam religion. This is probably associated with the fact that the maximum number of posts in our dataset belong to muslim, isis, jews, jihad and religion tags. Figure 7(a) also reveals that with an open platform to express religious opinions and sentiments, people make subjective and detailed posts about these religions on Tumblr.

6.2   Named Entities Based Features

As our previous study Agarwal and Sureka [2] reveals that the user behavior and the writing cues of an author changes with the emotions and sentiments expressed in a post. We observe that in different dimension of conflicting posts, users mention various entities that can be identified using the natural language processing methods. For example, in defensive posts, users mention the name of the people such prophets. In counter-statement and annoyance posts, they tag several communities and organizations such as political parties, religious communities or terrorist organizations. Figure 7(b) shows the distribution of

---

[9] http://www.alchemyapi.com/api/language-detection.

five named entities in various posts related to islamic, christian, hinduism and judaism religions. Figure 7(b) reveals a very small percentage of posts contain time information. While, date entity is mentioned in 10 to 15% of the posts. This is probably associated with the fact that people do mention about several incidents happening around the religious beliefs. Figure 7(b) also reveals that despite the subjectivity in Tumblr posts, due to the variation in word count of each post, only 10 to 20% of the posts contain person, location and organization names in the post. Further, the English translated post might change the syntax of the content leading to the inaccuracy in named entity recognition.

6.3 Linguistic Inquiry and Word Count (LIWC)

We use LIWC based features to extract the various emotional range of bloggers in religion based posts. Figure 8(a) reveals that on an average the maximum number of key-terms showing anxiety in their posts are approximately 10%. While, the relative percentage of terms showing anger in the post are comparatively higher in Hinduism posts. On a contradictory, in Islam and Christian posts, percentage of anger terms is lesser than Hinduism religion based posts while they have a large number of outliers. Similarly, despite having a low median in sadness terms, the number of outliers are reasonably higher in Islam and Judaism posts. Further, Fig. 8(b) shows that the large percentage of obscene and swear terms in religion based posts shows the conflicts among bloggers. Figure 8(b) also reveals that a lot of discussion in religion based posts is about women. For example, in all religion based posts in our experimental dataset contains an approximate of 10% women related key-terms. Our analysis also reveals that Islam, Christian and Judaism

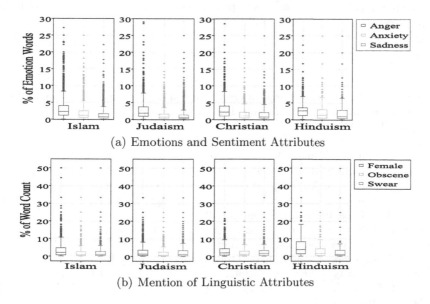

(a) Emotions and Sentiment Attributes

(b) Mention of Linguistic Attributes

Fig. 8. Distribution of LIWC features for Tumblr posts identified as religion posts

related posts have similar number of outliers mentioning female words, obscene and swear words showing the conflicts among these communities.

7   Conclusions and Future Work

With the unexpected emergence of religious influence in political and social activities, identification of collision in various religion and race communities in society has come out to be an important problem for the government, local forces and law enforcement agencies. We create a hypothesis that due to the popularity of websites and subjectivity in content, mining social media posts can fill the gaps of traditional and offline surveys. We create a dataset of all types of Tumblr posts consisting of religion based tags and publish our dataset for the research community. Based on the sentiments and opinions of 50 users, we define 9 dimensions of religion based posts that can lead to religious conflicts. We perform topic modeling on our data and classify the posts that belong to a religion. We further perform computational linguistics for constructing our feature vectors and conduct an empirical analysis on Tumblr posts. Our result reveals that despite the presence of ambiguity in content, computational linguistic approaches can be used as a base method for identifying collision in users' beliefs and religious sentiments. However, if more than one religions are being discussed in a post, it is challenging to identify the beliefs of an author for each religion. Therefore, it requires an improvement in order to disambiguate between conflicting posts such as sarcasm and insult, disgust and disappointment.

Future work includes the improvement of linguistic features and making them generalizable for very short and long posts. It further includes addressing the limitations of present study and developing an automatic solutions for classifying defined dimensions of religious conflicts.

References

1. Agarwal, S., Sureka, A.: A topical crawler for uncovering hidden communities of extremist micro-bloggers on Tumblr. In: 5th Workshop on Making Sense of Microposts (MICROPOSTS) (2015)
2. Agarwal, S., Sureka, A.: But I did not mean it!- intent classification of racist posts on Tumblr. In: Proceedings of European Intelligence and Security Informatics Conference (EISIC), IEEE (2016)
3. Agarwal, S., Sureka, A.: Religious beliefs on social media: large dataset of Tumblr posts and bloggers consisting of religion based tags, mendeley data, v1, (2016). http://dx.doi.org/10.17632/8hp.39rknns.1
4. Agarwal, S., Sureka, A.: Spider and the flies: focused crawling on Tumblr to detect hate promoting communities. arXiv preprint (2016). arXiv:1603.09164
5. Agarwal, S., Sureka, A., Goyal, V.: Open source social media analytics for intelligence and security informatics applications. In: Kumar, N., Bhatnagar, V. (eds.) BDA 2015. LNCS, vol. 9498, pp. 21–37. Springer, Heidelberg (2015). doi:10.1007/978-3-319-27057-9_2

6. Bourlai, E., Herring, S.C.: Multimodal communication on Tumblr: I have so many feels! In: Proceedings of the 2014 ACM Conference on Web Science, ACM (2014)
7. Cohen, J.: Freedom of expression. Philos. Public Affairs **22**(3), 207–263 (1993)
8. Kojetin, B.A., McIntosh, D.N., et al.: Quest: constructive search or religious conflict? J. Sci. Study Relig. **26**, 111–115 (1987)
9. Maynard, D., Bontcheva, K., et al.: Challenges in developing opinion mining tools for social media. In: Proceedings of the@ NLP can u tag# usergeneratedcontent (2012)
10. Swinyard, W.R., Kau, A.K., Phua, H.Y.: Happiness, materialism, and religious experience in the US and Singapore. J. Happiness Stud. **2**(1), 13–32 (2001)
11. Wilt, J.A., Grubbs, J.B., et al.: Anxiety predicts increases in struggles with religious/spiritual doubt over two weeks, one month, and one year. Int. J. Psychol. Relig. 1–9 (2016)
12. Yang, L.F., Ishak, M.S.A.: Framing interethnic conflict in malaysia: a comparative analysis of newspapers coverage on the hindu rights action force (HINDRAF). Int. J. Commun. **6**, 24 (2012)

Scalable IQRA_IG Algorithm: An Iterative MapReduce Approach for Reduct Computation

P.S.V.S. Sai Prasad[1(✉)], H. Bala Subrahmanyam[2], and Praveen Kumar Singh[3]

[1] School of Computer and Information Sciences,
University of Hyderabad, Hyderabad, India
saics@uohyd.ernet.in
[2] Quadratic Insights Pvt Ltd, Hyderabad, India
hothabalu777@gmail.com
[3] TCS Innovation Labs, Mumbai, India
singh.praveen2@tcs.com

Abstract. Feature Selection is an important preprocessing step in any machine learning model construction. Rough Set based feature selection (Reduct) methods provide efficient selection of attributes for the model without loss of information. Quick Reduct Algorithm is a key Reduct computation approach in Complete Symbolic Decision Systems. Authors have earlier implemented a scalable approach for Quick Reduct Algorithm as In-place MapReduce based Quick Reduct Algorithm using Twister's Iterative MapReduce Framework. Improved Quick Reduct Algorithm is a standalone extension to Quick Reduct Algorithm by incorporating Trivial Ambiguity Resolution and Positive Region Removal. This work develops design and implementation of distributed/parallel algorithm for Improved Quick Reduct Algorithm by incorporation of Trivial Ambiguity Resolution and Positive Region Removal in In-place MapReduce based Quick Reduct Algorithm. Experiments conducted on large benchmark decision systems have empirically established the significance of computational gain and scalability of proposed algorithm in comparison to earlier approaches in literature.

Keywords: Rough Sets · Reduct · Quick Reduct · Iterative MapReduce · Twister

1 Introduction

In the recent years, large amount of data is being captured every day and used in fields like science, space, industry etc. The amount of data generated per day is of the order of exabytes as per 2014 info-graphic report [1]. Hence, processing the generated data and extracting useful information for the application scenario has become the need of the hour. This knowledge discovery involves collecting data, cleaning the data, selecting useful features for the data and building a model for the application. Selecting a subset of relevant features for model building

© Springer International Publishing AG 2017
P. Krishnan et al. (Eds.): ICDCIT 2017, LNCS 10109, pp. 58–69, 2017.
DOI: 10.1007/978-3-319-50472-8_5

(Feature Selection) is a key preprocessing step involved in any machine learning model construction.

Rough Sets, introduced by Prof. Pawlak [11] is an emerging soft computing technique, useful for dealing with uncertainty and vagueness present in the data. Feature Selection (by Reduct Computation) is an important application of theory of Rough Sets, which provides an efficient way of selecting useful features for model building without loss of information. Reduct computation was successfully applied in several fields like Engineering, Business and Medicine [8]. Several efficient Reduct computation algorithms are proposed in Rough Set literature [6,15]. Out of these algorithms Sequential Forward Selection (SFS) based Reduct computation algorithms are suitable for scaling to large datasets. Quick Reduct Algorithm (QRA) is a key Reduct computation algorithm using SFS strategy. Extending QRA and incorporating the features of handling trivial ambiguity and positive region removal, IQRA_IG [12] was developed. It proved to be an efficient approach among standalone Reduct computation algorithms. The efficiency of IQRA_IG is because of the incorporation of positive region removal part into QRA.

In an attempt to improve the scalability, several MapReduce based distributed/parallel approaches for Reduct computation were developed in the recent years [13,16], using Hadoop MapReduce. Iterative MapReduce frameworks such as Twister [5], Apache Spark [17], Haloop [3] etc. offer better environment for iterative algorithms with in-memory computations. Twister [5] is an iterative MapReduce framework developed by Indiana university. Twister is a light weight MapReduce extension developed in Java and gives programmer a finer control in processing distributed datasets. A comparison of different MapReduce Programming models was made in [7] among Apache Spark, Hadoop, Twister, Haloop and MPI. Table IV in [7] shows that Twister works much faster than the remaining MapReduce frameworks in all the cases.

This motivated the authors to develop a Twister Iterative MapReduce based Quick Reduct Algorithm as IN_MRQRA in [14], which obtained good computational gains over Hadoop MapReduce based PAR Reduct algorithm [16]. With the objective of improving further the computational efficiency of IN_MRQRA, this work develops IN_MRIQRA_IG as a distributed/parallel algorithm for standalone IQRA_IG. IN_MRIQRA_IG is implemented by incorporating the features of handling trivial ambiguity and positive region removal into IN_MRQRA.

The rest of the paper is organized as follows: Sect. 2 contains basics of Classical Rough Sets, QRA, IQRA_IG, Twister framework and IN_MRQRA. Section 3 presents proposed implementation i.e. IN_MRIQRA_IG, Sect. 4 contains Experimental Analysis, Analysis of Results in Sect. 5 and Conclusion in Sect. 6.

2   Basics and Related Work

2.1   Basics

Definition 1. Complete symbolic decision [11] system is defined as:

$$DT = (U, C \cup \{d\}, \{V_a, f_a\}_{a \in C \cup \{d\}}) \tag{1}$$

where U: Set of objects, d: Decision attribute, C: Set of conditional attributes and for each a $\in C \cup \{d\}$, V_a is domain of a and $f_a : U \rightarrow V_a$ is value set for attribute a.

Definition 2. Rough set is defined over an approximation space $(U, IND(S))$ for any $S \subseteq C$. IND(S) is termed as Indiscernibility relation and is defined as:

$$IND(S) = \{(x, y) \in U^2 / f_a(x) = f_a(y), \forall a \in S\} \tag{2}$$

IND(S) is an equivalence relation and partition of U induced by IND(S) is denoted by $U/\text{IND}(S)$ and equivalence class of $y \in U$ is denoted by $[y]_s$.

Definition 3. A concept $T \subseteq U$ is approximated in $(U, IND(S))$ by a pair of lower and upper approximations. The lower and upper approximations are given by (3, 4)

$$\underline{S}(T) = \{y \in U/[y]_s \subseteq T\} \tag{3}$$

$$\overline{S}(T) = \{y \in U/[y]_p \cap T = \phi\} \tag{4}$$

Set T is crisp if $\underline{S} = \overline{S}$ otherwise it is said to be a Rough Set.

Definition 4. Positive region $POS_s(\{d\})$ contains objects classified to decision equivalence classes without ambiguity and Gamma measure defines the degree of dependency of $\{d\}$ on S. $POS_S(\{d\}), \gamma_S(\{d\})$ are defined as

$$POS_s(\{d\}) = \cup_{T \in U/IND(\{d\})} \underline{S}T \tag{5}$$

$$\gamma_s(\{d\}) = \frac{|POS_s(\{d\})|}{|U|} \tag{6}$$

Definition 5. Reduct is a subset of a features that are individually necessary and jointly sufficient in-order to maintain a property of a decision/information system. Reduct R is a minimal subset of conditional attribute set C such that

$$\gamma_R(\{d\}) = \gamma_C(\{d\}) \tag{7}$$

Attaining a minimum length reduct(R) is an NP-Hard problem [10]. Hence, Heuristic based Reduct computation approaches are proposed for obtaining it.

Quick Reduct Algorithm. Quick Reduct Algorithm (QRA) was proposed by Chouchoulas and Shen [4] and is a dependency function based SFS algorithm. It uses the greedy based approach for computing reduct following SFS strategy. In SFS strategy, reduct R is initialized to empty set and $\gamma_C(D)$ is computed. Gamma computation ($\gamma_C(D)$) is required to properly define end condition both for consistent and inconsistent decision systems. In every iteration, an attribute from $C - R$ which gives the maximum gain of gamma measure ($\gamma_{R \cup \{a\}}(D) - \gamma_R(D)$) is included to R. This process continues till the end condition (7) is reached.

Trivial Ambiguous Situation in QRA. When there is no gamma gain in an iteration of QRA, the selection of an attribute from $C - R$ becomes difficult and may lead to the inclusion of redundant attributes. This situation is known trivial ambiguous situation in QRA. Usually in QRA, an attribute with least value (the order is as present in the dataset) which is not included in $C - R$ is selected and included in R otherwise QRA will result in returning the subreduct.

Positive Region Removal. Objects that go into the positive region remain in the positive region throughout the iterations irrespective of the newly selected attributes. Hence any Reduct computation algorithm will not be affected if the objects that go into the positive region are not considered in the future selection of an attribute into R. This aspect of removing objects that go into positive region is called positive region removal.

IQRA_IG. Overcoming the trivial ambiguous situation embedding positive region removal into QRA, IQRA_IG was proposed in [12]. Trivial ambiguous situation in IQRA is dealt by using the secondary heuristic of Information Gain for selecting an attribute. In this scenario the attribute which gives maximum Information Gain is selected into R. After every iteration granules of $U/IND(R)$ newly entered into positive region are removed for further computations after updating the cardinality of positive region.

Twister. Twister [5] is an enhanced Iterative MapReduce programming model developed by Juliya Ekanayake as a part of his Ph.D work and is supported by SALSA team at Indiana University [5]. Twister's programming model is comprised of Driver, Mapper, Reducer, Combiner. Driver is the main function through which Mappers and Reducers are configured and the loop for MapReduce iterations are invoked. Initially the data is horizontally partitioned and stored in distributed locations in cluster. Driver configures Mappers in such a way that each Mapper is associated with a data partition and Mappers are made in-memory persistent objects till the completion of all iterations. In an iteration, Driver broadcasts the state of the iteration to all the Mappers. Each Mapper working with static data partition and broad-casted dynamic data produces a set of $< key, value >$ pairs. A shuffle and sort phase is invoked using a pub-sub broker and outputs from all Mappers are grouped by $< keys >$ and assigned to Reducers. Each reduce invocation in Reducer works on a single $< key >$ and associated list of *values* from all Mappers and generates aggregated $< key, value >$ pairs. Combiner acting on outputs from all Reducers, works as a global aggregation and computes the result of the iteration. Driver receiving the result from the Combiner checks for the end condition and in-case end condition is not reached a new iteration is initiated.

2.2   Related Work (IN_MRQRA Algorithm)

IN_MRQRA is an iterative MapReduce based QRA algorithm using Twister's framework. The input dataset is horizontally partitioned and distributed across the computing nodes. An iteration of MapReduceCombiner (MRC) is used for selecting the next best attribute using gamma measure. The computation of $\gamma_B(\{d\})$ for $B \subseteq C$ involves computing granules (equivalence classes)

$U/IND(B)$ and deriving consistent granules (granule going into lower approximation of any decision concept, i.e. all objects of granule corresponds to single decision class). The union of consistent granules results in $POS_B(\{d\})$. Computation of $\gamma_B(\{d\})$ requires only the cardinality of $POS_B(\{d\})$. Let $DT^i = (U^i, C \cup \{d\})$ denote the data partition made available to i^{th} partition where $U^i \subset U$.

In Driver, Reduct R is initialized to ϕ. Mappers are configured with data partitions. In each iteration, Driver broadcasts the current R value to all the Mappers. Because of horizontal partitioning, Mappers can only construct partial granules and the complete granule is constructed at Reducer level. In i^{th} Mapper working with DT^i and broad-casted R, partial granules $g' \in U^i/IND(R \cup \{a\})$ are constructed for all competing attributes $a \in C - R$. If g' is consistent a $< key, value >$ pair is generated where key $= < a, GS(g') >$ and value $= < |g'|,$ $d(g') >$. Competing attribute 'a' is included in key as the objective is to compute $\gamma_{R \cup \{a\}}(\{d\})$. $GS(g')$ denote granule signature of g' (unique value combination for satisfied by objects of g'). Only the cardinality of g' without the object information is included in value portion as it is sufficient for computing $\gamma_{R \cup \{a\}}(\{d\})$. $d(g')$ denote the unique decision value of objects of g'. In case g' is inconsistent $value = < 0, -1 >$.

Through shuffle and sort phase a reduce invocation of Reducer will receive list of values corresponding to unique key. Hence all the partial granule information for the same contesting attribute with the same granule signature across all Mappers is involved in one reduce invocation. In reduce method the list of values are aggregated for producing a single value corresponding to the resulting granule $g \in U/R \cup \{a\}$. The consistency of granule is determined from $d(g')$ component and in-case of consistency $|g'|$ components are added to result as $|g|$ in which case a $< key, value >$ pair is submitted to Combiner where $key = < a >$ and $value = |g|$. In-case of inconsistency the value portion is set to zero.

Combiner acting on all the $< key, value >$ pairs from Reducers computes $|POS_{R \cup \{a\}}(\{d\})| \ \forall a \in C - R$. From the resulting $POS_{R \cup \{a\}}(\{d\})$ the best attribute a^* and corresponding $\gamma_{R \cup a^*}(\{d\})$. Driver updates R with a^* and checks for the end condition (7) and continues the iterations if needed.

3   Proposed IN_MRIQRA_IG Algorithm

Extending IN_MRQRA as distributed/parallel algorithm, IN_MRIQRA_IG algorithm is proposed. This requires to embed aspects of positive region removal and trivial ambiguity resolution using IG heuristic into IN_MRQRA.

3.1   Incorporation of Positive Region Removal

Positive region removal process in IQRA_IG is effected by removal of $POS_R(\{d\})$ objects from DT. Adopting this process as it is to distributed framework of IN_MRQRA is not straight forward. Combiner in IN_MRQRA doesn't have information of objects going into positive region and works only with cardinality of consistent granules. Inclusion of object-id information in the *value* portion of partial granule information at Mapper will solve the problem but results as bottleneck for Combiner as it receives id information of $|U| * |C - R|$ size for all competing attributes $|C - R|$. That would significantly constrain the scalability of algorithm and utilizes significant bandwidth. In Combiner, after selection of next best attribute a^* we are only in requirement of objects in $POS_{R\cup\{a^*\}}(\{d\})$. Hence an additional phase of $POS_{R\cup\{a^*\}}(\{d\})$ computation is incorporated after updating of R by the newly selected attribute in Driver. This phase is named as GranuleGather and is described below.

GranuleGather. In the case Driver is to implement positive region removal process, Driver communicates R along with a flag indicator (named as JobIndicator) for computing $POS_R(\{d\})$ to the same Mappers involved in IN_MRQRA computations. Based on the JobIndicator Mapper constructs the partial granule information for only R attributes and works similar to the Mapper of IN_MRQRA i.e. the $< key, value >$ pairs resulting from i^{th} Mapper correspond to partial granules $(U^i/IND(R))$. Hence the resulting key portion contains only $GS(g')$. An important aspect of GranuleGather phase is the changing of objective of computing $POS_R(\{d\})$ to a simplified objective of collating consistent granule signatures of U/R. Passing object-id information was proved to be sufficient for small datasets and was resulting as stumbling block at the single synchronization point of Combiner for large datasets. As cardinality of granule signatures is smaller than cardinality of objects in POS, this motivated us to collate only granule signatures of U/R at Combiner. Having granule signatures of U/R we have the enough information for deriving objects of $POS_R(\{d\})$ in all data partitions. As the objective is to only derive consistent granule signatures of U/R, the information aspect of cardinality is omitted. So the $< key, value >$ pair committed from i^{th} Mapper for a partial granule $g' \in U/R$ is as follows. If g' is consistent then $key =< GS(g'), JobIndicator >$ and $value =< d(g') >$, otherwise $key =< GS(g'), JobIndicator >$ and $value =< -1 >$.

Reducer of IN_MRQRA is unchanged for GranuleGather phase except the key communicated to Combiner contains GS(g), JobIndicator and doesn't involve computation of cardinality of $|g|$. If resulting g is consistent the $< key, value >$ communicated to Combiner contains $< GS(g), JobIndicator >$ as key and $value$ as NULL. If it is inconsistent nothing is communicated to Combiner. Hence, Combiner receives all the granule signatures of consistent granules of U/R and collates them and returns it to Driver. As the job of effecting positive region removal is not complete, Driver initiates the next phase of POSRemoval described below.

POSRemoval. In this phase, JobIndicator is set for POSRemoval and Driver broadcasts $< JobIndicator, R, POSGranularSignatures >$ to all the Mappers. In i^{th} Mapper, using JobIndicator instruction, Mapper determines objects going into positive region by verifying whether the object matches with any of the consistent granule signatures based on R attributes. As Twister does not allow modification of static data, we have used a boolean flag array of size $|U^i|$ for denoting objects that are in positive region. During Mapper configuration, the array is initialized to false values representing all objects are not in positive region. In this POSRemoval phase objects identified to be in positive region will be remembered by setting the corresponding boolean array entries to true. In all other phases of Mapper, the computations are performed only on non-positive region objects.

After completion of POSRemoval process JobIndicator is reset to POS based attribute selection and proceeds with the corresponding execution, i.e. map task of IN_MRQRA algorithm.

POSGather phase involves an additional MapReduceCombiner iteration and invoking for each selection of new attribute into R will result in computational overhead and the gain obtained will not be significant in cases where the new attribute inclusion has resulted in only a slight increase of γ_R. Hence a threshold (α) is maintained by Driver and the process of POSRegion removal is initiated only after γ_R exceeds α. α is further incremented to become the new barrier for next POSRemoval process initiation. In our experiments α is initially set to 0.1 and whenever α barrier is crossed by γ_R it is reset to $\gamma_R + 0.1$.

The effect of POSRemoval results in different iterations of IN_MRIQRA_IG working with different reduced decision systems. Iterations between two POSRemoval phases work with the same decision system. In order to properly maintain $POS_R(\{d\})$ and $\gamma_R(\{d\})$, two additional variables GlobalPOSCount, CurrentPOSCount are maintained by Driver. GlobalPOSCount represents $|POS_R(\{d\})|$ and CurrentPOSCount represents Positive Region obtained in between two POSRemoval phases. Before going into POSRemoval phase, GlobalPosCount is updated by CurrentPosCount and CurrentPosCount is reset to zero. Incorporation of all these changes into IN_MRQRA results in embedding of positive region removal process.

3.2   Incorporation of Trivial Ambiguity Resolution

In IQRA_IG, trivial ambiguity situation occurs when next best attribute inclusion into R doesn't result in increase of γ. As positive region heuristic is unable to result in best attribute, the resolution process selects that attribute obtaining maximum information gain (minimum conditional information entropy) upon inclusion into R. Information entropy calculated on objects U with respect to decision attribute $\{d\}$ is defined as

$$H(U, \{d\}) = -\sum\nolimits_{k \in U/\{d\}} p(k) \ln(p(k)) \text{ where for any } Y \subseteq U, p(Y) = \frac{|Y|}{|U|}$$

Conditional Information entropy [2] of decision attribute $\{d\}$ with respect to attribute set $B \subseteq C$ is defined as

$$H(U, \{d\}/B) = -\sum\nolimits_{g \in U/B} p(g) * H(g, \{d\})$$

The occurrence of trivial ambiguous situation in IN_MRIQRA_IG is realized in an iteration of POS based attribute selection when $|POS_{R \cup a^*}(\{d\})|$ obtained from Combiner is equal to CurrentPosCount. Here, JobIndicator is set to IG base attribute selection and Driver broadcasts JobIndicator,R to all the Mappers. Based on JobIndicator, Mappers work towards Conditional Information Entropy (CIE) for all competing attributes $a \in C - R$. In i^{th} Mapper the frequency distributions of partial granule $(g' \in U^i / R \cup \{a\})$ into different decision classes is computed and communicated to Reducer in a $key, value$ pair where $key = < JobIndicator, GS(g', a) >$ and $value =$ frequency distribution of decision values in g'. In a reduce invocation the granule g contribution to CIE is computed as Partial CIE, which is equal to $-|g| * H(g, \{d\})$. From the list of values obtained at the Reducer containing frequency distribution of decision classes at partial granular level, frequency distribution of decision values (c_i), (i varies from 1 to n (number of decision values)) at granule level are obtained. The summation of resulting frequencies gives the cardinality of the granule. The PCIE is calculated using (8).

$$PCIE = -|g|(\sum_{i=1}^{n} \frac{c_i}{|g|} \ln\{\frac{c_i}{|g|}\}) \tag{8}$$

A $< key, value >$ pair is committed to Combiner where key is unchanged from input and $value$ is PCIE. The Combiner extracts the contesting attribute from key portion, and aggregates all PCIE's to form CIE. The Combiner then selects the attribute which gives minimum CIE (maximum IG) and sends the result to the Driver. Driver adds selected attribute to R without any updation to CurrentPosCount and sets the JobIndicator to work for POS based attribute selection.

Algorithm IN_MRIQRA_IG results from inclusion of above two features into IN_MRQRA algorithm. The resulting Driver for IN_MRIQRA_IG is given in Algorithm 1. Let MapReduceCombiner in Algorithm 1 be termed as MRC.

4   Experimental Analysis

4.1   Cluster Environment

A series of experiments with varied datasets are conducted on a cluster of 6 nodes. Each node has **Intel(R)Core(TM)i5-3750** Processor with clock frequency of 3.2 GHz, having 4 GB of RAM. Each node is installed with Open-Suse 13.2(Harlequin)(x86_64), Java 1.7.0_75, Twister, Apache Ant 1.9.3, Apache ActiveMQ 5.4.2. In our experiments one node is set as master and the remaining 5 nodes are set as slaves.

Dataset Description: Datasets used in our experiments are Mushroom, kddcup99. Mushroom is taken from UCI Machine Learning Repository and discretized. The source of kddcup99 is from [9]. Mushroom is duplicated 5000 times (M_5K) for comparing with results in [13]. We could not conduct comparative experiments with standalone IQRA_IG because the datasets could not be loaded into single system. The datasets are described in Table 1.

Algorithm 1. Driver of *IN_MRIQRA_IG*

Input Horizontally partitioned $DT(U, C \cup \{d\})$
Output Reduct (R)
Configure Mappers() // Load Mapper $'i'$ with U^i at remote locations
Configure Reducers() // Reducer objects are created at remote locations
JobIndicator = POSAttributeSelection
GlobalPosCount = 0, CurrentPosCount = 0, $\gamma_R = 0$, $\alpha = 0.1$
Compute γ_C with single MRC
repeat begin
    switch *JobIndicator* **do**
        case *POSAttributeSelection*
        Broadcast $< JobIndicator, R >$
        BlocktillCompletion() of MRC IN_MRQRA
        $(\ a^*, |POS_{R \cup \{a^*\}}(\{d\})|\ ) =$ Combiner.getPOSresults()
        if CurrentPosCount $== |POS_{R \cup \{a^*\}}(\{d\})|$ **then**
          JobIndicator = IGAttributeSelection
        else
          CurrentPosCount $= |POS_{R \cup \{a^*\}}(\{d\})|$
          $R = R \cup \{a^*\}$
          $\gamma_R = (CurrentPosCount + GlobalPosCount)/\ |U|$
        end if
        if $\gamma_R > \alpha$ **then**
          JobIndicator = GranuleGather ; $\alpha = \gamma_R + 0.1$
          GlobalPosCount = CurrentPosCount + GlobalPosCount
          CurrentPosCount = 0
        end if
        end
        case *IGAttribute selection*
        Broadcast $< JobIndicator, R >$
        BlocktillCompletion() of MRC using IGheuristic // Sec 3.2
        $a^* =$ Combiner.getIGresults() , $R = R \cup a^*$
        JobIndicator = POSAttributeSelection
        end
        case *GranuleGather*
        Broadcast $< JobIndicator, R >$
        BlocktillCompletion() of MRC using GranuleGather // Sec 3.1
        ConsistentGranuleSignatures = Combiner.getGranuleresults()
        JobIndicator = POSRemoval
        end
        case *POSRemoval*
        Broadcast $< ConsistentGranuleSignatures, JobIndicator, R >$
        Blocktillcompletion() of MRC using POSRemoval // Sec 3.1
        JobIndicator = POSAttributeSelection
        end
    endsw
    end
until($\gamma_R == \gamma_C$)
return R

Table 1. Description of datasets

Dataset	Objects	Features	Classes	Consistency
M_5k	40620000	23	2	Yes
kddcup99	4898431	41	23	No

4.2 Comparative Experiments with IN_MRQRA and PAR

IN_MRIQRA_IG is compared with IN_MRQRA [14] and PAR [16]. Algorithm described in [16] is a parallel attribute reduction algorithm in rough sets using Hadoop MapReduce Framework. Experiments in [14] are conducted in Twister environment with 4 nodes, each having 4GB of main memory and installed with OpenSuse-12.2(Linux 3.4 Kernel) having Intel(R) Core(TM) i5-2400 CPU @3.10GHz processor. Experiments in [16] are conducted using hadoop-0.20.2, here one node is taken as namenode and 10 nodes are considered as datanodes. Each node has 1 GB of main memory and 2.4 GHz CPU. Experiments in [14,16] are conducted using kdd99cup dataset. Comparative results are shown in Table 3.

4.3 Comparative Experiments with PAAR-DM Using M5K Dataset

Mushroom is replicated 5000 times (M5K) and a comparison is made with algorithms in [13]. Experiments in [13] are run on 17 node cluster where one node is set as master and the rest are put as slaves. Each node has 2 GB of main memory and is installed with Cygwin 2.697, Hadoop 0.20.2 and Java 1.6.20. In [13] several parallel attribute reduction algorithms in MapReduce were proposed based on different heuristics called positive region (PAAR-PR), boundary region (PAAR-BR), Information Entropy (PAAR-IE), Discernibility matrix (PAAR-DM). The computation times for the calculation of core attributes of experimented datasets were graphically represented in [13]. PAAR-DM performed best among the parallel algorithms for the reduct computation of M5K dataset and the approximated time for the algorithm is calculated from the Fig. 4 of [13]. The summary of comparative results is shown in Table 3. The cumulative available RAM of our cluster of six nodes could not support experimentation on remaining datasets used for experiments in [13]. For example, in [13], Gisette is replicated for 17 times (102000,5001) and our cluster could support Gisette repeated for 10 times (60000,5001).

5 Analysis of Results

The computational gain percentage of IN_MRIQRA_IG over IN_MRQRA, PAR and PAAR-DM algorithms is highly significant (around 90% for all datasets). Our earlier implementation of IN_MRQRA could perform better than PAR due to Twister's Iterative MapReduce support of higher granularity in Mapper construction. In our experiments with a 2 node cluster, it is observed that

Table 2. Comparative results by computation time (in sec) using kddcup99 dataset

kdd99	Objects	IN_MRIQRA_IG (6 nodes)	IN_MRQRA (4 nodes)	PAR (11 nodes)
20%	979686	39.92	444.298	939
60%	2939059	61.61	1294.646	3301
100%	4898431	68.84	1947.338	5050

Table 3. Comparison with PAAR-DM using M5K dataset

	IN_MRIQRA_IG (6 nodes)	PAAR-DM (17 nodes)
Computed time	76.09 s	4900 s
Reduct size	5	4
Reduct	5,20,18,13,19	5,20,22,21

In_MRQRA_IG has computed the result for kddcup99 in 99.738 s. This aptly illustrates that slightly better cluster configuration (with 6 nodes and 4 GB RAM) is not the primary reason for obtained computational gains. The significant gains obtained by IN_MRIQRA_IG are primarily due to successful incorporation of positive region removal into IN_MRQRA and also fusing several MapReduceCombiner tasks in a same MapReduceCombiner job by using JobIndicator, which avoids different MapReduceCombiner jobs to be initiated for different purposes (Table 2).

6   Conclusion

This work proposes IN_MRIQRA_IG algorithm, a distributed/parallel algorithm for IQRA_IG using Twister's Iterative MapReduce framework. IN_MRIRQA_IG is implemented by incorporation of positive region removal and trivial ambiguity resolution in IN_MRQRA. Trivial ambiguity resolution with IG makes IN_MRIQRA_IG algorithm an effective algorithm by allowing to gracefully overcome ambiguous situation. But the computational efficiency of IN_MRIQRA_IG was enhanced by positive region removal. There are several standalone Reduct algorithms in literature using positive region removal for efficiency. IN_MRIQRA_IG is the first algorithm to embed this aspect in distributed/parallel approach. Through GranuleGather, POSRemoval phases, this is achieved by utilizing the network bandwidth optimally since only granule signatures are gathered. Experimental results also establish the several orders of magnitude of computing efficiency achieved over existing MapReduce approaches. IN_MRIQRA_IG is a Reduct algorithm suitable for feature selection in big data scenario.

References

1. Amount of data generated as per 2014 reports. https://aci.info/2014/07/12/the-data-explosion-in-2014-minute-by-minute-infographic/
2. Anaraki, J.R., Eftekhari, M.: Rough set based feature selection: a review. In: 2013 5th Conference on Information and Knowledge Technology (IKT), pp. 301–306, May 2013
3. Bu, Y., Howe, B., Balazinska, M., Ernst, M.D.: Haloop: efficient iterative data processing on large clusters. Proc. VLDB Endow. **3**(1–2), 285–296 (2010)
4. Chouchoulas, A., Shen, Q.: Rough set-aided keyword reduction for text categorization. Appl. Artif. Intell. **15**(9), 843–873 (2001)
5. Ekanayake, J., Li, H., Zhang, B., Gunarathne, T., Bae, S.H., Qiu, J., Fox, G.C.: Twister: a runtime for iterative MapReduce. In: Hariri, S., Keahey, K. (eds.) HPDC, pp. 810–818. ACM (2010)
6. Hoa, N.S.: Some efficient algorithms for rough set methods. In: Proceedings IPMU 1996 Granada, Spain, pp. 1541–1457 (1996)
7. Jakovits, P., Srirama, S.N.: Evaluating MapReduce frameworks for iterative scientific computing applications. In: 2014 International Conference on High Performance Computing Simulation (HPCS), pp. 226–233 (2014)
8. Komorowski, J., Polkowski, L., Skowron, A.: Rough sets for data mining and knowledge discovery. In: Komorowski, J., Zytkow, J. (eds.) PKDD 1997. LNCS, vol. 1263, p. 393. Springer, Heidelberg (1997). doi:10.1007/3-540-63223-9_139
9. Lichman, M.: UCI machine learning repository (2013). http://archive.ics.uci.edu/ml
10. Nguyen, H.S., Skowron, A.: Boolean reasoning for feature extraction problems. In: Raś, Z.W., Skowron, A. (eds.) ISMIS 1997. LNCS, vol. 1325, pp. 117–126. Springer, Heidelberg (1997). doi:10.1007/3-540-63614-5_11
11. Pawlak, Z.: Rough sets. Int. J. Parallel Program. **11**(5), 341–356 (1982)
12. Sai Prasad, P.S.V.S., Raghavendra Rao, C.R.: Extensions to IQuickReduct. In: Sombattheera, C., Agarwal, A., Udgata, S.K., Lavangnananda, K. (eds.) MIWAI 2011. LNCS (LNAI), vol. 7080, pp. 351–362. Springer, Heidelberg (2011). doi:10.1007/978-3-642-25725-4_31
13. Qian, J., Miao, D., Zhang, Z., Yue, X.: Parallel attribute reduction algorithms using MapReduce. Inf. Sci. **279**, 671–690 (2014)
14. Singh, P.K., Sai Prasad, P.S.V.S.: Scalable quick reduct algorithm: iterative MapReduce approach. In: Marathe, M., Mohania, M.K., Mausam, J.P. (eds.) CODS, pp. 25:1–25:2. ACM (2016)
15. Thangavel, K., Pethalakshmi, A.: Dimensionality reduction based on rough set theory: a review. Appl. Soft Comput. **9**(1), 1–12 (2009)
16. Yang, Y., Chen, Z., Liang, Z., Wang, G.: Attribute reduction for massive data based on rough set theory and MapReduce. In: Yu, J., Greco, S., Lingras, P., Wang, G., Skowron, A. (eds.) RSKT 2010. LNCS (LNAI), vol. 6401, pp. 672–678. Springer, Heidelberg (2010). doi:10.1007/978-3-642-16248-0_91
17. Zaharia, M., Chowdhury, M., Franklin, M.J., Shenker, S., Stoica, I.: Spark: cluster computing with working sets. In: Proceedings of the 2nd USENIX Conference on Hot Topics in Cloud Computing, HotCloud 2010, p. 10. USENIX Association, Berkeley (2010)

Simulation of MapReduce Across Geographically Distributed Datacentres Using CloudSim

D.S. Jayalakshmi[1](✉) and R. Srinivasan[2]

[1] Department of Computer Science and Engineering,
MS Ramaiah Institute of Technology, Bangalore, India
jayalakshmids@msrit.edu
[2] Directorate of Research, SRM University,
Kattankulathur, Chennai, Tamil Nadu, India
rsv38@yahoo.co.in

Abstract. Analysis of geo-distributed Big Data has been recently gaining importance. This is addressed either by copying data to a single data centre, or by processing data locally at each datacentre and aggregating the outputs at a single datacentre. Both involve expensive data transfers over wide area networks (WAN). In this work, we analyzed different models proposed for distributed MapReduce in various papers and selected a feasible model to simulate Map Reduce across distributed data centers. We have designed an extension to CloudSim and CloudSimEx to support three methods of implementing geo-distributed MapReduce. A heuristic decision algorithm is devised based on input, intermediate, and output files sizes to select suitable execution path.

Keywords: MapReduce · CloudSim · Geo-distributed data centres · Optimal execution path

1 Introduction

Scientific research data, data from various social media, commercial enterprise data, etc. are generated and stored in datacentres across the globe due to any of the following reasons - data is stored near its place of generation, data is acquired by different organizations but yet are to be shared for a common goal, or data is replicated across datacentres for availability [1]. The biggest challenge is in organizing and coordinating large amount of computations to process distributed big data.

The MapReduce programming model uses a parallel, distributed algorithm to process large data sets on a cluster of commodity machines [2]. Apache Hadoop is the most popular, open-source implementation of MapReduce [3, 4]. The current Hadoop solutions fail to provide resource-aware job scheduling and task scheduling for multidatacentre Hadoop cluster instances that are running in a geographically distributed cloud, comprising of multiple autonomous and possibly heterogeneous datacentres. If Hadoop is used for MapReduce on geographically distributed data, the map and reduce phases might be run on nodes that are in different clusters and the JobTracker

© Springer International Publishing AG 2017
P. Krishnan et al. (Eds.): ICDCIT 2017, LNCS 10109, pp. 70–81, 2017.
DOI: 10.1007/978-3-319-50472-8_6

can assign Reduce task to a slave node that is far from the intermediate file, output of the Map phase. Another option is to bring the entire dataset to one location and then run MapReduce [5]. However, this is tedious and is highly time and resource consuming. This limitation prevents seamless resource utilization across datacentres, and can lead to unpredictably poor performance for Hadoop MapReduce jobs [6]. Therefore, a global MapReduce that finds an optimal path to use available resources effectively and in a distributed manner is of utmost importance [7].

Cloud resources in each physical data centre are managed independent of other datacentres. With an increase in the adoption and deployment of cloud computing across datacentres, it is critical to evaluate the performance of new applications, policies, etc. in such cloud environments. Currently, modeling and simulation has become a useful and powerful tool in cloud computing research community to deal with these issues. CloudSim [8], SPECI [9], DCSim [10] and several cloud simulators have been developed for performance analysis of cloud computing environments.

In this paper we propose an extension to CloudSim and CloudSimEx [11] to provide simulation environment for performing MapReduce across different datacentres. The extension tool should provide the same output as it does when the MapReduce engine is run at a single datacentre. We identify and model a suitable architecture for MapReduce over different datacentres and implement the identified architecture while providing suitable user interface to appropriately import input for the MapReduce to simulate distributed data.

The following sections are organized as follows. In Sect. 2 we review some papers which discuss different methods to implement MapReduce across datacentres and comparison of the different simulators available for cloud environment. The proposed extension to CloudSim and CloudSimEx based on G-MR is presented in Sect. 3. A brief review of G-MR and CloudSim is also presented in this section. In Sect. 4 we provide the implementation details and in Sect. 5 we discuss the results. In Sect. 6 we present conclusions and list the possible directions in which this work can be pursued further.

2   Geo-distributed MapReduce and Cloud Simulators

In this section we discuss different methods in which we can implement the MapReduce across datacentres which are geographically distributed and provide a brief review of CloudSim and CloudSimEx.

2.1   MapReduce Across Geographically Distributed Datacentres

A geographically distributed cloud should be capable of coordinating with multiple autonomous physical datacentres located in different geographical locations to seamlessly and transparently provision computing resources to customers. The authors in [6] provide an insight on improving Hadoop service provisioning in a geo-distributed Hadoop cluster which is a large cluster consisting of multiple sub clusters; each sub-cluster is from a different data centre and has its own namespace. They focus on the three optimization techniques - sub-cluster aware job/task scheduling, sub-cluster aware reduce output placement, and map input data pre-fetching.

Resilin, an elastic MapReduce model that can run across different clouds [12]. Resilin enhances the Elastic MapReduce (EMR) published by Amazon Web Services. Resilin allows users to choose the type of resources they require on Amazon EC2 as well as use private and scientific cloud also.

G-Hadoop [13] is a MapReduce framework that aims to enable large scale distributed computing across multiple clusters belonging to different administrative domains connected via a wide-area network. G-Hadoop replaces Hadoop's native distributed file system - HDFS with the Gfarm file system which uses a file based storage semantics. This avoids splitting files into blocks which significantly decreases the amount of metadata and hence inherently impacts latency and bandwidth in wide-area environments.

Hierarchical MapReduce framework described in [14] brings together computation resources from different clusters to run MapReduce jobs across them. The applications implemented in this framework adopt the Map-Reduce-Global Reduce model where computations are expressed as three functions: Map, Reduce, and Global Reduce. Two scheduling algorithms are introduced: Compute Capacity Aware Scheduling for compute-intensive jobs and Data Location Aware Scheduling for data-intensive jobs. These algorithms process data in their locations itself and thus does not perform well under conditions of an imbalanced replica distribution scenario. If data partitions are relatively large in proportion then the algorithms fails to balance the workload without further partitioning of the existing data partitions. Furthermore, the algorithms do not provide a runtime change.

2.2   G-MR

G-MR employs a novel algorithm named data transformation graph (DTG) algorithm that determines an optimized execution path for performing a sequence of MapReduce jobs on a geo-distributed data set [1]. G-MR optimizes for either the execution time, or the cost, based on characteristics of the data set, type of MapReduce jobs, and the data centre infrastructure.

G-MR provides a good compromise by determining and executing an optimized execution path that performs better than commonly used execution paths. There are three main execution paths for performing a MapReduce job on a geo-distributed data set which are identified as COPY, GEO, and MULTI execution paths [1].

- In COPY execution path, all the data is copied to a single data centre prior to executing a MapReduce job.
- In MULTI execution path, individual MapReduce jobs are executed in each of the data centres on corresponding inputs and then the results are aggregated in one of the datacentres. It is feasible to use this execution path only if the MapReduce job is associative allowing for automatic aggregation of results.
- In GEO execution path, MapReduce job is performed as a single geo-distributed execution with mappers and reducers randomly distributed across datacentres. It incorporates location or sizes of individual sub-datasets or the semantics of the job to decide on distribution.

2.3 Simulators for Cloud Computing

CloudSim: CloudSim supports system and behavior modeling of cloud components such as datacentres, VMs, load balancer, broker, etc. CloudSim quantifies the performance of scheduling and allocation policy in cloud infrastructure [8]. CloudSim is based on SimJava discrete event simulation engine and the GridSim toolkit that support high level software components for modeling multiple Grid infrastructures.

CloudSimEx: CloudSimEx is an extension to CloudSim that provides extended features such as Web Session modeling and MapReduce simulation and the implementation is designed to work as a standalone framework [11]. Though the implemented system cannot represent real world cloud systems by itself, the resulting system provides a perspective at MapReduce computing model. It takes into consideration the following features for implementing MapReduce on CloudSim: the workload may not be dependent on input file size, every separated Map has a Reduce operation, and reduce operation has to come after Map operation of corresponding input.

3 Extension to CloudSim

We provide an extension to CloudSimEx by employing MapReduce across multiple datacentres. In order to achieve this, a new architecture based on G-MR is proposed.

G-MR uses sampling of data to predict the optimal execution path. The DTG algorithm used is an exhaustive method and even with the suggested pruning can become unmanageable with increase in number of datacentres. The optimal path selection is done using Dijkstra's shortest path algorithm which has an $O(V^2)$ execution time for matrix representation of graph where V is the number of nodes. If adjacency list representation is used the complexity is $O(E \log V)$ where E is the number of edges in the graph. Hence in our implementation we have designed a simple heuristic to choose the optimal execution path for performing MapReduce jobs for each of the participating datacentres and implemented each of these execution paths. Following are the algorithms for each of these execution paths and the path choosing algorithm.

3.1   Proposed Decision Algorithm to Find Optimal Execution Path

Algorithm *GetSuitablePath* finds the execution path that is suitable for a given data-centre based on the size of the input data it has and is available for MapReduce, the intermediate data it is likely to generate and probable output data size. Such estimates of intermediate and output data sizes for a given input data size for a MapReduce operation are feasible in most cases based on the type of workload- high aggregation, zero aggregation and ballooning data, and data sources as discussed in [2].

If the input data size in a datacenter is small compared to estimated intermediate and output data sizes, the best execution path is COPY. The input data is transferred to the nearest data centre whose execution path is not COPY. The nearest data center for the given data center is that to where data can be transferred in minimum time. If the intermediate data size is smallest, then the chosen execution path is GEO; then the mapper can be run in respective datacentres and the intermediate data can be moved to the location of reducers. If both these conditions are not satisfied, MULTI is chosen. The execution path selected for a majority of participating, geographically distributed, data centres is taken for a MapReduce on input data sets spread over a number of datacentres.

Algorithm GetSuitablePath

Input:
> Input data size *ind* , intermediate data size *intd* and output data size *outd* for each datacenter ;

Output:
> Execution path *exp* to be implemented;

for each datacentret **do**
>> **if** (*ind* <*intd* **and** *ind* <*outd*) **then**
>>> *exp*=COPY;
>> **elseif** (ind > intd **and** outd > intd) **then**
>>> *exp*=GEO;
>> **else**
>>> *exp*=MULTI;
>> **endif**
> **end for**
> return *exp*;

3.2   Geo-distributed MapReduce Algorithm

The flow of the geo-distributed MapReduce is shown below in algorithm GEO_ DISTR_MAPREDUCE.

Algorithm GEO_DISTR_MAPREDUCE

Input:
> An xml file containing work details for each datacenter ;

Output:
> Map and Reduce Task details like submission time, status, cost, etc.;

read the datacentreconfig file.
for all dc in the datacentrelist **do**
> determine the suitable MR path using the algorithm GetSuitablePath()
> **if** the suitable path is COPY **then**

>> determine the nearest dc with MULTI or GEO path, to where the data can be transferred to.
>> **if** such a dc is found **then**
>>> set the sendmapto attribute of the dc to the nearest dc id.
>>> Set the waitformapfrom attribute of the nearest dc to the former
>> dc id
>> **end if**

> **end if**
> set the finish time for all dc=-1
end for
for all dc in the dclist **do**
> **if** dc.suitableMRType==COPY **then**
>> call Copy_MR
> **else if** dc.suitableMRType==GEO **then**
>> call Geo_MR
> **else if** dc.suitableMRType==MULTI **then**
>> call Multi_MR
> **end if**
end for
if there are more than one datacenters left with data to be further processed **then**
> select suitable data center with more data then others
> start reduce phase two
end if

The suitable execution path each of the datacentres participating in MapReduce execution is determined using GetSuitablePath(). If majority of datacentres are COPY, then the MapReduce execution path is chosen as COPY and data from all participating datacentres is transferred to the datacenter with the largest input data. If majority of datacentres are GEO then Map phase is executed in each of the participating data-centres. The intermediate data is transferred to the data centre that has the largest intermediate data size where a reduce phase is executed. If both these conditions fail, the execution path is taken as MULTI. Individual Map Reduce jobs are executed in each datacentre on corresponding inputs and the outputs are aggregated in the data-center with the largest output data size.

4   Implementation

This section discusses the framework implementation. The framework is entirely coded in Java. We have used the Map Reduce package provided in CloudSimEx and the main objective of our extensions to CloudSim and CloudSimEx are to provide the COPY, MULTI, GEO execution path alternatives to perform MapReduce across multiple data centres.

4.1   Modifications to Existing CloudSim Code

We have suitably modified the existing CloudSim [8] and CloudSimEx [11] codes. Simulation.java is the entry point to the simulation at each data centre as per the CloudSimEx design. We have included an extra feature in Simulation.java to take care of the case where the data centre has to wait for data from other data centres before starting MapReduce. The submission time and input data size are suitably modified to accommodate the data transfer. MapReduce engine has an added responsibility of creating an output class that contains the result of simulation at each data centre, which is later used in the aggregation phase.

4.2   Package GeoDistrMapReduce Classes

Figure 1 shows the overview of the high level classes and the relation between them. Classes in the CloudSim framework package that are relevant to our implementation are shown. The classes such as DatacentreBroker, Datacentre, MapReduceEngine that need modification to suit our work are shown outside the package. We have created a package called GeoDistrMapReduce that contains the following classes that interacts with various classes of different packages in CloudSim and CloudSimEx:

1. cloneJob - It has methods to assign values to Map and Reduce Tasks.
2. cloneMap - Declaring parameters for Map tasks.
3. cloneReduce - Declaring parameters for Reduce tasks.
4. CopyMRSimulation - This class implements COPY execution path algorithm discussed in the previous section.
5. DatacentreConfig - Defines configuration file parameters for datacentres.
6. DecisionAlgorithm - Implements the GetSuitablePath() algorithm defined in the previous section.
7. GeoMRSimulation - This class implements GEO execution path algorithm discussed in the previous section.
8. GroupManager - It has methods to read the dataconfig file, get number of datacentres, get the data transfer time and speed (between data centres), get the type of MR, get workfile, and select suitable datacentre. It runs the decision algorithm.
9. MultiMRSimulation - This class implements Multi execution path algorithm discussed in the previous section.

10. OutputClass - This class has five member variables i.e. cost, budget, finishtime, outputsize, and dcID for map and reduce phases that happen in each data centre. It has get() and set() methods for these member variables.

Group Manager: GroupManager is the master entity that interacts with the client by reading the DatacenterConfig file. The sequence of activities is shown in the sequence diagram in Fig. 2. GroupManager runs the Decision Algorithm described in Sect. 3.2 to determine the suitable MapReduce path for each of the data centers listed in the DatacenterConfig file and starts the corresponding execution path at each data center. GroupManager is implemented as a Java class that calls the main methods of the CopySimulation, MultiSimulation or GeoSimulation classes for each data center in the DatacenterConfigFile. The main methods in these classes, in turn call the MapReduce method of the CloudSimEx package. GroupManager initiates the Map Reduce by first reading the xml based DataCenterConfig file.

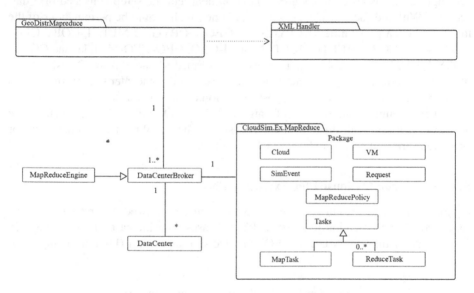

Fig. 1. Package GeoDistrMapReduce and related classes

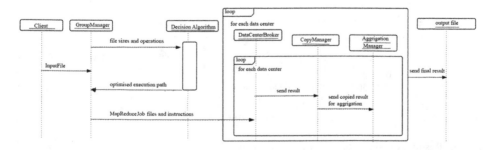

Fig. 2. Sequence of events initiated by GroupManager

4.3 Package XMLHandler Classes

The XMLHandler package assists in reading and writing of XML files such as the input files and the intermediate files. Handlers have been provided to read and write Experiment, Job, DatacentreConfiguration, etc. The input file name and operation to be performed are submitted to the scheduler, which does the computation on the given input after finding the data centres where the input file blocks are located and also decides on which optimized execution path to be employed. It consists of the following classes: (i) DatacentreConfigReader - used to read Datacentreconfig.xml file, (ii) ExperimentParser - used to read experiment files, (iii) JobParser - used to read Job files, (iv) WriteExperiment - used to write Experiment files, and (v) WriteJob - used to write Job files.

5 Results and Discussion

The algorithm was tested in CloudSim environment and the setup consisted of 3 datacentres. With 3 datacentres, the possible execution paths could be permutations of the following seven possibilities: COPY-COPY-GEO, COPYGEO-MULTI, COPY-GEO-GEO, COPY-COPY-MULTI, MULTI-MULTI-GEO, GEO-GEO-MULTI, and COPY-COPY-MULTI. (Refer Table 1). Tests were performed to check if the DecisionAlgorithm chooses the most appropriate MapReduce type and datacenter to perform various operations. The efficiency of the proposed decision algorithm was tested by conducting a number of simulations of each of naïve COPY, GEO and MULTI as well as the decision algorithm with different input data sizes. The simulation were optimized for execution time and cost as defined in CloudSimEx.

5.1 Simulation Optimized for Execution Time

Figure 3 shows the results of the simulation runs optimized for execution time. As expected, the execution time for COPY increases with increase in input data size. The execution time for MULTI, GEO, and decision algorithm (DA) are comparable

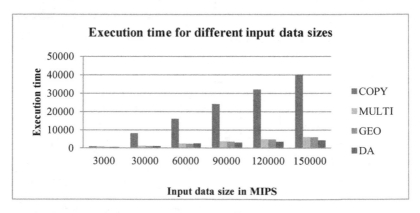

Fig. 3. Results of simulation – execution time v/s different input data sizes in Million Instructions per Second (MIPS)

though GEO has smaller execution time. The reason could be that MULTI requires an extra aggregation/reduce phase whereas in GEO the intermediate data are transferred to a single datacenter where the reduce phase is executed. The decision algorithm based DA has the least execution times.

Table 1. Different possible execution paths for 3 datacenters (DC) and the MapReduce type chosen by decision algorithm

Data centres			MapReduce type inference
DC1	DC2	DC3	
COPY	GEO	MULTI	DC1 transfers the data to DC3 where Map Reduce phases for MULTI and COPY execution paths takes place. In DC2 Map phase for GEO happens. The final reduce phase of MULTI and reduce phase of GEO happens in DC3
COPY	COPY	GEO	DC1 and DC2 transfers data to DC3 where three Map phases of each of the datacentres happen the Reduce phase of GEO happens in DC3
COPY	GEO	GEO	DC1 transfers the data to DC2 where Map phase for GEO and COPY execution paths takes place. In DC3 Map phase for GEO happens. The reduce phase of both GEO happens in DC3
COPY	COPY	MULTI	DC1 and DC2 transfer data to DC3 where three MapReduce phases of each of the two COPY and MULTI paths happens and final Reduce phase of MULTI happens in DC3
MULTI	MULTI	GEO	MapReduce for MULTI happens in both DC1 and DC2 and Map phase of GEO happens in DC3. The final reduce phase of DC1 and DC2 and the reduce phase of DC3 together happens in DC1
GEO	GEO	MULTI	Map phase of GEO happens in DC1 and DC2 and MapReduce for MULTI happens in DC3. Reduce phase for GEO and final Reduce phase for MULTI happens in DC1
COPY	MULTI	MULTI	DC1 transfers the data to DC2 where MapReduce for both COPY and MULTI happens. In DC3 MapReduce phase for MULTI happens and the final reduce phase happens in DC3

5.2   Simulation Optimized for Execution Cost

Figure 4 shows the results of the simulation runs optimized for cost. For each of the execution paths, cost increases as input data size increases. The cost is mainly contributed by the amount of data transfers involved. The cost for COPY increases with increase in input data size as the data from all the participating datacentres needs to be transferred to single datacentre. The costs for MULTI and GEO are similar. These execution paths are chosen when the input data size is large avoiding transferring them across datacentres. Further, GEO is chosen when intermediate data size is small whereas in MULTI only the output data is moved. Hence costs of these two execution paths in our simulation runs are the same. The decision algorithm performs in a manner comparable to MULTI and GEO with slightly less cost.

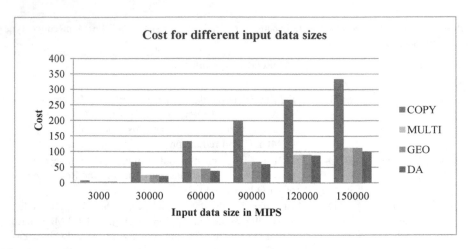

Fig. 4. Results of simulation – cost v/s different input data sizes in Million Instructions per Second (MIPS)

6   Conclusion and Future Work

The work described in this paper has been developed with the aim of addressing the problem of handling distributed data. We have successfully implemented an extension to CloudSim and CloudSimEx to simulate MapReduce for geographically distributed data based on G-MR [1]. The three alternatives for performing MapReduce on distributed data across data centers, namely- Copy MR execution path, Multi MR execution path and Geo MR execution path is implemented. However our work differs from the [1] in that our implementation is simulation-based whereas [1] is on physical clusters. The DTG in [1] uses edge weights indicating cost of execution path which are obtained from actual sampling of data. In our work we use a simple heuristic based on input data size to determine the optimal execution path. An algorithm to select the appropriate execution path for each of the datacenters by considering the various data sizes is successfully designed and implemented. We have tested the efficiency of the proposed model and it is observed that the decision algorithm implemented proves to be advantageous over naïve implementation of COPY, MULTI or GEO execution paths. The implementation assumes that the input data partitions at each of the datacenters do not have any replicas in other datacenters. The work can be extended to handle the replicated data across datacenters to avoid single point of failure.

References

1. Jayalath, C., Stephen, J., Eugster, P.: From the cloud to the atmosphere: running mapreduce across data centers. IEEE Trans. Comput. **63**(1), 74–87 (2014)
2. Dean, J., Ghemawat, S.: MapReduce: simplified data processing on large clusters. Commun. ACM **51**(1), 107–113 (2008)
3. Shvachko, K., Kuang, H., Radia, S., Chansler, R.: The Hadoop distributed file system. In: Proceedings of the 2010 IEEE 26th Symposium on Mass Storage Systems and Technologies (MSST) (MSST 2010), 1–10. IEEE Computer Society, Washington, D.C. (2010)
4. Hadoop MapReduce. http://hadoop.apache.org/. Accessed 13 Feb 2016
5. Cardosa, M., Wang, C., Nangia, A., Chandra, A., Weissman, J.: Exploring MapReduce efficiency with highly-distributed data. In: Proceedings of the Second International Workshop on MapReduce and its Applications (MapReduce 2011), pp. 27–34. ACM, New York (2011)
6. Zhang, Q., Liu, L., Lee, K., Zhou, Y., Singh, A., Mandagere, N., Gopisetty, S., Alatorre, G.: Improving Hadoop service provisioning in a geographically distributed cloud. In: Proceedings of the 2014 IEEE International Conference on Cloud Computing (CLOUD 2014), pp. 432–439. IEEE Computer Society, Washington, D.C. (2014)
7. Wang, L., et al.: MapReduce across distributed clusters for data-intensive applications. In: 2012 IEEE 26th International on Parallel and Distributed Processing Symposium Workshops and Ph.D. Forum (IPDPSW), Shanghai, pp. 2004–2011 (2012)
8. Calheiros, R.N., Ranjan, R., Beloglazov, A., De Rose, C.A.F., Buyya, R.: CloudSim: a toolkit for modeling and simulation of cloud computing environments and evaluation of resource provisioning algorithms. Softw. Pract. Exper. **41**(1), 23–50 (2011)
9. Sriram, I.: SPECI, a simulation tool exploring cloud-scale data centres. In: Jaatun, M.G., Zhao, G., Rong, C. (eds.) CloudCom 2009. LNCS, vol. 5931, pp. 381–392. Springer, Heidelberg (2009). doi:10.1007/978-3-642-10665-1_35
10. Keller, G., Tighe, M., Lutfiyya, H., Bauer, M.: DCSim: a data centre simulation tool. In: 2013 IFIP/IEEE International Symposium on Integrated Network Management (IM 2013), Ghent, pp. 1090–1091 (2013)
11. Alrokayan, M., Vahid Dastjerdi, A., Buyya, R.: SLA-aware provisioning and scheduling of cloud resources for big data analytics. In: Proceedings of 2014 IEEE International Conference on Cloud Computing in Emerging Markets (CCEM), pp. 1–8. IEEE (2014)
12. Iordache, A., Morin, C., Parlavantzas, N., Feller, E., P. Riteau, P.: Resilin: elastic MapReduce over multiple clouds. In: Proceedings of 2013 13th IEEE/ACM International Symposium on Cluster, Cloud and Grid Computing (CCGrid), Delft, pp. 261–268 (2013)
13. Wang, L., Tao, J., Ranjan, R., Marten, H., Streit, A., Chen, J., Chen, D.: G-Hadoop: MapReduce across distributed data centers for data-intensive computing. Future Gener. Comput. Syst. **29**(3), 739–750 (2013)
14. Luo, Y., Plale, B.: Hierarchical MapReduce programming model and scheduling algorithms. In: Proceedings of the 2012 12th IEEE/ACM International Symposium on Cluster, Cloud and Grid Computing (ccgrid 2012) (CCGRID 2012), pp. 769–774. IEEE Computer Society, Washington, D.C. (2012)

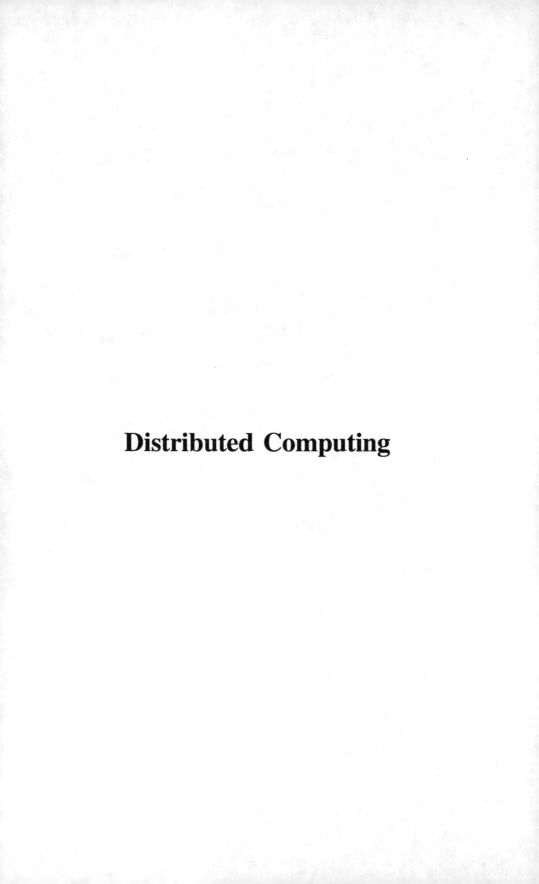

Distributed Computing

Revamping the Frequency and Computational Time of RTOS Task – Power Dissipation

Sharma Saravanan[1]([⊠]) and Sameera Shaik[2]

[1] School of Electronics, Vignan University, Guntur, Andhra Pradesh, India
Sharma_ece@vignanuniversity.org
[2] Department of Computer Science, Vignan University,
Guntur, Andhra Pradesh, India
Sks_cse@vignanuniversity.org

Abstract. Optimizing the frequency of a homogeneous multi-core platform for a Real Time Operating System (RTOS) increases the power utilization factor. The level of consistency of RTOS is concerning the amount of time taken to complete the execution of the hard real time task. Multi-core platforms need special techniques for process management and power management. DPM is one of the techniques designed to achieve the power efficiency in which all the cores have to operate at the same speed simultaneously which leads to the lack of flexibility for power management. This article, proposes an algorithm, dynamic computational energy aware where computing time of a task is increased based on the requirement in order to achieve exceptional power efficiency by considering multi-low power states.

Keywords: Optimization · Homogenous processor · Utilization factor · DPM

1 Introduction

A real time system is a system intended to serve real-time application requests. It must be able to process data in real time, without any service or buffering delays. Processing time requirements are measured in tenths of seconds or shorter. One of the major challenges in a real-time system is the efficient usage of energy. A key characteristic of a Real-Time Operating Systems (RTOS) is the level of its consistency concerning the amount of time it takes to accept and complete an application's tasks; the variability is jitter. Hard real-time operating system has less jitter than a soft real-time system. The design is not high throughput, but rather a guarantee of a soft or hard performance category. An RTOS that can usually or generally meet a deadline is a soft real-time OS, but if it can meet a deadline deterministically it is a hard real-time OS [1].

In CMOS-based technology, the energy consumption of a processor over a time interval is an increasing convex function of frequency. For RTOS, the major development requires Low energy consumption, long battery life and low heat dissipation in order to achieve exceptional utilization of the processor. Dynamic Voltage Scaling and Dynamic Power Management are the existing techniques for energy consumption. In these techniques, all the cores have to operate at the same speed simultaneously which leads to the lack of flexibility for power management. This paper focuses on cluster

P. Krishnan et al. (Eds.): ICDCIT 2017, LNCS 10109, pp. 85–93, 2017.
DOI: 10.1007/978-3-319-50472-8_7

based multi-core homogenous processor; the cores are grouped into clusters in which the cores operate at same speed. The approach stated in this paper is also applicable for non-cluster based real time multi-core processor [1].

In this article, the algorithm in described into two parts; first part consists of the heuristic approach for allocation of the hard real time task set to the cores which is the initial solution. Secondly, the proposed algorithm is employed for optimizing the frequency of the multi-core processor which in turn increases the utilization.

The organization of this paper is as follows, Sect. 2 describes the related technologies for power consumption. In the Sect. 3, the basic terminologies and the system model is described. The Sect. 4 explains the initial solution of the hard real time task allocation followed by Sect. 5 the proposed algorithm is explained and shows how the algorithm is working on the real time periodic task sets. Finally, before concluding the paper in the Sect. 7, the Sect. 6 shows the experimental results.

2 Related Work

For the real-time systems, DVS mainly focuses on power management whereas DPM concentrates on scheduling the processes. Existing studies on DPM and DVS are divided into three different categories, the DVS-only, DPM-only and DVS/DPM-combined approaches, as they work in contradict to each other. One of the DVS-only algorithms (full polynomial time approximation algorithm) with polynomial complexity is based on the operating system and compiler where the decision of frequency adjustment is made by means of the inserted code instruments in the application. To reduce the energy consumption at runtime, a dynamic speed adjustment scheme and a dynamic slack reclaiming algorithm are presented where the later works with complexity of $O(1)$ [1].

The DPM-only algorithm works on device usage scheduling as mentioned above. An online DPM algorithm has been proposed in association with Earliest Deadline First (EDF) to create large device idle intervals which can be achieved by task procrastination. To get the optimal solution for power management, a heuristic algorithm is proposed where an artificial task period is introduced. A dynamic counter approach is proposed which decides the number of upcoming events and therefore bounds the future workload. The shutdown policy can be safely applied based on this information [2].

In the context of system-wide energy efficient real-time scheduling, DVS and DPM are applied for the processors and devices respectively. Many algorithms are proposed based on critical speed and frame-based task model. The concept of critical speed is introduced since power consumption increases if a task runs under this speed and moreover these algorithms work only with a fixed real-time schedule EDF.

Energy efficient real-time scheduling approaches can be divided into three different categories, per-core, full-chip and cluster-based approaches. A per-core DVS algorithm has been proposed by assuming the frame-based task model and ideal processor where different power characteristics of tasks are taken into consideration. In case of full-chip platforms, most work concentrates on balanced task partition. The dynamic repartitioning algorithm is proposed based on existing partition, which tries to balance the task load on different cores by considering dynamic slack and to reduce the number of cores a dynamic core scaling scheme was proposed as well [1].

In recent times, more focus has been put on the cluster-based multi core platforms and various algorithms were proposed discussing the problem of clustering the cores into DVS domains. The authors, who introduced a fundamentally alternate means for cluster-based multi-core processor, believe that performance of a core designed for a dedicated frequency/voltage domain is much better than a core designed with run-time DVS capabilities. In contrast, in this paper a new approach called *Dynamic Computational Energy Aware Algorithm* is proposed for energy consumption in order to increase the utilization of the processor by extending the execution time of hard real time periodic task in such a way it reduces the idle time of the processor [3].

3 Terminologies

(a) **Processor Model**

The processor model that is considered is cluster based multi-core processor which states that the multiple cores in the processor are grouped to form the cluster. The cores in the same cluster operate at the same frequency whereas the cores in the outside of the cluster operate at the different frequency referred as heterogeneous frequency. In this context, each processor is assumed to operate at any speed in $[S_{min}; S_{max}]$, The number of CPU cycles executed in a time interval is linear of the processor speed and the energy consumed for a processor in the execution of a task at the processor speed s for t time units is P(s) [1, 4].

(b) **Task Model**

Tasks consider for analysis are periodic and independent in executions. A periodic task is an infinite sequence of task instances, referred to as jobs, where each job of a task comes in a regular period. Each task z is associated with its initial arrival time (denoted as C_i), its computation requirement in CPU cycles (denoted as ci), and its period (denoted as p_i). Note that C_i denotes the maximum number of CPU cycles required to complete the execution of any job of τ_i. Given a set of tasks Γ, the hyper-period of Γ, denoted as L, is defined as the least common multiple (LCM) of the periods of tasks in Γ [5].

Let the relative deadline of each task τ_i be equal to its period pi. That is, the arrival time of j + 1 task and dead of j-th instant of the task z_i. The task set is donated with $\Gamma = \{\tau_1, \tau_2, \ldots \tau_n\}$, where τ_i is the ith task of the processor. T_i is the maximum execution time of the task or deadline of the task [4].

4 Initial Solution

The initial solution is based on the Largest Task First (LTF) algorithm. Largest task first algorithm *[defines in Algorithm 1(LTF)]* allocates the tasks to the cores in non-increasing order of their execution time and loads of the processors. Let us consider the task of $\Gamma = \{\tau_1, \tau_2, \ldots \tau_n\}$ with the computational time of C_i and period of the task is P_i, the utilization of the processor for the specific real time task τ_i is the ratio of the computational time to the total period of the task is C_i/P_i. The task set is rearranged in non-increasing order of loads of the processor denoted as $T = \{T_1, T_2, \ldots T_N\}$ and the loads of the nth processor core are denoted by l_n. The loads of the nth processor is the summation of the all the loads of the task allocated to that particular processor in the order of $T = \{T_1, T_2, \ldots T_n\}$ where $T_1 > T_2$ and $T_2 > T_3 \ldots T_{N-1} > T_N$ [1, 6].

The task allocated to the processor in sorted order and the processors executes the given task at the critical operating frequency C_0. If the load is less than the critical speed i.e., $l_n < C_0$, then the utilization of the processor is not equal to maximum utilization factor. The major constraint of the LTF, is the lower bound of optimal energy consumption solution. To avoid the local optimal solution, the Sect. 5 derives the efficient global optimal solution for large number task set by optimizing the operating frequency of the cluster based multi-core homogeneous processor [7].

ALGORITHM 1. LTF

i.   Input : periodic task set $\Gamma = \{\tau_1, \tau_2, \ldots \tau_n\}$

ii.   Calculate the loads l_n by C_i/P_i of all tasks.

iii.   Sort all in non-increasing order in $T = \{T_1, T_2, \ldots T_N\}$

iv.   Assign a critical speed C_0.

v.   Find the initial utilization of the all the core.

vi.   For $i = 1$ to $|T|$ do
        Find **smallest** l_n
        Assign τ_i to processor l_n
        Return

vii.   Calculate the utilisation of the core in the critical speed C_0.

viii.   **Check U{T} is maximum or not.**

Fig. 1. Largest task first algorithm

5   Dynamic Computational Energy Aware Algorithm

In this section, dynamic computational energy aware algorithm is used to optimize the computational time of the task allocated to the processor by the Largest Task First solution. The main idea of DCEA algorithm is to iteratively improve the utilisation of the processor by optimizing the computational time of the task so that homogenous frequency of the core is altered. The iteration is continued till the global solution obtained and saturation of the utilisation factor. There are two main steps for optimizing the computational time of the real time task,

(a) Allocation of task using LTF
(b) Calculating utilisation of the processor

(a) **Allocation of task using LTF**
     The process in the multitasking is, initial task allocation to the processor which is done by the largest task allocation explained in Fig. 1. The input to the LTF is the hard real-time periodic task set and operating frequency of the processor. The final solution of the LTF is utilisation of the cores after allocating the task which is not the global optimum solution for energy consumption. The output of the Largest Task First is considered as initial solution for the main algorithm and from this, iteration starts deriving optimum computational time for consumption of energy.

(b) **Slow down the frequency and Calculating utilisation of the processor**
     Utilisation of the processor should be maximum for a effective reduction of energy consumption i.e., $U\{T\} = 1$. The utilisation of the processor model has to be calculated for each iteration and has to check whether it has attained its maximum value or not. Slow downing the computational time of the task leads to reduction of operating frequency of the multi-core processor so that the utilisation factor is increased. Utilisation is the ratio of optimized computational time to the total period of the task. Optimizing execution time of the task has to be continued until the utilization is converged or it attains the maximum value.

ALGORITHM 2. DCEA

Input: Frequency **F**

i.   Task allocated to all the core using LTF algorithm

ii.   Calculate the utilisation **U{T}** of all cores by $\sum_{n=1}^{m} I_n$.

iii.   Find the minimum utilisation among the cores $U_{min}\{T\}$.

iv.   Let $U_{min}\{T\}$ -> **slow down factor** S_f.

v.   Compute **new execution time** C_{ni} using **slowdown factor** by C_i/S_f.

vi.   Calculate **new slowdown factor** S_{nf} and **frequency** by $S_{nf}*F$.

vii.   **Repeat** the process from **(ii) until U{T} gets** saturated.

viii.   **END**

Fig. 2. Dynamic computational energy aware algorithm

Figure 2 illustrates the dynamic computational aware approach for energy consumption and attaining the maximum utilisation. The value of new utilisation is compared each and every time with current one. The aim is to apply the DCEA algorithm in runtime and the algorithm is iteratively improves the utilisation since the real time systems with periodic tasks are iterative in execution of each task only in the particular hyper period. The iteration in the algorithm is for one hyper period, for every other hyper period iteration has to be initialized from LTF algorithm. Henceforth, in the DCEA approach there is no task migration is occurring since the processor is homogenous core.

Figure 3 illustrates the flow of dynamic computational energy aware algorithm, the process starts with defining the task sets and number of cores before deriving the initial solution and the slow down factor for the DCEA algorithm (Fig. 4).

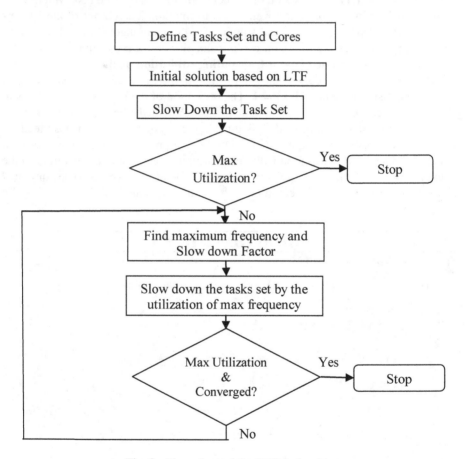

Fig. 3. Flow chart of the DCEA algorithm

6   Experiments and Results

Total number of cores: **3**
Total number of tasks: **5**
Configurations of task τ_1 = **[5 5 2]**
Configurations of task τ_2 = **[14 14 3]**

Configurations of task τ_3 = **[30 30 8]**
Configurations of task τ_3 = **[20 20 3]**
Configurations of task τ_3 = **[40 40 6]**

6.1   LTF Results

The value of C_i (computational requirement) **[2 3 8 3 6]**
    The value of p_i **[5 14 30 20 40]**
Core1 Utilization: 0.4   **Core2 Utilization: 0.416**   **Core3 Utilization: 0.364**

6.2   Dynamic Computational Energy Aware Algorithm

Frequency: 20 MHz

Old execution
Task 1: 2   Task 4: 3
Task 2: 3   Task 5: 6
Task 3: 4

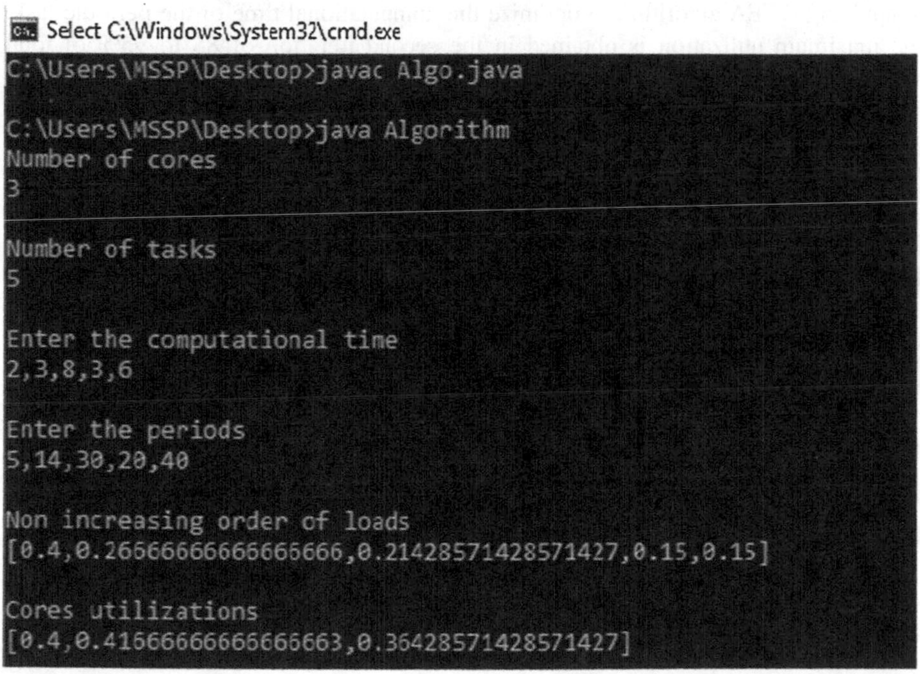

Fig. 4. Results of initial solution

Core1 utilization: 0.4	Core2 utilization: 0. 416		Core3 utilization: 0. 364
Old execution	New execution	Slow down factor	Frequency
Task 1: 2	2.11	0.95	19 MHz
Task 2: 3	3.16	0.95	19 MHz
Task 3: 8	11	0.7238	14.5 MHz
Task 4: 3	3.2	0.9375	18.75 MHz
Task 5: 6	7.8	0.7692	15.38 MHz
Maximum frequency: 19 MHz		Slow down factor: 0.95	
Core1 utilization: 0.422	Core2 utilization: 0. 524		Core3 utilization: 0. 355
Old execution	New execution	Slow down factor	Frequency
Task 1: 2	4.76	0.42	8 MHz
Task 2: 3	7.12	0.42	8 MHz
Task 3: 8	18	0.442	8.88 MHz
Task 4: 3	7.12	0.42	8 MHz
Task 5: 6	14.2	0.422	8.44 MHz
Maximum frequency: 8.8 MHz		Slow down factor: 0.444	

Core1 Utilization: 0.952   Core2 Utilization: 0.856   Core3 Utilization: 0.711

The results show that the utilization of the multi-core processor has been increased by applying DCEA algorithm to optimize the computational time of the periodic task. The maximum utilization is obtained in the second iteration of 85 to 95% of total utilisation of the processor by attaining maximum utilisation, the energy consumption in dormant mode and waking up from idle mode [8].

7 Conclusion

The continuous increase of system complexity and the advanced technology towards cluster based multi-core processor platforms; the problem of energy efficiency becomes more and more complex. This paper focuses on increasing the utilisation of the processor by optimizing the speed of the hard real-time tasks on cluster-based multi-core processor platforms. The proposed dynamic computational energy aware algorithm and its online execution increase the utilisation of the processor by 35% than the previous algorithms. This paper explores energy-efficient allocation of periodic real-time tasks in homogeneous multiprocessor environments in which the power consumption resulting from leakage current is non-avoidable. Eventually, through the experimental results DCEA approach shows its great efficiency and higher utilisation factor.

References

1. He, D., Mueller, W.: A heuristic energy aware approach for hard real time systems on multi-core platforms. Microprocess. Microsyst. **37**, 858–870 (2011)
2. Chen, J.-J., Hsu, H.-R., Kuo, T.-W.: Leakage–aware energy efficient scheduling of real-time tasks in multiprocessor systems. In: Proceedings of the 12th IEEE Real-Time and Embedded Technology and Applications Symposium, 2006, pp. 408–417 (2006)

3. Kulcsár, G., Erdélyi, F., Hormyák, O.: Multi-objective optimization and heuristic approaches for solving scheduling problems. IEEE Trans. Antennas Propag. **48**(11), 127–132 (2000). Department of Information Engineering, University of Miskolc, Hungary
4. Mostafa, S.M., Kusakabe, S.: Towards reducing energy consumption using inter-process scheduling in preemptive multitasking OS. In: 2016 International Conference on Platform Technology and Service (PlatCon), Jeju, pp. 1–6 (2016). doi:10.1109/PlatCon.2016. 7456832
5. Ning, J., Liu, C., Wang, H., Chen, Q.: Self-balanced motion planning for humanoid robot based on dynamic multitasking mechanism. In: 2016 IEEE 13th International Conference on Networking, Sensing, and Control (ICNSC), Mexico City, pp. 1–6 (2016). doi:10.1109/ ICNSC.2016.7478979
6. Gupta, A., Ong, Y.S., Feng, L.: Multifactorial evolution: toward evolutionary multitasking. IEEE Trans. Evo. Comp. (2015, accepted)
7. Jafarizadeh, M., Zakerolhosseini, A.: Performance analysis of processing load distribution in camera networks for multi-target tracking. In: 2015 9th Iranian Conference on Machine Vision and Image Processing (MVIP), Tehran, pp. 236–241 (2015). doi:10.1109/ IranianMVIP.2015.7397544
8. Chen, J., Hsu, H., Kuo, T.: Leakage-aware energy-efficient scheduling of real-time tasks in multiprocessor systems. In: Proceedings of the 12th IEEE RTAS, Washington, DC, USA, pp. 408–417 (2006)

CO$_2$ Penalty and Disaster Aware Data Center and Service Placement for Cost Minimization

Rishi Sharma, Ranu Vikram, Bala Prakasa Rao Killi$^{(\boxtimes)}$,
and Seela Veerabhadreswara Rao

Department of Computer Science and Engineering,
Indian Institute of Technology Guwahati, Assam 781039, India
{s.rishi,v.ranu,k.bala,svrao}@iitg.ernet.in

Abstract. Data center placement and service placement within a data center are the two most fundamental problems concerning cloud network design. In an ideal world, data centers should be placed in such a manner that there should be no data loss or service disruption, the costs incurred are minimum possible amounts, latency is minimized and it operates in a "green" way, i.e., minimal CO$_2$ emissions and runs on green energy. The service/content within a data center must be placed at locations that minimize content loss in case of any disaster, minimum latency for various requests, and also optimize available resources at hand. In this paper, we propose a data center and service placement problem that is aware of both CO$_2$ emissions and content loss due to disaster(s). The objective is to minimize the total cost which includes operational and setup cost of data center, and penalty associated with CO$_2$ emissions and expected content loss. This problem is modeled as a multi-objective optimization problem. Results show that the total cost incurred tend to increase with the number of disaster events and the setup and operational expenditures tend to increase with the number of software components. Furthermore, results also show that, for a given number of software components, CO$_2$ penalty of the CO$_2$ aware placement is less compared to the CO$_2$ unaware placement.

Keywords: Content loss penalty · CO$_2$ penalty · Data center and service placement · Multi-objective optimization

1 Introduction

Cloud computing, also known as on-demand computing, is essentially a form of distributed/network computing. We distribute the resources that are available to us in a network environment, and which are made available to services on-demand basis. This acts as a model for retrieval of computing resources in an on-demand fashion. The recent surge in cloud computing facilities can be owed to making both data storage and computation capabilities available to private and enterprise users at low cost and saving them the burden to first invest heavily in acquiring infrastructure. This relies upon the basic concept of pooling of

© Springer International Publishing AG 2017
P. Krishnan et al. (Eds.): ICDCIT 2017, LNCS 10109, pp. 94–104, 2017.
DOI: 10.1007/978-3-319-50472-8_8

resources to develop a scalable and coherent economic model. Cloud computing also focuses on most effective distribution of resources. This involves dynamic reallocation of resources to improve QoS, such as improving data locality. This takes us into the area of service and resources placement.

Data center placement and service placement within a data center are the two most fundamental problem concerning cloud network design. Service placement deals with determining placement location for a service/content among given data center locations, so as to minimize content loss, in case of any disaster, minimum latency for various requests, and also optimize available resources at hand. Different requirements of resources by different services is also taken into account, while considering optimal utilization of resources during service placement. With the emerging cloud network, small organizations lease cloud infrastructure and services from giant cloud providers like Amazon. However big firms need to set up their own cloud network for which they need to consider the fundamental problem of data center placement along with service placement. Data center placement deals with selecting locations for setting up data centers among given set of viable locations, such that factors such as cost, CO$_2$ emissions, and renewable energy are optimized. Most of the major cloud service providers pick/select data center locations based upon various factors, such as energy availability and efficiency, land available for development purposes, workforce availability, physical location of user market, etc.

Data center placement is a large and long-term investment on resource providers side. Thus, it becoming more and more important for them, to take into account the chances of natural and man-made disaster to strike a data center. These disasters, such as natural (tornadoes, earthquakes, etc.) and man-made (Chemical, biological, radiological, or nuclear attacks) should be influential factors, while deciding locations for setting up data centers as disruption caused by them are both correlated and cascading in nature, leading to huge downtime in services and/or data loss [1,2]. Amazon, a major cloud provider experienced huge data loss and disruption of service of several websites for days, due to the above mentioned reasons, despite making use of different physical locations to isolate failures [3]. Similarly in 2012, Alaska Airlines services were disrupted due to two Sprint fiber-optic cuts. These real world examples, and inherent flaw of not taking into account disaster awareness, while deciding data center placement prompted to focus on these issues. Estimate of number of data centers in the world is in the range of half-million and this is rising. This will and does pose a huge problem related to energy sustainability as mostly traditional energy sources, such as coal, oil, and other non-renewable resources are used to power data centers, which leads to spending of a limited resource and huge CO$_2$ penalties. In an ideal world, data centers should be placed in such a manner that, there should be no data loss or service disruption, costs incurred are minimum possible amounts, latency is minimized and it operates in a "green" way, i.e., minimal CO$_2$ emissions and runs on green energy. This is not possible in our real world scenarios, as all of the desired factors are competing in nature and optimizing one leads to determent of others.

In this paper, we propose a data center and service placement problem that is aware of CO_2 emissions and content loss due to disaster(s). More specifically, it selects the locations for setting up data centers from given set of viable locations, such that factors such as cost, CO_2 emissions, content loss are optimized. The objective is to minimize the total cost which includes operational and setup cost of data center, and penalty associated with CO_2 emissions and expected content loss. However, it is not possible to optimize all of the above factors simultaneously, as all of the desired factors are competing in nature and optimizing one leads to determent of others. Thus, we formulated it as a multi-objective optimization problem.

This paper is organized into various sections, first of which is Introduction. Literature survey on the data center placement is presented in Sect. 2. After that, we formulate our problem in Sect. 3. In Sect. 4, we discuss the results that are obtained after solving the problem using CPLEX optimization studio. The last and final section concludes the paper.

2   Related Work

The data center placement problem has its origin in operation research and there also exists thorough work on it. A disaster aware data center placement iss formulated as an integer linear program (ILP) in [4]. The authors defined a metric representing risk that takes into account expected content loss of a data center, in case it is struck by a disaster. Risk is defined as a linear combination of reachability loss and unavailability in the event of a disaster. The objective is to minimize the summation of product of risk involved with a particular disaster and probability of occurrence of that particular disaster over all candidate locations, content, nodes and probable list of disasters. A disaster resilient design of cloud network that maintains backups of virtual machines (VMs) on different physical data center locations is proposed in [5]. The problem is modeled as a distribution of primary and backup servers for a particular network topology with the intended goal of ensuring that backups do not fail at the same time as that of primaries. The objective is to jointly maximize primary servers included and minimize the number of backup servers required to run the dynamic backup service used.

The problem of minimizing the cost of data center placement along with capacity provisioning is considered in [6,7]. However, the dynamic nature of requests that come from users is not taken into account while modeling the problem, because of which they cannot be applied in real life scenarios. The routing of requests and resource allocation scheme depends on the placement of the data centers and the performance (in terms of Quality of Service) of a data center placement scheme depends on the routing of requests. Because of this interdependency, both the problems need to be looked upon simultaneously. The problem of data center and service placement along with capacity provisioning and the request flow control considering the dynamic nature of requests is presented in [8]. For considering the dynamic nature of requests, the authors

Table 1. List of variables used in the formulation

Variable	Meaning
x_d	A binary variable which is 1 if data center is placed at location $d \in D$; 0 otherwise
y_c^d	A binary variable which is 1 if software component $c \in C$ is placed at data center $d \in D$; 0 otherwise
s_d	Number of servers required in data center $d \in D$
n_d	Number of network switches required in data center $d \in D$
w_d	IT equipments average power consumption in data center $d \in D$

divided the whole day into different time slots and considered request generation rate in that time slot for each user. The problem is formulated as a mixed integer linear program (MILP) with objective to minimize the overall cost.

A renewable energy aware data center placement problem is proposed in [10] that maximizes consumption of renewable energy by placing data centers at appropriate location among given data center candidate location. Energy expenditure due to both running a data center (DC) itself and VM migration from one DC to another is taken into account. Both operational expenditure (OPEX) and capital expenditure (CAPEX) is considered along with availability of renewable energy. The problem is modeled as an mixed integer linear programming (MIP) with an objective to minimize both non-renewable energy consumption and number of data centers, while also making sure that constraints related to maximum network latency and minimal network availability are also satisfied. The problem of minimizing the cost of data center placement without compromising on QoS is proposed in [9]. Issue of CO$_2$ penalty is taken into account. Factors such as energy cost, server cost, capital and operational expenditure is taken into account while determining the total cost. They have also taken into account the CO$_2$ emissions. The problem is modeled as a mixed integer linear program.

Different from the aforementioned works, in this paper we propose a data center and service placement problem that is aware of both CO$_2$ emissions and content loss due to disaster(s). The objective is to minimize the total cost which includes operational and setup cost of data center, and penalty associated with CO$_2$ emissions and expected content loss.

3   Problem Formulation

The network is represented by a graph $G^N(V^N, E^N)$ where V^N is the set of potential data center locations and access nodes and E^N is the set of paths between data centers and source nodes. We denote the set of potential data center locations and set of access or source nodes from where services are accessed with $D(\in V^N)$ and $S(\in V^N)$ respectively. Let C be the set of software components which needs to be hosted on cloud network. We denote the expected content loss

Table 2. List of parameters used in the formulation

Parameter	Meaning
V^N	Set of potential data center locations and access nodes
$D \in V^N$	Set of potential data center locations
$S \in V^N$	Set of access or source nodes from where services are accessed
E^N	Set of paths between data centers, and source nodes
E_{sd}	Set of link disjoint paths between source node $s \in S$ and destination node $d \in D$
C	Set of software components which needs to be hosted on cloud network
L_c	Expected content loss of software component $c \in C$
m_c^1	Replicas of component $c \in C$ to be placed on cloud
m_d^2	Maximum number of machines(servers + switches) that can be accommodated in data center $d \in D$
m^3	Maximum number of servers that a LAN switch can connect
e^1	Power consumption of a network switch
e_d^2	Maximum power available at data center $d \in D$
e_d^3	Power Usage effectiveness of data center $d \in D$
e_d^4	CO_2 emissions in data center $d \in D$
e_c^5	Software component $c \in C$ replica average power consumption
e_c^6	Software component $c \in C$ replica peak power consumption
B	Set of disaster events
X_d^b	A binary value which is 1 when the data center $d \in D$ is damaged because of disaster event $b \in B$; 0 otherwise
Y_{kds}^b	A binary value which is 1 when the route $k \in E_{sd}$ between source node $s \in S$ and data center $d \in D$ is damaged because of disaster event $b \in B$; 0 otherwise
P_{ds}^b	Probability of data center $d \in D$ being unavailable or unreachable from access node $s \in S$ because of disastrous event $b \in B$
P_d^b	Probability of data center $d \in D$ being unavailable because of disastrous event $b \in B$
P_{kds}^b	Probability of the route $k \in E_{sd}$ between source node $s \in S$ and data center $d \in D$ being damaged because of disastrous event $b \in B$; 0 otherwise
D_s^c	A binary value which is 1 if source node $s \in S$ requests from software component $c \in C$
p^1	Network switch cost
p^2	Server cost
p_d^3	CAPEX of data center $d \in D$
p_d^4	OPEX of data center $d \in D$
p_d^5	Cost of a electricity unit in data center $d \in D$
p_d^6	CO_2 penalty
p_c^7:	Content loss penalty for software component $c \in C$

of software component $c \in C$ with L_c. Furthermore, we denote the set of link disjoint paths between source node $s \in S$ and destination node $d \in D$ with E_{sd}.

The set of variables and parameters used in the formulation are presented in Tables 1 and 2 respectively.

3.1   Objective Function

Given a network topology of available data center location candidates with known setup and operation costs for them, a set of services, and a set of possible disaster zones with given damage probabilities, the goal is to assign DCs and services to the candidate locations such that total cost is minimized. We considered two types of costs known as direct and indirect cost.

$$\min z = \min\{c^D + c^I\} \tag{1}$$

where c^D is the direct cost which includes network switch costs, server costs, setup and operational cost of data center, and energy cost. c^I is the indirect cost which includes the penalty associated with CO_2 emissions (6) and expected content Loss (7).

$$c^D = c^C + c^O \tag{2}$$

$$c^I = c^{CO_2} + c^{Loss} \tag{3}$$

$$c^C = \sum_{d \in D} p^1 n_d + \sum_{d \in D} p^2 s_d + \sum_{d \in D} p_d^3 x_d \tag{4}$$

$$c^O = \sum_{d \in D} p_d^4 x_d + \sum_{d \in D} p_d^5 (w_d \cdot 365 \cdot 24 \cdot 10^{-6}) e_d^4 \tag{5}$$

$$c^{CO_2} = \sum_{d \in D} p_d^6 (e_d^5 \cdot 10^{-6})(w_d \cdot 365 \cdot 24 \cdot 10^{-3}) e_d^4 \tag{6}$$

$$c^{Loss} = \sum_{c \in C} \sum_{b \in B} \sum_{s \in S} \sum_{d \in D} p_c^7 (L_c \cdot J_{dcs}^b \cdot P_{ds}^b) \tag{7}$$

Here c^C and c^O are the capital and operational expenditure of the data centers. The first term on the right hand side of (4) is the cost incurred by the LAN switches, routers and links between data centers. The second term on the right hand side of (4) is the cost of servers installed across all the data centers. The right most term of (4) is the cost incurred in setting up a data center which requires infrastructure for keeping servers, cooling system and internal network between servers. The first term on the right hand side of (5) is the operational cost of data center which includes cost of manpower, and other stuff required for the maintenance of data center. The right most term of (5) is the cost of total energy consumed across all the data centers. It is calculated by summing up the average power consumption across all the data centers. The power consumed by non IT equipments such as cooling system is calculated using Power Usage Effectiveness (PUE) of the data centers. The cost factor associated with unit amount of CO_2 emission is c^{CO_2}. Overall CO_2 emission is calculated from the total power consumption by the data center. The penalty associated with the content loss is c^{Loss}. Total cost is calculated by taking weighted sum of all these costs. The weights can be assigned according to the user's priority. Therefore, the objective is to minimize the weighted sum of all these costs.

$$\min z = \min\{\alpha c^S + \beta c^O + \gamma c^{CO_2} + \delta c^{Loss}\} \tag{8}$$

3.2 Constraints

$$\sum_{d \in D} y_c^d = 1 \quad \forall c \in C \tag{9}$$

$$y_c^d \leq x_d \quad \forall c \in C, \quad \forall d \in D \tag{10}$$

$$s_d = \sum_{c \in C} m_c^1 y_c^d \quad \forall d \in D \tag{11}$$

$$m^3 n_d \geq s_d \quad \forall d \in D \tag{12}$$

$$s_d + n_d \leq m_d^2 \tag{13}$$

$$w_d = e^1 n_d + \sum_{c \in C} e_c^5 m_c^1 y_c^d \quad \forall d \in D \tag{14}$$

$$e^1 n_d + \sum_{c \in C} e_c^6 m_c^1 y_c^d \leq e_d^2 \quad \forall d \in D \tag{15}$$

$$x_d \in \{0, 1\} \quad \forall d \in D \tag{16}$$

$$y_c^d \in \{0, 1\} \quad \forall d \in D, \forall c \in C \tag{17}$$

$$s_d \in W \quad \forall d \in D \tag{18}$$

$$n_d \in W \quad \forall d \in D \tag{19}$$

$$w_d \in \mathbb{R}_{\geq 0} \quad \forall d \in D \tag{20}$$

Constraint (9) and (10) together guarantees that every software component is mapped to exactly one data center that is active (opened). Constraint (11) ensures that the total number of servers in a data center is exactly equal to the number of software components that are mapped to it. Constraint (12) guarantees that, for every data center $d \in D$, the total number of switch ports is greater than or equal to the number of servers required in the data center. Constraint (13) ensures that, for every data center $d \in D$, the sum of number of switches and servers is less than or equal to the maximum number of machines(servers + switches) that can be accommodated in the data center. The average power consumption of a data center is determined by (15). The sum of power consumed by the all the network switches in a data center and software components that are placed in the data center must be less than the peak power consumption of the data center, which is ensured by (15). Constraints (16)–(20) ensures that the decision variables takes values from the respective domain.

4 Simulation Results

We evaluated our proposed formulation on a hypothetical graph of cloud network. The graph consisted of 20 nodes with 5 source nodes and rest are viable data centers. The data center capacity is decided such that all should be of different sizes. The capacities are randomly generated between 2 to 20. The maximum power capacity of data centers' is set to a random value between 10 kW to 100 kW keeping in mind the increasing sizes of data centers. The power usage effectiveness(PUE) is set to 1.08. Electricity charges of all data centers are different and generated randomly between 20 to 80. Setup and operational costs of all data centers are set to same value which are 12/year and 0.24/year respectively. Network switch cost and server cost is set to 1000/unit. Maximum number of servers that can be connected through a LAN switch is set to 10. Power consumption of such a network switch is set to 400W. CO_2 emissions is measured in g/kWh for each data center and are randomly generated between 30 to 200.

Number of software components to be hosted on network are varied from 5 to 30. The number of replicas of each component are randomly generated between 2 to 6. Average power consumption of each software components is generated between 70 to 150. Peak power consumption of each software components is set to a random value between 150 and 300. The importance metric of each software components are a random value between 3 and 7. CO_2 penalty and Content loss penalty per unit are set to 200 and 500 respectively. We generated the integer linear programming input file using MATLAB [11] and solved it using the CPLEX tool [12]. Each of the instance is executed for 10 different times and the average over all iterations are presented in the graphs.

The effect of number of software components on the setup and operational expenditure is presented in Fig. 1. We altered services/software components to be placed, such that service placement approach need to be altered. The most fundamental observation is that, the setup and operational expenditures tend to increase with the number of software components. This can be explained, simply owing to the fact that our placement approach needs to assign each of the software component to some data center and this increases the setup and operational costs.

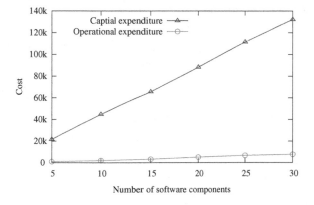

Fig. 1. Effect of the number of software components on the setup and operational cost

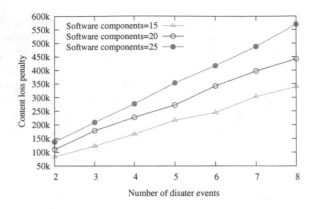

Fig. 2. Effect of the number of disaster events on the content loss penalty

The effect of number of disaster events on the content loss penalty is presented in Fig. 2. The number of disaster events are varied from 2 to 8. We can observe that, for a given number of software components, the content loss penalty tend to increase with the number of disaster events. This can be explained, simply owing to the fact that there are high chances of content loss when the number of disaster events are more. We can also observe that the for a given number of disaster events, the content loss penalty tend to increase with the number of software components.

The effect of number of disaster events on the total cost is presented in Fig. 3. We varied the number of disaster events from 2 to 8. We can observe that, for a given number of software components, the total cost incurred tend to increase with the number of disaster events. This can be attributed to the fact that the content loss penalty increases with the number of disaster events and the total cost itself is a function of content loss penalty. We can also observe that the for a given number of disaster events, the total cost incurred tend to increase with the number of software components.

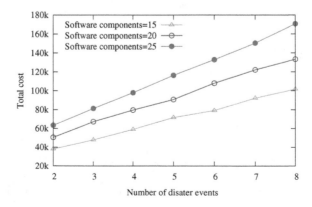

Fig. 3. Effect of the number of disaster events on the total cost

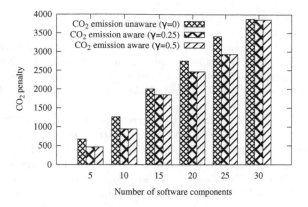

Fig. 4. Effect of CO_2 awareness on the CO_2 penalty

The effect of CO_2 awareness on the CO_2 penalty is shown in Fig. 4. We varied the number of software components from 5 to 30. We can observe that, for a given number of software components, CO_2 penalty of the CO_2 aware placement is less compared to the CO_2 unaware placement. We can also observe that the CO_2 penalty increases with the number of software components.

5   Conclusion

In this paper, we proposed a data center and service placement problem that is aware of CO_2 emissions and content loss due to disaster(s). The objective is to minimize the total cost which includes operational and setup cost of data center, and penalty associated with CO_2 emissions and expected content loss. We formulated it as an mixed integer linear program. Results show that the total cost incurred tend to increase with the number of disaster events and the setup and operational expenditures tend to increase with the number of software components. Furthermore, results also show that, for a given number of software components, CO_2 penalty of the CO_2 aware placement is less compared to the CO_2 unaware placement.

References

1. Habib, M.F., et al.: Design of disaster-resilient optical datacenter networks. J. Lightwave Technol. **30**(16), 2563–2573 (2012)
2. Dikbiyik, F., et al.: Minimizing the disaster risk in optical telecom networks. In: Optical Fiber Communication Conference and Exposition (OFC/NFOEC), pp. 1–3 (2012)
3. http://www.datacenterknowledge.com/archives/2013/01/15/amazon-toadd-capa city-to-us-east-region/
4. Ferdousi, S., et al.: Disaster-aware data-center and content placement in cloud networks. In: IEEE International Conference on Advanced Networks and Telecommuncations Systems (ANTS), pp. 1–3 (2013)

5. Couto, R.S.: Server placement with shared backups for disaster-resilient clouds. Comput. Netw. **93**(3), 423–434 (2015)
6. Greenberg, A., et al.: The cost of a cloud: research problems in data center networks. ACM SIGCOMM Comput. Commun. Rev. **39**(1), 68–73 (2008)
7. Le, K., et al.: Intelligent placement of datacenters for internet services. In: 31st International Conference on Distributed Computing Systems (ICDCS), pp. 131–142 (2011)
8. Chen, S., Wang, Y., Pedram, M.: Concurrent placement, capacity provisioning, request flow control for a distributed cloud infrastructure. In: Design, Automation, Test in Europe Conference, Exhibition (DATE), pp. 1–6 (2011)
9. Yu, W., et al.: Renewable-energy-aware data center placement in optical cloud networks. In: Optical Fiber Communication Conference, pp. 1–3 (2015)
10. Larumbe, F., Sanso, B.: A tabu search algorithm for the location of data centers and software components in green cloud computing networks. IEEE Trans. Cloud Comput. **1**(1), 22–35 (2013)
11. MATLAB version 8.5.0.197613 (R2015a). The Mathworks Inc., Natick, Massachusetts (2015)
12. IBM ILOG CPLEX. http://www-01.ibm.com/software/integration/optimization/cplex-optimizer

Virtual Machines

PMM: A Novel Prediction Based VM Migration Scheme in Cloud Computing

Srimoyee Bhattacherjee[1]($\boxtimes$), Uttiya Sarkar[2], Sunirmal Khatua[2],
and Sarbani Roy[1]

[1] Department of Computer Science and Engineering,
Jadavpur University, Kolkata, India
b.srimoyee@gmail.com, sarbani.roy@cse.jdvu.ac.in
[2] Department of Computer Science and Engineering,
University of Calcutta, Kolkata, India
sarkar.uttiya@yahoo.com, skhatuacomp@caluniv.ac.in

Abstract. Massive technological advancements has promoted rise in energy costs, cloud computing being one of the key contributors. The cloud datacenters consume huge amount of energy which lead to carbon emissions, detrimental for our environment. Design of resource scheduling, load balancing and migration schemes for virtual machines (VM) in the cloud environment is one of the ways by which energy consumption can be minimized. This work proposes a prediction based VM migration approach (PMM) and explores how the proposed approach can affect the total energy consumption of a datacenter; with the aim to make the technology more environment friendly. PMM has been designed keeping the concept of the well-known Markov chain model in mind. Substantial amount of simulation has been conducted in this work to conclude how a prediction based resource management technique can play vital role in influencing the energy consumption of a cloud datacenter, in comparison to the existing and popular minimization of migrations (MM) policy.

Keywords: Cloud · Datacenter · Energy consumption · Migration · Prediction · History data

1 Introduction

Over the past decade, a new branch of distributed computing has made its way into the world of computing, more commonly known as cloud computing. It has taken computing to different heights through the variety of services it can provide to its consumers. The users can reap benefits out of this technology without having any profound knowledge about it. The various benefits that a cloud user (an individual or a business) might get are flexibility, security, capacity and reduction of cost. With such enormous advantages, cloud computing is now a boom. IT giants like Google, Amazon, IBM, Microsoft, to name only a few, have been providing cloud services to its customers which have been widely accepted.

© Springer International Publishing AG 2017
P. Krishnan et al. (Eds.): ICDCIT 2017, LNCS 10109, pp. 107–117, 2017.
DOI: 10.1007/978-3-319-50472-8_9

The sharp rise in the usage of the cloud services has led to rise in energy consumption. The large number of datacenters that have been built all over the world by the cloud service providers has been continuously contributing to the increasing energy costs. The research community has been found to be concerned about the energy use of these datacenters, along with the allied emission of greenhouse gases and other air pollutants. The energy required by these datacenters accounts to 1–2% of the total global energy use, which is quite alarming. A report by NRDC [1] states that datacenters are one of the nation's largest and fastest-growing populations of consumers of electricity. It was observed in 2013 that the amount of electricity consumed by around 3 million computer rooms was enough to power all the households in New York City for two years. This is almost equal to the yearly output of 34 large coal-fired power plants. According to the report published by the Lawrence Berkeley National Laboratory, the power consumption of datacenters has become twice between 2000 and 2005. It now contributes to around 1.2% of American electricity consumption [2,3]. Greenpeace [4] has talked about analogous scenarios and has also pointed out that the growth rate of energy consumed by datacenters is 12% every year. Though cloud computing is referred as the new, green model for our IT infrastructure needs, there are barely any companies providing data that can be used to verify and validate such claims. Hence the energy issue in cloud computing should be taken care of immediately. The main contribution of this work is the design of a prediction based VM migration scheme using Markov chain model which reduces total energy consumption of the cloud environment.

The flow of this paper is as follows: Sect. 2 presents a brief overview of existing works in this domain, Sect. 3 formulates the prediction based VM migration scheme (PMM). The results and their corresponding discussions have been made in Sect. 4. Section 5 concludes this work, while giving a future direction to the same.

2   Related Work

Currently, a lot of research is being conducted addressing the energy saving issues and building an energy efficient cloud network has become of utmost importance to the research community due to the adverse effect of the carbon emissions on our environment. This inclination towards building a green cloud network is obvious from the several research works that are being carried out in this domain. It has been shown in [5] that energy can be reduced by consolidation of VMs based on current utilizations along with QoS maintenance. Efficient migration techniques are required to reduce energy in this method. In [6], it has been again discussed how efficient VM migration and dynamic VM consolidation methods have been able to reduce energy consumption significantly. An efficient resource management technique for virtualized Cloud datacenters has been proposed by the researchers in [7]. Their goal is continuous VM consolidation that influences live migration and switches off idle nodes which leads to reduced power consumption, while providing required Quality of Service. A similar approach in minimizing energy consumption of a cloud datacenter has been noted in [8]. Two energy-aware task consolidation heuristics which showcase their energy saving capabilities has been presented in [9]. These heuristics have maximized resource utilization by considering both active and idle energy consumptions. The various VM consolidation strategies and their effect in energy consumption along with the process of live migration have been explored in [10]. In [11], power and energy models along with energy efficient VM placement and migration policies (discussed in detail in Sect. 3) have been proposed. While most of the existing researches have proposed different heuristics to reduce energy consumption in a cloud environment, [12] has developed a linear integer program to design an exact allocation algorithm teamed with an efficient exact VM migration algorithm. The algorithms in [12] have been able to perform better when compared to best fit heuristic.

The above discussion clearly points out how VM consolidation and migration can be beneficial in saving energy in cloud computing and how this domain of research has gained considerable amount of popularity. Unlike existing works where VM migrations are initiated as soon as SLA (in terms of availability and Quality of Service) is violated, PMM policy takes such decisions if SLA is violated currently and also in the future, estimated from the predictions, thereby minimizing the number of VM migrations and making an accurate migration decision.

3   Formulation of the Proposed Prediction Based VM Migration Scheme

3.1   Background

This work chiefly deals with designing an energy aware prediction based VM migration policy for migrating VMs amongst hosts, when required. Exhaustive literature survey helped in identifying that Beloglazov et al. have presented energy efficient VM placement and VM migration policies in [11]. The Modified Best Fit Decreasing (MBFD) algorithm in [11] proposes an energy efficient virtual machine placement algorithm on physical machines in a cloud environment. The well-known bin packing problem has been used to form the MBFD algorithm. MBFD finds out upon placement on which host, a particular VM consumes least energy among all the available hosts and allocates it accordingly. To calculate the power ($P(u)$) and energy (E) consumed by a host, MBFD uses the Eqs. 1 and 2 respectively.

$$P(u) = k * P_{max} + (1 - k) * P_{max} * u \tag{1}$$

and,

$$E = \int_t P(u(t)) \tag{2}$$

where, a fully utilized server consumes a maximum power P_{max}, an inactive server consumes a fraction of P_{max} denoted by k and u is the CPU utilization. $u(t)$ stands for CPU utilization which is a function of time. Energy E is calculated by integrating the power function over time t. Three different threshold based migration techniques namely, the Minimization of Migrations policy (MM), the Highest Potential Growth policy (HPG) and the Random Choice policy (RC) have been proposed in [11]. Of these three policies, the MM policy gives the best performance i.e. generates least amount of energy. It selects the minimum number of VMs needed to migrate from a host to lower the CPU utilization below the upper utilization threshold if the upper threshold is violated. In case the lower threshold is violated, all the VMs from the host are migrated to other available hosts, turning off the underutilized host which saves energy. The reallocation of VMs is done using MBFD algorithm. In this work, we have applied prediction on the existing MM policy to make the migration policy more energy efficient.

3.2   Markov Chain Based Prediction: The Theory Behind PMM

A Markov Chain is a process in which the outcome of a given experiment can affect the outcome of the next experiment.

Let there be a set of states, $S = s_1, s_2 \ldots \ldots, s_r$. Any process can start from any of these states and can move to any other state, each move being referred to as a step. The transition probability p_{ij} is defined as the probability of transition from s_i to s_j in a chain and it does not depend on the previous states of the chain. The starting state is specified by an initial probability distribution, defined on S. This is usually done by denoting a particular state as the starting state. If a Markov chain has r states, then,

$$p_{ij}^2 = \Sigma_{k=1}^r p_{ik} p_{kj} \tag{3}$$

If P is the transition matrix of a Markov chain, the ij-th entry $p_{ij}(n)$ of the matrix P_n gives the probability that the Markov chain, starting in state s_i, will be in state s_j after n steps.

In MM Policy [11], when a host's utilization exceeds the upper threshold specified, one or more VMs (with minimum utilization) whose migration would reduce the host's utilization below the upper threshold, are migrated and placed on one or more hosts where they consume least power (based on MBFD algorithm). It is also checked that the target hosts' utilizations do not exceed the upper threshold on placement of the incoming VMs. Similarly, if a host's utilization comes below the specified lower threshold, all the constituent VMs are migrated to suitable hosts (based on MBFD algorithm) and the concerned host is turned off. Thus in MM policy, migration takes place each and every time the upper and lower thresholds get violated.

Prediction has been used in this work to minimize the number of VM migrations, in case of upper threshold violation i.e. one or more VMs will not be migrated as soon as upper threshold is violated. Based on past behavior of the host and its constituent VMs, it will be predicted whether the upper threshold will be violated in the near future. If yes, migration will be initiated, otherwise not. This minimizes the number of migrations which eventually lead to energy savings. Here, using Markov chain model, many states are defined based on the VMs' utilizations. Based on past behavior, a state transition matrix is constructed (Fig. 1). Each entry in the state transition matrix denotes the probability of transition from one state to the other. From the transition matrix, it can be found out to which state the current state might reach. Based on the prediction, migration decisions will be taken. Hence, Markov chain model has been appropriate in modeling this problem.

3.3 Proposed Algorithm: PMM

The minimum number of VMs required to migrate from a host to lower the CPU utilization below the upper utilization threshold if the upper threshold gets violated presently and is also found to be violated in the future time frame based on predicted VM utilization values is selected by the prediction based minimization of migrations (PMM) policy.

Let V_j be a set of VMs currently allocated to the host j. Then $P(V_j)$ is the power set of V_j. The policy finds a set $R \in P(V_j)$ defined in 4.

Algorithm 1. Prediction based Minimization of Migrations (PMM)

INPUT: host, upperThreshold, NoOfStates (denoted by n), windowSize(denoted by w), Simulator specific interval after which host utilization to be predicted(denoted by i)

OUTPUT: Migration decision (denoted by isMigrated)

1: **for each** vm $\in$ host.vmList **do**
2:     vm.isMigrated $\leftarrow$ false
3:     vm.UtilHistory $\leftarrow$ getVmutilization
4:     $S_c \leftarrow$ buildStateMatrix (vm.PresentUtil, n)
5:     T$\leftarrow$ buildTransitionMatrix
6:     SetTimer(w)
7:     **while** Timer() **do**
8:         nextState $\leftarrow$ NextpredictedState(T,S_c)
9:         T $\leftarrow$ UpdateTransMatrix(T,nextState)
10:        host(Timer()).update(vm(Timer()))
11:        host.nextState()
12:    **end while**
13: **end for**
14: isMigrated $\leftarrow$ host.isMigrated(w,i)
15: **return** isMigrated

$$
R = \begin{cases}
\{s | s \in P(V_j), \\
\quad U_j - \sum U_a(V) < UpperThreshold, |s| \rightarrow min\}, & \text{if } U_j < UpperThreshold \\
& \text{and} \\
& U_j(predicted) > UpperThreshold \\
& \text{for atleast } w/(i*2) \text{ cases;} \\
V_j, & \text{if } U_j < LowerThreshold; \\
\phi, & \text{Otherwise.}
\end{cases}
\tag{4}
$$

Where U_j is the current CPU utilization of the host j; and $U_a(V)$ is the fraction of the CPU utilization allocated to the VM V. w and i are the window size and Simulator defined interval respectively. The pseudo code for PMM policy is presented in Algorithm 1 which determines whether to migrate a VM from an over utilized host or not.

3.4   An Example Showing the Creation and Updation of Transition Matrix in PMM

A state diagram has been presented here and updation will be done on the basis of history data and prediction model. Let us consider a state transition sequence $s_1 s_2 s_2 s_3 s_1 s_3 s_3 s_1 s_2 s_3 s_2 s_2 s_3 s_1 s_3 s_3$. Figures 1 and 2 represent initial and updated transition matrices respectively.

Let us assume that the current state is s_3. Now, the TM will be updated in a manner such that all the numerator values are incremented by $1/(n-1)$, except current position of that row. All the denominator values of s_3's row are increased by 1 to create the next transition matrix.

Figures 3 and 4 represent the initial and updated state diagrams.

$$
TM = \begin{bmatrix} 0 & 1/2 & 1/2 \\ 0 & 1/2 & 1/2 \\ 1/2 & 1/6 & 1/3 \end{bmatrix}
\qquad
TM = \begin{bmatrix} 0 & 1/2 & 1/2 \\ 0 & 1/2 & 1/2 \\ 3/7 & 1.5/7 & 2.5/7 \end{bmatrix}
$$

Fig. 1. Initial transition matrix   **Fig. 2.** Updated transition matrix

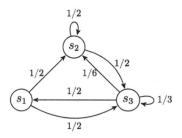

Fig. 3. Initial state diagram

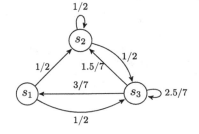

Fig. 4. Updated state diagram

4 Results and Discussions

We have implemented the above mentioned policy in *CloudSim 3.0.3* toolkit concatenated with *eclipse*. Here we have simulated a datacenter which has 800 hosts and n number of VMs are to be allocated among the hosts. The number of VMs depends on the PlanetLab workload file used for simulation. Each host has 1 CPU core with performance equivalent to 1000, 2000 or 3000 MIPS, 8 GB RAM, and 1 TB storage capacity. Each VM has 1 CPU core with 250, 500, 750 or 1000 MIPS, 128 MB RAM and 1 GB storage. The hosts are homogeneous in nature and follow the power model as mentioned in Eq. (1), where maximum power P_{max} is taken to be 250 W.

Case I (PMM_{sw_1}): Every time the upper threshold gets violated, instead of immediately migrating one or more VMs as in MM policy in [11], the future behavior of the constituent VMs of the host will be predicted based on previous behavior (for a time period of 1 h). Within this time period (1 h), if upper threshold gets violated, migration will be immediately initiated. After this time period (1 h) is over, in case of upper threshold violation, Algorithm 1 will be applied. When $CurrentTime > slidingWindowSize$ (12 h), the sliding window will slide forward in such a way so that the size of the *slidingWindow* remains unchanged, i.e. to create a Transition matrix, the distance between the starting point of the history data of a VM and the current position is always the size of the Sliding Window. Based on the history data, the constituent VMs' utilizations will be predicted for a certain time frame (say, 15 min, 30 min or 1 h). If within that time frame, the host's utilization, based on its constituent VMs' utilizations, violates the upper threshold for 50% or more times, migration will be initiated. This will be done using Algorithm 1 after creating state and transition matrices Here, we have taken the *slidingWindowSize* to be 12 h as Cloudsim 3.0.3 operates on a basis of 24 h and to get large data set, the history data is formed based on 12 h behavior.

Case II (PMM_{sw_12}): In this case, the future behavior of the constituent VMs of the host will be predicted based on previous behavior (for a time period of 12 h). Within this time period (12 h), if upper threshold gets violated, migration will be immediately initiated. After this time period (12 h) is over, the approach will be similar to that of case 1 and migration decisions will be taken accordingly.

Case III (PMM_{no_sw}): In this case, the concept of sliding window is not used. As done in case 1, the future behavior of the constituent VMs of the host will be predicted based on previous behavior (for a time period of 1 h). Within this time period of 1 h, if upper threshold gets violated, migration will be immediately initiated. But after 1 h, if at any time instance a host's utilization exceeds the upper threshold, based on the history data, the constituent VMs' utilizations will be predicted for a certain time frame (say, 15 min, 30 min or 1 h). If within that time frame, the host's utilization, based on its constituent VMs' utilizations, violates the upper threshold for 50% or more times, migration will be initiated. This will be done using Algorithm 1 after creating state and transition matrices.

The future predictions, every time the upper threshold gets violated, will be done based on the updated matrices followed by again updating them based on migration decisions. This is done over the entire time period i.e. 24 h. Hence as time progresses, the prediction becomes more accurate due to large history data set.

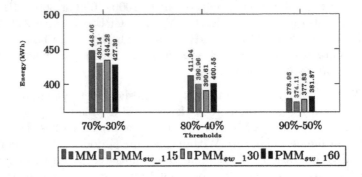

Fig. 5. Comparative analysis of energy consumption for MM and PMM$_{sw\_1}$ (with sliding window) policies at different thresholds for workload W

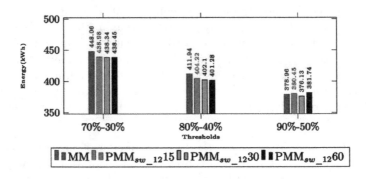

Fig. 6. Comparative analysis of energy consumption for MM and PMMsw_12 (with sliding window) policies at different thresholds for workload W

From Figs. 5, 6 and 7, it is clearly visible that all the variations of PMM generates less energy than MM in maximum of the cases. But from Fig. 7, it can be concluded that PMM$_{no\_sw}$ when applied, always reduce energy consumption of the cloud network when compared to existing MM. But there are cases in PMM$_{sw\_1}$ and PMM$_{sw\_12}$ where they do not always yield better result than MM. In case of PMM$_{sw\_1}$ and PMM$_{sw\_12}$, the size of the history data set is small in comparison to PMM$_{no\_sw}$ which might lead to inaccurate predictions and hence energy consumption gets increased in few cases.

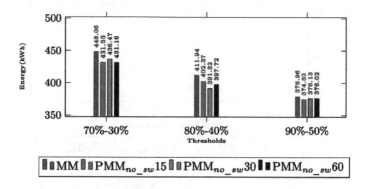

Fig. 7. Comparative analysis of energy consumption for MM and PMM$_{no\_sw}$ (without sliding window) policies at different thresholds for workload W

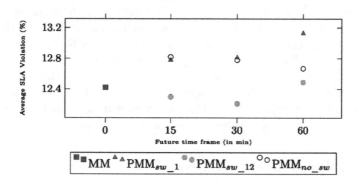

Fig. 8. Comparative analysis of average SLA violation for MM and PMM policies for (70%–30%) for workload W

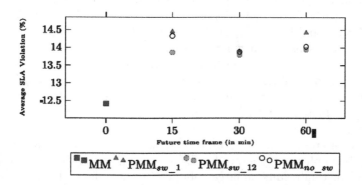

Fig. 9. Comparative analysis of average SLA violation for MM and PMM policies for (80%–40%) for workload W

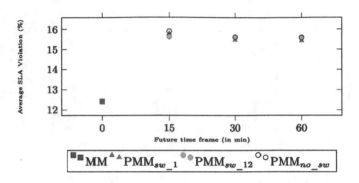

Fig. 10. Comparative analysis of average SLA violation for MM and PMM policies for (90%–50%) for workload W

Figures 8, 9 and 10 represent the average SLA violations of the different policies. It is clearly shown that though PMM policies reduce the energy consumption over MM policy, the SLA violations are increased. But the deviations of the SLA violations are in the range of 6 to 25%, which is acceptable. So the PMM policies can afford to pay penalty due to increasing SLA violations for reaching the broader goal of reducing energy consumption of the datacenters.

To reach the above conclusion about the nature of the results, simulations have been carried out with multiple PlanetLab workloads available in *Cloudsim 3.0.3* and the nature of the results have come out to be similar.

5   Conclusion and Future Scope

The detailed study and implementation of the allocation and migration policies for VMs could show us how efficient resource management strategies could lead to reduction of energy consumption in a cloud computing environment.

The proposed PMM policy takes migration decisions based on history data generated from the VMs' behavior in the near past. Again, the history data set for PMM_{sw_1} and PMM_{sw_12} is always generated depending on the behavior of the VMs in the past 12 h whereas PMM_{no_sw}'s history data set gradually becomes large. This is the reason why PMM_{sw_1} and PMM_{sw_12} policies fail to perform as desired in all the cases. However, the proposed algorithm PMM have been implemented on a homogeneous host environment. The efficacy of the same will also be evaluated in future by implementing PMM on a heterogeneous set of hosts.

To make the results more accurate and save more energy, learning mechanisms may be applied to generate history data for long durations (1–6 month). Based on prediction results on large volume of history data, the migration decision can be taken which will be more accurate and energy efficient.

The proposed PMM policy is a greedy approach that follows the problem solving heuristic to find out the optimum solution for allocation and migration of VMs at each stage. Hence, the methods discussed to minimize total energy consumption are not optimal. To get the optimal solution, this work can be further extended to formulate and solve an IPP(Integer Programming Problem) that will minimize the total energy consumption while providing the required Quality of Service and also take exact VM allocation and migration decisions.

Acknowledgements. The research of the first author is supported by DST - Inspire Fellowship vide Reference No. DST/INSPIRE Fellowship/IF140873.

References

1. Delforge, P., Whitney, J.: Scaling up energy efficiency across the data center industry: evaluating key drivers and barriers. NRDC 1–35 (2014). https://www.nrdc.org/sites/default/files/data-center-efficiency-assessment-IP.pdf
2. Beloglazov, A., Buyya, R., Lee, Y.C., Zomaya, A.: A taxonomy and survey of energy-efficient data centers and cloud computing systems. Adv. Comput. **82**(2), 47–111 (2011)
3. Barroso, L.: The price of performance. ACM Queue **3**(7), 53 (2005)
4. Cook, G., Horn, J.V.: How dirty is your data? A look at the energy choices that power cloud computing. Greenpeace Int. 1–36 (2011). http://www.greenpeace.org/international/Global/international/publications/climate/2011/Cool%20IT/dirty-data-report-greenpeace.pdf
5. Beloglazov, A., Buyya, R.: Energy efficient resource management in virtualized cloud data centers. In: Proceedings of the 2010 10th IEEE/ACM International Conference on Cluster, Cloud and Grid Computing, pp. 826–831 (2010)
6. Beloglazov, A., Buyya, R.: Optimal online deterministic algorithms and adaptive heuristics for energy and performance efficient dynamic consolidation of virtual machines in cloud datacenters. Concurr. Comput.: Pract. Exp. **24**(13), 1397–1420 (2012)
7. Beloglazov, A., Buyya, R.: Energy efficient allocation of virtual machines in cloud data centers. In: 2010 IEEE/ACM10th International Conference on Cluster, Cloud and Grid Computing (CCGrid), pp. 577–578 (2010)
8. Buyya, R., Beloglazov, A., Abawajy, J.: Energy-efficient management of data center resources for cloud computing: a vision, architectural elements, and open challenges. In: Proceedings of the 2010 International Conference on Parallel and Distributed Processing Techniques and Applications (2010)
9. Lee, Y.C., Zomaya, A.Y.: Energy efficient utilization of resources in cloud computing systems. J. Supercomput. **60**(2), 268–280 (2012)
10. Ye, K., Huang, D., Jiang, X., Chen, H., Wu, S.: Virtual machine based energy-efficient datacenter architecture for cloud computing: a performance perspective. In: Proceedings of the 2010 IEEE/ACM International Conference on Green Computing and Communications & International Conference on Cyber, Physical and Social Computing, pp. 171–178 (2010)
11. Beloglazov, A., Abawajy, J., Buyya, R.: Energy-aware resource allocation heuristics for efficient management of data centers for Cloud computing. Future Gener. Comput. Syst. **28**(5), 755–768 (2012)
12. Ghribi, C., Hadji, M., Zeghlache, D.: Energy efficient VM scheduling for cloud datacenters: exact allocation and migration algorithms. In: 13th IEEE/ACM International Symposium on Cluster, Cloud and Grid Computing (CCGrid), pp. 671–678 (2013)

Bid Selection for Deadline Constrained Jobs over Spot VMs in Computational Cloud

Sharmistha Mandal, Sunirmal Khatua$^{(\boxtimes)}$, and Rajib K. Das

University of Calcutta, Kolkata, India
sharmistha.cse@gmail.com, {sunirmal.khatua.in,rajib.k.das}@ieee.org

Abstract. Spot instance is an attractive pricing option to the cloud service users. But to use the spot instances, the cloud service users (CSU) have tos select an appropriate bid. The total cost of using spot instances and time to complete the user's job are both determined by the bid chosen. Thus, selection of appropriate bid for spot instances is a critical problem for the CSUs because of the unpredictable nature of spot prices. The problem is more challenging when there is a deadline constraint. The Dynamic Bidding Algorithm (DBA) was considered to be an effective approach in this field. In this paper, we show that by combining a greedy approach for bidding with effective use of checkpointing, the total cost of using spot instances can be reduced further without violating the deadline constraint. To measure the cost of our solutions and those given by DBA with the optimum we have formulated an IPP for the given problem. In formulating the IPP it is assumed that spot prices at all future times are known. Experimental results based on some actual spot and on-demand price data show that the cost of our solution is comparable to those given by IPP. It is also observed that the cost decreases as the deadline to complete the job is extended.

Keywords: Cloud computing · Spot instances · Deadline constrained job · Cost optimization · Dynamic bidding policy · Checkpointing

1 Introduction

The on-demand availability and auto scaling of computational resources make cloud computing technology the most preferable choice for deploying a large scale distributed application. The computational resources in cloud are generally offered in the form of Virtual Machines (VMs) with different CPU, memory, bandwidth etc. The VMs offered by Amazon EC2 [10], one of the most popular public cloud service provider (CSP), are called instances. The non trivial quality of service (QoS) and cost for an instance are determined by the instance type [7] and purchasing option [8]. The amount of virtual resources allocated to an instance depends on its instance type while its purchasing option decides the cost and availability of that instance. Amazon EC2 provides 55 instance types with different computing, memory and storage capabilities to fit different

© Springer International Publishing AG 2017
P. Krishnan et al. (Eds.): ICDCIT 2017, LNCS 10109, pp. 118–128, 2017.
DOI: 10.1007/978-3-319-50472-8_10

use cases. However, they provide only 3 purchasing options namely on-demand, reserved and spot. On-demand instances let one pay for compute capacity by the hour with no long-term commitments or upfront payments. Such instances are charged at high hourly rate compared to other purchasing options. One can avail significant discount on hourly charge by using reserved instances. However, reserved instances require an extra payment for one time reservation charge. On the other hand, spot instances provide the ability for customers to purchase compute capacity with no upfront payment and at a variable hourly rate.

Generally, spot instances are available at much lower cost compared to on-demand instances. This makes spot instances a lucrative option for running an application in cloud. However, since the spot price depends on demand and availability of a specific spot instance type, at some point of time one may need to pay much higher cost compared to on-demand instances. To limit such a high cost, users need to specify the upper limit (called bid) on the hourly rate of usage. When the users bid exceeds the current spot price, the requested spot instance is launched and is available until the spot price exceeds the specified bid (called out-of-bid). Clearly, spot instances are inherently unreliable in nature where the cost and reliability depend on the defined bid. Therefore, one needs to use spot instances with proper analysis of the past spot prices to determine the optimal bid. In this paper, we have discussed various bidding strategies in order to minimize the cost of running a deadline constrained job in spot instances.

The rest of the paper is organized as follows. Various characteristics of spot instances and the problem statement of this work is specified in Sect. 2. Section 3 discusses various bid selection strategies. The performance of these strategies are evaluated in Sect. 4. Some related works in the literature are presented in Sect. 5. Finally, this paper concludes with a direction of future work in Sect. 6.

2   Motivation and Problem Statement

The various characteristics of Amazon EC2 spot instances [9] that make them an important choice for cost reduction are summarized below:

1. Spot instances are available for computation as long as the spot price is below the user defined bid as shown in Fig. 1.
2. Spot instances are terminated (becomes unavailable) without any notification to the user whenever the current spot price exceeds the user's bid.
3. The price per instance-hour for a spot instance is set at the beginning of each instance-hour. Any change to the spot price will not be reflected until the next instance-hour begins.
4. The CSP will not charge the last partial hour if the spot instance is terminated due to out-of-bid situation. However it will charge the full hour if the user terminates the instance forcefully.
5. Since on-demand instances are always available, user's bid should not exceed the on-demand cost.

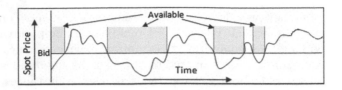

Fig. 1. Availability vs bid for spot instances

Motivated by these characteristics of spot instances, the problem addressed by this work can be stated as

Given a job, and the type of instances on which it should run, and the deadline within which the job is to be completed, determine the amount to be bid at each hour, so that the cost of completing the job is minimized.

3   Bid Selection Strategies

In this section, we discuss various strategies for selecting bids in order to minimize the cost of executing the deadline constrained jobs using spot instances. First of all, we formulate an Integer Programming Problem (IPP) to determine optimal bids. Then, we describe in brief the existing dynamic bidding strategy as proposed in [12]. Finally, we propose a novel greedy approach to determine the bids effectively.

3.1   Optimal Bidding Strategy

While attempting to get the optimal solution, we assume that the spot prices are known beforehand. One straightforward way to get at the optimal solution for a job with deadline of D hours and computation requirement of C hours is as follows:

1. Find the first minute price for each of the next D hours
2. Compute the sum of the minimum C of those prices.

Since the cost of running a job is determined by the spot price at the beginning of the hour, by selecting the bid amount to be any high value for those C hours, and a very low value for the remaining hours, one can expect to get a minimum total cost.

But this approach does not take into account that one can get computation for a fraction of an hour if a job gets out-of-bid before an hour is completed, and no cost is incurred for that computation. If spot price reaches a peak value at time t_p within an hour, by selecting a bid just smaller than the peak value one can get $t_p - 1$ amount of computation absolutely free as discussed in Sect. 2. This realization leads us to formulate an IPP for computing the optimal cost which exploits this characteristic of spot instances.

For the IPP we use the following parameters

1. $s_i, 1 \leq i \leq D$ are the spot prices at the first minute of the ith hour
2. $f_i, 1 \leq i \leq D$, are the free minutes obtainable in the ith hour

We use a binary variable $x_i, 1 \leq i \leq D$, where

$x_i = 1$, implies that the job never became out-of-bid in the ith hour
$x_i = 0$, implies that the job became out-of-bid after f_i minutes.

The IPP can now be stated as

minimize z = $\sum_i (x_i s_i)$
subject to, $60x_i + f_i(1 - x_i) \geq 60C$

In order to calculate f_i one needs to find the peak price in the ith hour and then find the time when that peak price occurs first within that hour.

3.2 Dynamic Bidding Strategy

In [12] the authors propose the dynamic bidding strategy to determine the bid. They formulate the problem of minimizing the average computation cost as a finite-time stochastic dynamic program. The proposed dynamic bidding algorithm (DBA) applies the following optimality equation to determine the bid for each hour of computation using dynamic programming.

$$B_t = B_{t+1} - (1 - p)F(B_{t+1})[B_{t+1} - G(B_{t+1})] \tag{1}$$

In Eq. 1, B_t represents the bid for time stage t, p is the probability that spot price at time stage t remains same as its previous time stage $(t - 1)$. $F(.)$ is the distribution function of the spot prices and $G(.)$ is the distribution function of the time duration until a new realization of the spot price occurs. $G(.)$ is geometrically distributed with mean $1/(1 - p)$.

3.3 Greedy Bidding Strategy

We have taken a simple approach for selecting the bid. Since, a job can always be completed without interruption using on-demand-instance, and we can always opt for it when the deadline becomes tight (remaining computation hour equals deadline), we should not bid higher than the on-demand rate, at any time. At any given minute t, the amount bid is the value of spot price 3 min earlier (time to retrieve the current spot price), provided it is less than the on-demand price. If the current spot price is less than or equal to bid, spot instance is considered available and computation of the job proceeds. The boolean variable *avail* remains true while computation is in progress and Δt keeps the number of minutes the job has completed. Whenever spot price exceeds the bid value, *avails* is set false to indicate that the spot instance is no longer available, and Δt is reset to zero implying that computation has to resume from the last taken check point.

Algorithm 1. GetBid

---

input : time t, on-demand price S_{od}
output: Appropriate Bid bid, Availability $avail$
begin
  if $prices[t-3] < S_{od}$ **then**
    $bid \leftarrow prices[t-3]$;
    $avail \leftarrow true$;
  else
    $bid \leftarrow 0$;
    $avail \leftarrow false$

Algorithm 2. GreedyBid

---

input : Computation Hour C, Deadline in minutes T, On-demand Price S_{od},
        Checkpoint Interval Δc, Checkpoint Overhead δc .
output: Appropriate Bid bid, Cost $cost$.
begin
  $t \leftarrow 1$; $\Delta t \leftarrow 0$; $c \leftarrow C \times 60$; $cost \leftarrow 0$
  $avail \leftarrow false$;
  while $t \leq T \ AND \ c > 0$ **do**
    if $c = T - t$ **then**
      $cost \leftarrow cost + S_{od} * \lceil \frac{c}{60} \rceil$; return;

    if $avail = false$ **then**
      $bid \leftarrow$ GetBid(t); **if** $avail = true$ **then**
        $sp \leftarrow prices[t]$
    else
      if $price[t] > bid$ **then**
        $avail \leftarrow false$; $\Delta t \leftarrow 0$

      else
        $\Delta t \leftarrow \Delta t + 1$;
        if $\Delta t \% \Delta c = 0$ **then**
          $c \leftarrow c - \Delta c + \delta c$; take checkpoint

        if $\Delta t = 60$ **then**
          $cost \leftarrow cost + sp$; $\Delta t \leftarrow 0$;
          $bid \leftarrow$ GetBid(t);
          if $avail = true$ **then**
            $sp \leftarrow prices[t]$
  $t \leftarrow t + 1$;

It is assumed that spot prices are kept in an array *prices* and at any given minute t only the spot prices up to time t are available.

Algorithm 2 depicts the proposed greedy bidding strategy. The main features of the GreedyBid algorithm are as follows:

1. Satisfying deadline: This is ensured by comparing the remaining computation c with the remaining time $T - t$ where T is the deadline. Since running a job on spot instances gives no guarantee of completion (due to *out-of-bid* events), when c becomes equal to $T - t$, only way of ensuring the jobs completion is to run it with on-demand instances. In that case, the cost of job execution is current cost plus on-demand cost × remaining hours.
2. Check point: A check point is taken as per the predefined checkpoint interval. If the job gets out-of-bid later on, the execution can resume from the last check point taken. Another advantage of check point is that if a job gets out-of-bid before Δt becomes 60, there is no cost incurred by the user, but executions completed before the last check point remain useful.
3. After completing one hour of execution i.e. when Δt becomes equal to 60, cost is increased by the spot price at the first minute of that hour, and a new bid is chosen by algorithm GetBid. Also Δt is reset to zero.

Thus, the greedy bidding strategy considers the most recent spot price as the bid for the next hour and takes checkpoints to save the partially computed jobs.

4   Simulation Results

We have simulated all the bidding strategies discussed in the previous section with Amazon EC2 instances using JDK 1.7 and GLPK 4.47 (GNU Linear Programming Kit) [28]. In this section, a comparative study of the bidding strategies is presented in details.

Since Amazon EC2 spot prices depend on instance types (small, medium, large etc.), operating systems and the geographical regions (Asia Pacific (Sydney), US East(Virginia) etc.), we have considered the spot instances with different types, OS and regions for the simulation. We obtain the real spot prices of these spot instances from [11]. The corresponding on-demand prices(S_{od}) are taken from [10] as on April, 2015. The checkpoint interval is considered to be 15 min while 3 min is considered for the checkpoint overhead(δc). We have taken the result for 20 different windows on every spot price history with 100 VM-hour computation (C) and various deadlines (10% to 100% of computation). Finally, the average of these 20 windows is considered for the basis of comparison.

First of all, we have compared the results of different bidding strategies with randomly generated spot prices as used in [12]. The checkpoint is taken at the end of each computation hour. The result is depicted in Fig. 2. Here, we observe that GreedyBid outperforms DBA and provides better result with tight deadline.

Figures 3 and 4 provides the comparison with real spot prices for a linux based m3.2xlarge instance in the Asia Pacific (Sydney) region. In Fig. 3, the result considers the checkpoint to be taken at the end of each hour while in Fig. 4 the checkpoint is considered to be taken after every 15 min. In both the cases, GreedyBid outperforms DBA in terms of total monetary cost. We also

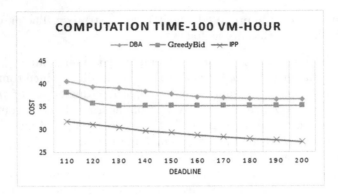

Fig. 2. Comparison of DBA, GreedyBid and IPP with random spot prices

observe that the cost is further reduced with fine grained checkpointing. This is due to the high probability of saving a partially completed jobs free of cost during an out-of-bid event.

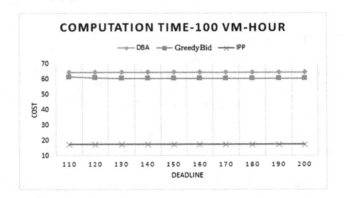

Fig. 3. Comparison of DBA, GreedyBid and Optimal (IPP) strategies with Asia Pacific (Sydney)/Linux/m3/2xlarge spot prices

A comparative study of the bidding strategies for a linux based m3.xlarge instance in the US East (Virginia) region with hourly and 15 min checkpointing are depicted in Figs. 5 and 6 respectively. Here we observe a significant gain in terms of cost reduction with GreedyBid strategy. This gain is further magnified with increase in the deadline. With fine grained checkpointing, GreedyBid provides optimal solution with deadline more that 40% of the computation time.

Therefore, GreedyBid algorithm provides the best result for cost minimization with deadline constrained jobs. Nevertheless, GreedyBid algorithm is simple and very fast compared to DBA since it does not require to analyze the history of spot prices.

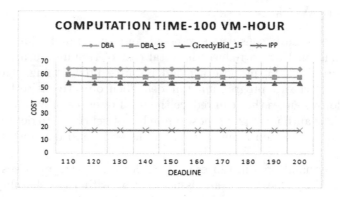

Fig. 4. Comparison of DBA, DBA_15, GreedyBid_15 and Optimal (IPP) strategies with Asia Pacific (Sydney)/Linux/m3/2xlarge spot prices

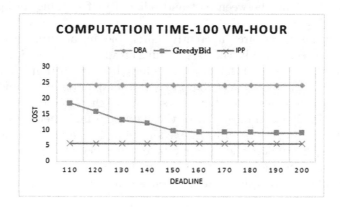

Fig. 5. Comparison of DBA, GreedyBid and Optimal (IPP) strategies with US East (Virginia)/Linux/m3/xlarge spot prices

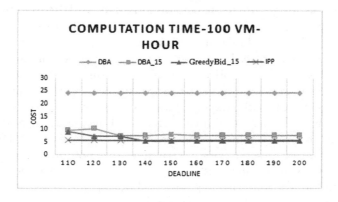

Fig. 6. Comparison of DBA, DBA_15, GreedyBid_15 and Optimal (IPP) strategies with US East (Virginia)/Linux/m3/xlarge spot prices

5   Related Work

Many researchers have considered reserved and spot purchasing options [8] offered by Amazon EC2 to reduce the total cost of running an application in cloud. Chaisiri et al. [3] propose a cloud resource provisioning algorithm by formulating a stochastic programming model. Their objective is to find a reservation plan for resources that can reduce the total resource provisioning cost for a consumer. The authors in [2] propose a number of heuristics to determine optimal amount of reservation required to meet the estimated demands for virtual machines.

On the other hand, spot instances are considered to be the most cost-effective option for a CSU. One important issue to deal with the reliability of spot instances is to decide the bid value properly. In [4], a feedback control based mechanism based on spot price history is proposed to determine the bidding decision. A hybrid model of on-demand and spot pricing schemes is considered in [5] and [6] to balance between cost and reliability of running an application in cloud.

Since, spot instances are inherently unreliable in nature, checkpointing schemes are required to handle the jobs running on spot instances. Some schemes that apply predictive methods for spot prices have been studied in [1]. They have also shown how work migration can improve task completion in the midst of failures while maintaining low monetary costs. A novel checkpointing scheme have been proposed in [2] which outperforms the checkpointing schemes in [1].

This paper considers the spot instances for running deadline constrained jobs. The authors in [12] propose the dynamic bidding strategy to determine the bid for deadline constrained jobs in spot instances. The bidding strategy, introduced in this paper, outperforms the strategy proposed in [12].

6   Conclusion and Future Work

Determining optimal bid is a challenging issue for running deadline constraint jobs with spot instances. In this paper, we formulate an IPP to determine the optimal bid for spot instances. However, we need to find heuristics to solve this issue since IPP is NP-hard in nature and requires the future prices to be known in advance. In the literature, DBA is effectively used to determine the bids by analysing the history of spot prices and using dynamic programming. In this paper, we propose a greedy approach to solve the issue of determining bid for spot instances more efficiently. Experimental results show the effectiveness of the proposed GreedyBid algorithm compared to DBA. Fine grained checkpointing is also introduced to further improve the performance of the GreedyBid algorithm.

This work considers serial jobs for running on spot instances. It can be extended in future to consider the effect of parallel jobs on GreedyBid algorithm. Also we can consider the effect of novel checkpointing scheme, proposed in [2], with the bidding strategies discussed in this paper. The work can also be extended in future to consider reserved instances along with spot instances for deadline constrained jobs in cloud.

References

1. Yi, S., Andrzejak, A., Kondo, D.: Monetary cost-aware checkpointing and migration on amazon cloud spot instances. IEEE Trans. Serv. Comput. 5(4), 512–524 (2012)
2. Khatua, S., Sur, P.K., Das, R.K., Mukherjee, N.: Heuristic-based resource reservation strategies for public cloud. IEEE Trans. Cloud Comput. (TCC) (2014). doi:10. 1109/TCC.2014.2369434
3. Chaisiri, S., Bu-Sung, L., Niyato, D.: Optimization of resource provisioning cost in cloud computing. IEEE Trans. Serv. Comput. 5(2), 164–177 (2012)
4. Li, Z., Kihl, M., Robertsson, A.: On a feedback control-based mechanism of bidding for cloud spot service. In: 7th International Conference on Cloud Computing Technology and Science (CloudCom), Vancouver, BC, pp. 290–297 (2015). doi:10. 1109/CloudCom.2015.76
5. Sadashiv, N., Dillip Kumar, S.M., Goudar, R.S.: Hybrid spot instance based resource provisioning strategy in dynamic cloud environment. In: International Conference on High Performance Computing and Applications (ICHPCA), Bhubaneswar, pp. 1–6 (2014). doi:10.1109/ICHPCA.2014.7045296
6. Lu, S., et al.: A dynamic hybrid resource provisioning approach for running large-scale computational applications on cloud spot and on-demand instances. In: International Conference on Parallel and Distributed Systems (ICPADS), Seoul, pp. 657–662 (2013). doi:10.1109/ICPADS.2013.117
7. Amazon EC2 Instance Types. http://aws.amazon.com/ec2/instance-types/
8. Amazon EC2 Purchasing Options. http://aws.amazon.com/ec2/purchasing-options/
9. Amazon EC2 Spot Instances. http://aws.amazon.com/ec2/spot-instances/
10. Amazon EC2 Public Cloud Provider. http://aws.amazon.com/ec2/
11. Spot Price History. http://timetric.com/dataset/amazon-web-services-aws-spot-price/
12. Zafer, M., Song, Y., Lee, K.: Optimal bids for spot VMs in a cloud for deadline constrained jobs. In: IEEE 5th International Conference on Cloud Computing (2012)
13. Song, Y., Zafer, M., Lee, K.: Optimal bidding in spot instance market. In: IEEE INFOCOM, Orlando, FL, March 2012
14. Hajjat, M., Sun, X., Sung, Y.-W.E., Maltz, D., Rao, S., Sripanidkulchai, K., Tawarmalani, M.: Cloudward bound: planning for beneficial migration of enterprise applicationsto the cloud. In: Proceedings of the ACM SIGCOMM 2010 Conference on SIGCOMM, SIGCOMM 2010. ACM, New York (2010)
15. Chohan, N., Castillo, C., Spreitzer, M., Steinder, M., Tantawi, A., Krintz, C.: See spot run: using spot instances for mapreduce workflows. In: 2nd USENIX Workshop on Hot Topics in Cloud Computing (2010)
16. Liu, H.: Cutting mapreduce cost with spot market. In: 3rd USENIX Workshop on Hot Topics in Cloud Computing (2011)
17. Ganapathi, A.S.: Predicting and optimizing system utilization and performance via statistical machine learning. Ph.D. thesis, EECS Department, University of California, Berkeley (2009)
18. Ko, S.Y., Hoque, I., Cho, B., Gupta, I.: Making cloud intermediate data fault-tolerant. In: Proceedings of the 1st ACM Symposium on Cloud Computing, SoCC. ACM (2010)

19. Krawczyk, S., Bubendorfer, K.: Grid resource allocation: allocation mechanisms and utilisation patterns. In: AusGrid 2008: Proceedings of the Sixth Australasian Workshop on Grid Computing and e-Research. Australian Computer Society (2008)

20. Raman, R., Livny, M., Solomon, M.: Matchmaking: distributed resource management for high throughput computing. In: HPDC 1998: Proceedings of the 7th IEEE International Symposium on High Performance Distributed Computing. IEEE Computer Society (1998)

21. Isard, M., Prabhakaran, V., Currey, J., Wieder, U., Talwar, K., Goldberg, A.: Quincy: fair scheduling for distributed computing clusters. In: SOSP 2009: Proceedings of the ACM SIGOPS 22nd Symposium on Operating Systems Principles (2009)

22. Den Bossche, R.V., Vanmechelen, K., Broeckhove, J.: Cost-efficient scheduling heuristics for deadline constrained workloads on hybrid clouds, Antwerp, Belgium (2011)

23. Yao, M., Zhang, P., Li, Y., Jie, H., Li, C.L.-Y.: Cutting your cloud computing cost for deadline-constrained batch jobs. In: IEEE ICWS 2014, pp. 337–344 (2014)

24. Li, T., Chen, W., Li, Z., Liu, Z.: Deadline oriented resource broker for cloud computing. In: ISCI 2015 (2015)

25. Bertsekas, D.P.: Dynamic Programming and Optimal Control, vol. 1. Athena Scientific, Belmont (2005)

26. Amies, A., Sluiman, H., Tong, Q., Liu, G.: Infrastructure as a service cloud concepts. In: Developing and Hosting Applications on the Cloud. IBM Press. ISBN 978-0-13-306684-5

27. Boniface, M., et al.: Platform-as-a-service architecture for real-time quality of service management in clouds. In: 5th International Conference on Internet and Web Applications and Services (ICIW), pp. 155–160. IEEE, Barcelona (2010). doi:10.1109/ICIW.2010.91

28. GNU Linear Programming Kit (GLPK) (2014). http://www.gnu.org/software/glpk

An Efficient Request-Based Virtual Machine Placement Algorithm for Cloud Computing

Sanjaya K. Panda[1(✉)] and Prasanta K. Jana[2]

[1] Department of Computer Science and Engineering and Information Technology, Veer Surendra Sai University of Technology, Burla 768018, India
sanjayauce@gmail.com
[2] Department of Computer Science and Engineering, Indian Institute of Technology (ISM), Dhanbad 826004, India
prasantajana@yahoo.co.in

Abstract. The energy efficiency of cloud computing has drawn gigantic attention due to the explosive growth of cloud services. Moreover, this growth extends the capacity of various resources of the datacenters. As a circumstance, the amount of carbon footprints generated from the datacenters is sharply increased. Therefore, the objective is to use the datacenter's resources proficiently without compromising the user requirements such that energy consumption is minimized. The recent studies have shown that the user requirements are provided in the form of virtual machines (VMs) which are deployed in the physical machines (PMs) of the datacenters based on the resource utilization or decreasing order of the VM capacity. However, these studies have not considered the capacity of the user requests. In this paper, we propose a request-based VM placement (RVMP) algorithm by considering the capacity of the requests. The proposed algorithm assigns the user requests to the VMs and further assigns the used VMs to the PMs based on the capacity of the requests and VMs respectively. Our simulation results on five different datasets, which are generated using Monte Carlo method, show that RVMP improves performance in terms of the number of used VMs and PMs, average PM utilization and energy consumption of PMs compared to state-of-the-art algorithms.

Keywords: Cloud computing · Virtual machine placement · Datacenter · Physical machine · Request · Energy consumption · Resource utilization

1 Introduction

The growth of cloud computing is massively increasing due to on-demand service, scalability, operational efficiency, cost saving and energy efficiency [1, 2]. Therefore, many companies migrate to the cloud systems for their business benefits. As per Google analysis [3], a company saves about 68% to 87% of energy by migrating to the cloud. On the other hand, the cloud service providers (CSPs) extend their capacity of datacenters to accommodate a large influx of users. However, the expansion of the datacenters leads to high energy consumption and generation of carbon footprints [4].

© Springer International Publishing AG 2017
P. Krishnan et al. (Eds.): ICDCIT 2017, LNCS 10109, pp. 129–143, 2017.
DOI: 10.1007/978-3-319-50472-8_11

According to the NRDC report [5], 91 billion kilowatt-hours (kWh) of electricity are consumed annually by US datacenters and it is expected to reach about 140 billion kWh by 2020. However, the consumption is reduced to 39 billion kWh by taking technical initiatives such as increasing server utilization, power management and scaling virtualization which save $ 3.8 billion per year. Alternatively, the electricity consumption of the datacenters is dominated by processor and memory [6, 7].

In IaaS cloud, the user requirements are delivered by creating the VMs which are placed in the PMs of the datacenters [8]. This VM placement is a challenging issue and a well-known NP-Hard problem [9, 10] as the objective is to minimize the number of PMs, such that the energy consumption is minimized. Therefore, many efforts [4, 6, 7, 9–11] have been made to find an efficient VM placement algorithm. Most of these algorithms are reported that the VMs are mapped to PMs based on the current resource utilization or decreasing order of the VM capacity. However, they have not considered the capacity of user requests which increase the number of used PMs and energy consumption. This phenomenon inspires us to consider the capacity of user requests for reducing considerable amount of energy. Therefore, we propose a request-based VM placement (RVMP) algorithm that minimizes the energy consumption of the datacenters by minimizing the number of used VMs and PMs. The key idea of RVMP is to sort the requests, VMs and PMs in non-increasing order of their capacity. Then we follow one of the two procedures, namely basic placement (BRVMP) and optimal placement (ORVMP) to place the requests to the VMs and further place the used VMs (i.e., a subset of VMs) to the PMs. These procedures make the unused VMs and PMs to be switched off. As a result, energy consumption is drastically reduced. The key contributions of this paper are as follows. (1) We present a VM placement algorithm to reduce the energy consumption of datacenters. (2) We show how RVMP can produce optimal placement of the requests and VMs. (3) We compare the proposed algorithm with five state-of-the-art algorithms. From now onwards, we use resources for requests, VMs or PMs, when there is no ambiguity.

The structure of this paper is as follows: Sect. 2 discusses the related work and research challenges for VM placement. Section 3 presents the cloud system and energy model followed by VM placement problem. Section 4 provides a detailed discussion of the proposed algorithm with an example. Section 5 shows the simulation results and comparisons. We conclude with some notable remarks in Sect. 6.

2   Related Work

As the idle resources of the datacenters are drawing a significant amount of power, energy consumption is a critical issue for the recent development of cloud computing. One of the possible solutions is to properly utilize the active resources by minimizing the number of idle resources. Therefore, many practitioners [4, 6, 7, 9–11] have proposed efficient VM placement algorithms to improve the energy efficiency of the datacenters. Ahmad et al. [12] have presented an extensive survey on server consolidation for datacenters. They have found that improper VM placement, frequent VM migration and agreement violation are the key issues of the consolidation. Beloglazov et al. [7] have presented an energy-aware allocation algorithm, called modified best fit decreasing (MBFD) to deliver the quality of service. However, capacity of user requests is also an equally important parameter which is not considered in this algorithm. Lin et al. [10] have proposed a dynamic round robin (RR) algorithm for VM consolidation. They have modeled the consolidation problem by taking the arrival and execution time of the VMs. However, the capacity of PMs is not considered in this approach. Song et al. [11] have modeled the resource provisioning problem as modified on-line bin packing problem (BPP). The objective of this problem is to minimize the number of servers (or bins) without overloading the resources. Here, they have assumed that the PMs are homogeneous in their capacity. Trivella et al. [13] have viewed the load balancing problem in multi-dimensional BPP. It balances the trade-off between the average load of the bins and the individual load. Like [11], this problem has also considered the homogeneous bins. Recently, Esfandiarpoor et al. [4] have proposed our MBFD (OBFD) VM placement algorithm and showed it in the form of bin packing problem. Therefore, the well-known algorithms, first fit decreasing (FFD), RR and BFD can be used to place the VMs to PMs. However, the above works were not considered the capacity of user requests.

The proposed algorithm is completely different from [4, 7] with respect to following novel ideas. (1) Our algorithm uses the non-increasing order to sort the resources in compare to decreasing order of VMs and PMs as used by [4, 7]. (2) The algorithm assigns the used VMs to the PMs to reduce the energy consumption in contrast to all VMs to PMs as used by [4, 7]. (3) We generate the results with a large set of requests, VMs and PMs in compared to [4, 7]. Our simulation results show the energy efficiency of the RVMP over FFD, RR, BFD, MBFD and OBFD algorithms.

3 Models and Problem Statement

3.1 Cloud System and Energy Model

In our proposed cloud model, we consider an IaaS cloud system. In this type of system, a datacenter consists of a set of physical servers, storage devices, memory and network to provide services to the users. When a user requests for a service, the CSP finds a suitable VM based on the capacity of the request. However, several requests can be placed to the same VM. Without loss of generality, we assume that the VMs are different types and characteristics. Subsequently, the used VMs are placed in the PMs of the datacenter. It is noteworthy to mention that multiple VMs can be placed in the same PM and the PMs are varying capacity. We have assumed that the capacity of resources, i.e., requests, VMs, PMs are represented in the form of million instructions per second (MIPS) and they are determined before the placement takes place [4].

In a datacenter, the resources such as processor or CPU, storage and network are the measurable components of power consumption. However, the processor leads in power consumption than the other components. Typically, the processor usage is proportional to the load of the system [7] and the idle power consumption of a server is roughly 70% of the power consumption of a fully utilized server [7, 14]. Thus the idle servers need to switch off (or sleep mode) for reducing a substantial amount of power. They may be awakened when the running servers are fully utilized. Therefore, the power model of a server (P) is mathematically expressed as follows [7].

$$P = \lambda \times P_{max} + (1-\lambda) \times P_{max} \times P_U \qquad (1)$$

where λ = the power used by the idle server (i.e., 70%), P_{max} = the maximum power used for a fully utilized server, P_U = the processor utilization. Therefore, the energy consumption (E) for a period $[a, b]$ can be calculated as follows [7].

$$E = \int_a^b P(t)\, dt = [\dot{P}(t)]_a^b = \dot{P}(b) - \dot{P}(a) \qquad (2)$$

where $P(t)$ denotes the processor utilization over time t, $\dot{P}(t)$ is the integral of $P(t)$ and $\dot{P}$ (b) and $\dot{P}(a)$ are the value of the integral at $t = b$ and $t = a$ respectively. Note that the above energy model is similar to the energy model used in [7]. However, we describe here for the completeness of our paper.

3.2 Problem Statement

Consider a set U of n user requests with its corresponding capacity set CU, a set V of m VMs with its corresponding capacity set CV and a set P of M PMs with its corresponding capacity set CP. Here, the capacity is considered in dynamic requested MIPS. The MIPS value of a request U_i, $1 \leq i \leq n$, a VM V_j, $1 \leq j \leq m$ or a PM P_k, $1 \leq k \leq M$ denotes how much power and speed this request, VM or PM makes the system busy at the higher end. The problem is twofold, which is defined as follows. It first maps the user requests to the VMs. Mathematically, $f\colon U \rightarrow V$ where f is the mapping function. Secondly, it maps the used VMs $V' \subseteq V$ to the PMs. Mathematically, $g\colon V' \rightarrow P$. This problem is subjected to the following constraints.

(a) $\sum_{i=1}^m CV_i \leq \sum_{j=1}^M CP_j$, (b) $\sum_{k=1}^n (CU_k \times F_{kj}) \leq CV_j$, $1 \leq j \leq m$

where $F_{kj} = \begin{cases} 1 & \text{if user requests } k \text{ is placed to VM } j \\ 0 & \text{Otherwise} \end{cases}$

(c) A user request U_l, $1 \leq l \leq n$ is not placed on a given VM V_j, $1 \leq j \leq m$ if

$$\left(\sum_{k=1}^{l-1} (CU_k \times F_{kj})\right) + CU_l > CV_j$$

(d) A user request cannot be migrated from one VM to another VM, preempted and/or shared between VMs at any cost.

4 Proposed Algorithm

4.1 Request-Based Virtual Machine Placement Algorithm

The request-based virtual machine placement (RVMP) algorithm is a deployment algorithm for cloud computing systems. The objectives of this algorithm are as follows. (a) Minimize the energy consumption of the datacenter (b) Minimize the number of used VMs and PMs. For this, it undergoes a two-phase process, namely the placement of user requests to VMs (Phase 1) and placement of used VMs to PMs (Phase 2). The pseudo code for the proposed algorithm is presented in Fig. 1.

Algorithm: Request-Based VM Placement (RVMP)

Inputs: (1) A set of user requests U and their corresponding load set CU
        (2) A set of VMs V and their corresponding capacity set CV
        (3) A set of PMs P and their corresponding capacity set CP

Outputs: (1) Placement of user requests to VMs   (2) Placement of VMs to PMs
Phase 1: Placement of user requests to VMs

1. Sort the set U in the non-increasing order of MIPS and store the sorted sequence in U
2. Sort the set V in the non-increasing order of MIPS and store the sorted sequence in V
3. **Call** *BASIC-PLACEMENT(U, V, n, m, CU, CV)*
   // This procedure returns a set of VMs $V' = \{V_1, V_2, V_3,..., V_{m'}\}$,
     $V' \subseteq V$ and their corresponding capacity set CV'

Phase 2: Placement of VMs to PMs

4. Sort the set P in the non-increasing order of MIPS and store the sorted sequence in P
5. **Call** *BASIC-PLACEMENT(V', P, m', M, CV', CP)*
   // This procedure returns a set of PMs $P' = \{P_1, P_2, P_3,..., P_{M'}\}$,
     $P' \subseteq P$ and their corresponding capacity set CP'

Fig. 1. Pseudo code for RVMP algorithm

4.1.1 Phase 1: Placement of User Requests to VMs

In this phase, RVMP first sorts the user requests and VMs in the non-increasing order of their capacity (Line 1 and Line 2 of Fig. 1). Then it calls Procedure 1 to place the sorted requests to the VMs (Line 3) which is shown in Fig. 2. Note that we refer this procedure as BRVMP. In this procedure, we first check whether the capacity of the first VM is sufficient enough for the user request (Line 3 of Procedure 1). If it is so, then it places the user requests to that VM (Line 4) and updates the capacity of that VM (Line 5). Otherwise, it continues to check the next VM (Line 2). If the capacity of the VM is fully occupied by one or more requests, then it is excluded from the set of VMs (Lines 6–8). Here, the inner for loop iterates for m times in the worst case (Lines 2–11) whereas outer for loop iterates for n times (Lines 1–12). Note that *place_xm* will represent *place_vm* in Phase 1 and *place_pm* in Phase 2.

Procedure 1: *BASIC-PLACEMENT(X, Y, p, q, CX, CY)*
1. **for** $i = 1, 2, 3,\ldots, p$
2.   **for** $j = 1, 2, 3,\ldots, q$
3.   **if** $place\_xm[j] == 0$ && $CY[j] \geq CX[i]$
4.   Place X_i to Y_j
5. $CY[j] = CY[j] - CX[i]$
6.   **if** $CY[j] == 0$
7. $place\_xm[j] = 1$
8.   **endif**
9.   break
10.   **endif**
11.   **endfor**
12. **endfor**
13. **Return**

Fig. 2. Pseudo code for basic placement RVMP algorithm

Lemma **4.1:** *The time complexity for the process of sorting of user requests, VMs or PMs is* $O(p^2)$*.*

Proof: Let n, m and M be the total number of user requests, VMs and PMs respectively. Prior to place the requests to the VMs, they are sorted in the non-increasing order of their capacity which requires two loops with n iterations each. As a result, it takes $O(n^2)$ time (Step 1, Fig. 1). In the similar fashion, the VMs and PMs are sorted and they take $O(m^2)$ and $O(M^2)$ time respectively (Step 2 and Step 4). Therefore, the time complexity is $O(n^2)$ by assuming $p = max(n, m, M)$.

Lemma **4.2:** *The time complexity of Procedure 1 is* $O(pq)$*.*

Proof: In Procedure 1, the inner for loop iterates q times in the worst case (Steps 2–11). As a result, it takes $O(q)$ time. However, the outer for loop iterates p times (Steps 1–12). Therefore, the time complexity is $O(pq)$.

4.1.2   Phase 2: Placement of VMs to PMs

In this phase, RVMP first sorts the PMs in the non-increasing order of their capacity (Line 4 of Fig. 1). Then it calls the Procedure 1 to place the used VMs of Phase 1 (i.e., V') into the PMs (Line 5). Note that the Procedure 1 is common for both the phases. Here, we check the capacity of the first PM to place the VM (Line 3 of Procedure 1). If the PM has enough capacity to keep the VM, then the VM is placed to that PM (Line 4) and the capacity is updated (Line 5). Otherwise, we continue with the next PM (Line 2). Once the capacity of the PM is fully housed with VMs, the PM is excluded from the mapping set (Lines 6–8). This procedure returns a set of PMs and their corresponding capacity set to the main algorithm (Fig. 1) (Line 13).

Theorem 4.1 *The time complexity of the proposed algorithm BRVMP is O(kn2).*

Proof: Step 1 and Step 2 take $O(n^2)$ and $O(m^2)$ time (Phase 1 of Fig. 1). Subsequently, it calls Procedure 1 which requires $O(pq) = O(nm)$ time. Step 4 takes $O(M^2)$ time and Step 5 takes $O(pq) = O(mM)$ time (Phase 2 of Fig. 1). However, both phases iterate, say k times. Therefore, the time complexity of the proposed algorithm is $\underbrace{k \times [O(n^2) + O(m^2) + O(mn)]}_{\text{Phase1}} + \underbrace{k \times [O(M^2) + O(mM)]}_{\text{Phase2}} = O(kn^2)$ by assuming $n \gg m \gg M$.

4.2   An Illustration

Consider an example that consists of six user requests, six VMs and three PMs as shown in Table 1(a)–(c). The specification of the user requests, the maximum capacity of the VMs and PMs (in MIPS) are shown in the even column of Table 1.

Table 1. An example with (a) six user requests, (b) six VMs and (c) three PMs.

U	CU	V	CV	P	PM
U_1	150	V_1	1000	P_1	1700
U_2	200	V_2	600		
U_3	300	V_3	500	P_2	850
U_4	350	V_4	700		
U_5	150	V_5	250	P_3	900
U_6	300	V_6	400		
(a)		(b)		(c)	

The proposed RVMP algorithm first sorts the requests, VMs and PMs in the non-increasing order. It makes the requests in the order of U_4, U_3, U_6, U_2, U_1 and U_5, the VMs in the order of V_1, V_4, V_2, V_3, V_6 and V_5 and the PMs in the order of P_1, P_3 and P_2 respectively. Then it follows a two-phase process.

In Phase 1, the first user request U_4 requires 350 MIPS and the capacity of VM V_1 is 1000 MIPS. As the capacity of the VM is more than the user request, request U_4 is placed to VM V_1 and the remaining capacity of VM V_1 is 650 MIPS. Next the second user request U_3 requires 300 MIPS and it is placed to the same VM as the capacity is more than the request. Here, the remaining capacity of VM V_1 is updated to 350 MIPS. Similarly, the user request U_6 is placed to VM V_1 and the updated capacity is 50 MIPS. Next the user request U_2 needs 200 MIPS. However, the remaining capacity of VM V_1 is not sufficient enough to keep the request U_2. Therefore, it assigns to the next available VM which is VM V_4 and the remaining capacity of VM V_4 is updated to 500 MIPS. In the similar way, user requests U_1 and U_5 are placed to VM V_4 and the remaining capacity is 200 MIPS. The Gantt chart for Phase 1 is shown in Table 2.

Table 2. The Gantt chart for the placement of user requests to VMs

V_1	$0 \sim 350$	$350 \sim 650$	$650 \sim 950$	$950 \sim 1000$
User request	U4	U3	U6	*
V4	$0 \sim 200$	$200 \sim 350$	$350 \sim 500$	$500 \sim 700$
User request	U2	U_1	U5	*

In Phase 2, the proposed algorithm places the used VMs (i.e., V_1 and V_4) to the PMs. The first VM V_1 requires 950 MIPS and the capacity of PM P_1 is sufficient enough to keep the VM V_1. Therefore, the VM V_1 is placed to PM P_1 and the remaining capacity of PM P_1 is 750 MIPS. The next VM V_4 needs 500 MIPS and it is placed in the same PM as the remaining capacity is more than the VM. Now the remaining capacity of PM P_1 is 250 MIPS. Therefore, the utilization of P_1 is 85.29% (i.e., $(1450/1700) \times 100$) and the energy consumption is 6572 units of energy per time (i.e., $175 + (75 \times 85.29)$). The Gantt chart for Phase 2 is shown in Table 3.

Table 3. Gantt chart for the placement of VMs to PMs

P_1	$0 \sim 950$	$950 \sim 1450$	$1450 \sim 1700$
VM	V_1	V4	*

We also present the placement of VMs to PMs (*PVP*) and utilization of PMs (i.e., U_P) for all the existing algorithms in Table 4. Here, MBFD algorithm is unable to place VM V_1 to one of the PMs and energy consumption is 8956 units of energy per time. Except MBFD, all other algorithms require three PMs to place the six VMs as they have not considered the capacity of the requests. However, the proposed algorithm needs only one PM. The energy consumption of all the existing algorithms (except MBFD) is 10819 units of energy per time, which is 65% (approx.) more than BRVMP. The illustration clearly shows the efficacy of the proposed algorithm.

Table 4. Comparison of placement of VMs to PMs and PM utilization for FFD, RR, BFD, MBFD and OBFD algorithm

	FFD		RR		BFD		MBFD		OBFD	
	PVP	UP	PVP	UP	PVP	UP	PVP	UP	PVP	Up
P_1	V1, V4	29.41%	V1, V4	29.41%	V1, V4	29.41%	V6, V4	38.24%	V1, V4	29.41%
P2	V2, V5	41.18%	V2, V5	41.18%	V2, V5	41.18%	V3	35.29%	V2, V5	41.18%
P3	V3, V6	66.67%	V3, V_6	66.67%	V3, V_6	66.67%	V5, V2	38.89%	V3, V_6	66.67%

We notice the following observations. (1) The pair of VMs (V_1, V_3) is a good choice than the pair (V_1, V_4) for BRVMP. Therefore, we present Procedure 2 (see Sect. 4.3) for the optimal selection of the VMs which results 96.67% utilization of PM P_1. (2) The VMs V_4, V_3 and V_5 are the best choice than the pair (V_1, V_4). However, it is unable to place the request U_5. (3) The VMs V_2, V_3 and V_6 are the alternative choice of the pair (V_1, V_4). However, it is also not feasible to place the request U_5.

4.3 Optimal Placement for RVMP (ORVMP)

The ORVMP improves the placement by selecting those VMs and PMs that are very close to the requirement of requests and VMs respectively. To select such things, we propose Procedure 2 (Fig. 3) which substitutes Procedure 1. Note that *xm_selection* will represent *vm_selection* in Phase 1 and *vm_selection* in Phase 2.

Procedure 2: *OPTIMAL-PLACEMENT(X, Y, p, q, CX, CY)*

1. $total\_mi = \sum_{i=1}^{p} CU$

2. Set $\tau = 1$
3. **Call** *ONE-PLACEMENT(q, Y, CY, total_mi)*
4. **if** the above placement is infeasible
5.   Set $\tau = 2$
6.   **Call** *TWO-PLACEMENT(p, q, X, Y, CX, CY, total_mi)*
7. $\vdots$
8. **endif**
9. **for** $i = 1, 2, 3, \ldots, p$
10.   **for** $j = 1, 2, 3, \ldots, \tau$
11.   **if** $CY[xm\_selection[j]] \geq CX[i]$
12.   Place X_i to Y_j
13. $CY[xm\_selection[j]] = CY[xm\_selection[j]] - CX[i]$
14.   break
15.   **endif**
16.   **endfor**
17. **endfor**
18. **Return**

Fig. 3. Pseudo code for optimal placement RVMP

In Phase 1, this procedure determines the total capacity of the user requests (Line 1). Then, it finds a single VM to place all the requests by calling Procedure 3 (Line 2 and Line 3). In procedure 3 (see Fig. 4), it selects a VM such that the remaining MIPS of that VM is minimum after placing all the requests (Lines 5–8 of Procedure 3). If it fails to find a VM, then it checks for placement of two VMs by calling Procedure 4 (Lines 4–6). In Procedure 4 (see Fig. 5), it selects a pair of VMs to place the requests such that the remaining MIPS is minimum (Lines 14–20 of Procedure 4). If it again fails to find two VMs, then it checks for three VMs and this procedure is repeated until it finds a set of VMs that accommodate all the requests (Line 7 and Line 8). On the other hand, it places the requests to the VMs when it finds a suitable VM placement (Lines 9–17). Note that this procedure is also same for Phase 2.

Procedure 3: *ONE-PLACEMENT*(q, Y, CY, total_mi)
1. Set *min_remaining_mips* = ∞
2. **for** *j* = 1, 2, 3,..., *q*
3.   **if** *CY*[*j*] ≥ *total_mi*
4.   *remaining_mips* = *CY*[*j*] – *total_mi*
5.   **if** *remaining_mips* < *min_remaining_mips*
6.   *min_remaining_mips* = *remaining_mips*
7.   *xm_selection*[1] = *j*
8.   **endif**
9.   **endif**
10. **endfor**
11. **Return**

Fig. 4. Pseudo code for the optimal placement of a single VM (or PM)

Procedure 4: *TWO-PLACEMENT*(p, q, X, Y, CX, CY, total_mi)
1. Set *min_remaining_mips* = ∞
2. **for** *j* = 1, 2, 3,..., *q* – 1
3.   **for** *k* = *j* + 1, *j* + 2, *j* + 3,..., *q*
4.   Set *capacity_mips*1 = *CY*[*j*], *capacity_mips*2 = *CY*[*k*], *placement* = 0
5.   **if** *capacity_mips*1 + *capacity_mips*2 ≥ *total_mi*
6.   **for** *i* = 1, 2, 3,..., *p*
7.   **if** *capacity_mips*1 ≥ *CX*[*i*]
8.   *capacity_mips*1 = *capacity_mips*1 – *CX*[*i*]
9.   **else**
10.   *capacity_mips*2 = *capacity_mips*2 – *CX*[*i*]
11.   **endif**
12.   *placement* = *placement* + 1
13.   **endfor**
14.   **if** *placement* == *p*
15.   *remaining_mips* = *capacity_mips*1 + *capacity_mips*2
16.   **if** *remaining_mips* < *min_remaining_mips*
17.   *min_remaining_mips* = *remaining_mips*
18.   *xm_selection*[1] = *j*, *xm_selection*[2] = *k*
19.   **endif**
20.   **endif**
21.   **endif**
22.   **endfor**
23. **endfor**
24. **Return**

Fig. 5. Pseudo code for the optimal placement of a pair of VMs (or PMs)

Lemma 4.3: *The time complexity of Procedure 2 is $O(q^\tau p)$.*

Proof: Let τ be the number of VMs or PMs required for optimal placement. Step 1 takes $O(p)$ time. Then, it calls the Procedure 3 which takes $O(q)$ time (Step 3). If this placement is infeasible, then it calls the Procedure 4 which takes $O(q^2 p)$ time (Step 6). Similarly, the placement of τ requires $O(q^\tau p)$ time. Step 9 to Step 17 take $O(\tau p) = O(p)$ time as $p >> \tau$. Therefore, the time complexity is $O(p) + O(q) + [O(q^2 p) + \dots + O(q^\tau p)] + O(p) = O(q^\tau p)$.

Lemma 4.4: *The time complexity of Procedure 3 is $O(q)$.*

Proof: Step 1 takes constant time. To check whether a single resource can place all the user requests, Steps 3–9 require $O(1)$ time. However, this process is repeated for all the resources which require $O(q)$ time (Steps 2–10). Therefore, the time complexity of Procedure 3 is $O(q)$.

Lemma 4.5: *The time complexity of Procedure 4 is $O(q^2 p)$.*

Proof: Step 1 takes $O(1)$ time. To check whether a pair of the resources can place all the user requests, Steps 4–21 require $O(p)$ time. On the other hand, $O(q^2)$ time is required to find the all possible pairs of VMs (Steps 2–23). Therefore, the time complexity of Procedure 4 is $O(q^2) \times O(p) = O(q^2 p)$.

Theorem 4.2 *The time complexity of the proposed algorithm ORVMP is $O(km\tau n)$.*

Proof: The ORVMP (refer Fig. 1) also sorts the user requests and VMs. Thus the complexity remains same for sorting as BRVMP. Next, it calls Procedure 2 which further calls Procedure 3 or Procedure 4 which requires $O(q) = O(m)$ or $O(q^2 p) = O(m^2 n)$ time. But, it requires $O(q^\tau p) = O(m^\tau n)$ time for placement of τ in Phase 1. The above process is repeated, say k times for both phases. Therefore, the time complexity of proposed algorithm is $\underbrace{k \times [O(n^2) + O(m^2) + O(m^\tau n)]}_{\text{Phase1}} + \underbrace{k \times [O(M^2) + O(M^\tau m)]}_{\text{Phase2}} =$
$O(km^\tau n)$ by assuming $n >> m >> M$.

5 Simulation Results

5.1 Simulation Setups and Datasets

The simulation runs were carried out using MATLAB R2014a version 8.3.0.532, running on Windows 7 edition with the system configuration of Intel (R) Core (TM) i3-2330 M CPU @ 2.20 GHz 2.20 GHz processor, 4 GB RAM and 64-bit operating system. The performance of the proposed algorithm is evaluated through a series of simulation run with some datasets generated using Monte Carlo method. In each run of the simulation, we used an instance of the generated datasets whose general structure is $ix\_a\_b\_c$. Here, ix denotes the instance number (i.e., $ix \in \{i1, i2, i3, i4, i5\}$), a denotes the number of requests, b denotes number of VMs and c denotes the number of PMs. For the diversity of simulation runs, we select the instances as $i1$ to $i5$, the number of requests as 100 to 10000, the number of VMs as 10 to 1000 and the number of PMs as 5 to 500. Moreover, we use the MATLAB random function to generate the parameters such as requests, capacity of VMs and capacity of PMs of the datasets in the range of [1–20], [100–200] and [100–1000] respectively. Here, [d–e] indicates the lower (d) and upper limit (e) (both inclusive) of the parameter.

5.2   Results and Discussion

We ran the instances of the five different datasets for FFD, RR, BFD, MBFD, OBFD, and the proposed BRVMP algorithm. These algorithms are evaluated using four performance metrics, namely the number of used VMs (P_1), number of used PMs (P_2), average PM utilization (P_3) and energy consumption of PMs (P_4) and the average value of the five instances are shown in Tables 5 and 6. We also present the pictorial comparison of energy consumption in Fig. 6. Here, P_3 is calculated by dividing the sum of the utilization of PMs and the number of PMs. Note that energy consumption is calculated by assuming $k = 70\%$ and $P_{max} = 250$ W as given in [4, 7].

Table 5. Comparison of number of used VMs and number of used PMs for FFD, RR, BFD, MBFD, OBFD and BRVMP algorithm

Dataset	FFD		RR		BFD		MBFD		OBFD		BRVMP	
	P_1	P_2	P_1	P_2	P_1	P_2	P_1	P_2	P_1	P_2	P_1	P_2
100_10_5	10	4	8	5	10	4	10	4	10	5	7	2
500_50_25	50	16	45	24	50	19	50	16	50	25	32	8
i000_i00_50	100	28	87	48	100	37	100	29	100	50	64	13
5000_500_250	500	144	433	239	500	186	500	147	500	250	309	62
i0000_i000_500	1000	286	872	481	1000	370	1000	289	1000	500	623	125

Table 6. Comparison of average PM utilization and energy consumption of PMs for FFD, RR, BFD, MBFD, OBFD and BRVMP algorithm

Dataset	FFD		RR		BFD		MBFD		OBFD		BRVMP	
	P_3	P_4	P_3	P_4	P_3	P_4	P_3	P_4	P_3	P_4	P_3	P_4
i00_i0_5	82	2.27e+04	57	2.13e+04	83	2.64e+04	79	2.18e+04	68	2.49e+04	69	1.18e+04
500_50_25	90	1.09e+05	56	1.06e+05	92	1.32e+05	88	1.08e+05	60	1.17e+05	87	5.08e+04
i000_i00_50	91	1.98e+05	53	1.99e+05	92	2.60e+05	89	2.00e+05	59	2.30e+05	92	9.09e+04
5000_500_250	93	1.03e+06	55	1.03e+06	94	1.34e+06	91	1.02e+06	61	1.19e+06	94	4.51e+05
i0000_i000_500	93	2.04e+06	55	2.06e+06	94	2.67e+06	91	2.02e+06	60	2.34e+06	95	9.09e+05

The simulation results clearly indicate that all the instances of five different datasets (i.e., 25 out of 25 instances) give better performance for the proposed algorithm BRVMP than all the existing algorithms. It is important to note the following things. (1) Except RR algorithm, all other algorithms use about [43%–62%] more VMs than the proposed algorithm BRVMP. However, RR fails to place all the VMs to PMs.

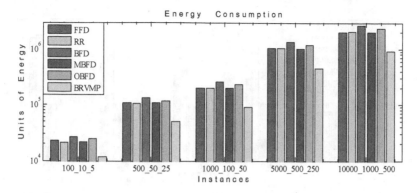

Fig. 6. Comparison of energy consumption for all the existing and proposed algorithms

(2) The existing FFD, RR, BFD, MBFD and OBFD algorithms use about [100%–132%], [150%–285%], [100%–200%], [100%–137%] and [150%–303%] more PMs than BRVMP. (3) These existing algorithms give approximately 2%, 42%, 1%, 4% and 37% less average PM utilization than BRVMP. (4) They also produce about [92%–128%], [80%–128%], [124%–197%], [85%–126%] and [111%–164%] more energy consumption than the proposed algorithm. Note that these approximate percentage values are subjected to the generated datasets. The rationality behind the better performance of BRVMP is that it monitors the VMs based on the user requests and further monitors the PMs based on the VMs. Thus, the number of used VMs and PMs is drastically reduced. It is noteworthy to mention that we have not explicitly shown the average VM utilization and energy consumption of VMs as they are associated with the average PM utilization and energy consumption of PMs.

We also compare the BRVMP and ORVMP algorithm using five different datasets, as shown in Table 7 (also in Fig. 7). It is obvious to see that the ORVMP outperforms BRVMP in all the performance metrics, (especially, energy consumption). The rationality behind this is that ORVMP selects a subset of VMs (or PMs) such that the minimum remaining capacity of those VMs are minimized. Note that ORVMP is feasible on the smaller value of τ. For larger value, BRVMP is reasonable.

Table 7. Comparison of the proposed BRVMP and ORVMP algorithm

Dataset	P_1		P_2		P_3		P_4	
	RVMP	ORVMP	RVMP	ORVMP	RVMP	ORVMP	RVMP	ORVMP
10_2_1	2	2	1	1	80	80	6.18e+03	6.18e+03
20_4_2	2	2	2	1	69	93	1.07e+04	7.13e+03
30_6_3	5	5	3	2	80	84	1.84e+04	1.29e+04
40_8_4	5	5	4	3	77	83	2.39e+04	1.92e+04
50_10_5	7	7	4	3	83	88	2.57e+04	2.04e+04

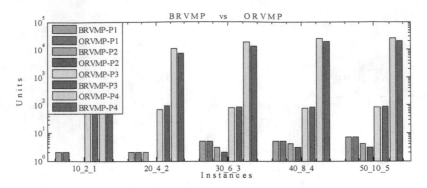

Fig. 7. Comparison of performance metrics (P_1 to P_4) for BRVMP and ORVMP algorithm

6 Conclusion

We have proposed a VM placement algorithm called RVMP for cloud computing systems. The basic placement of RVMP (BRVMP) has been shown to require $O(kn^2)$ time for n user requests and k iterations. On the contrary, the optimal placement of RVMP (ORVMP) has been shown to require $O(km^\tau n)$ time for m VMs and τ^{th} placement. We have performed an extensive simulation on the proposed algorithm and compared the results with state-of-the-art algorithms using five different datasets. Our simulation results show that the proposed RVMP outperforms than existing algorithms in terms of four performance metrics. Further, we have compared the basic and optimal placement of RVMP and found that ORVMP outperforms BRVMP. In the future, we plan to investigate cost-based VM placement.

References

1. Dayarathna, M., Wen, Y., Fan, R.: Data center energy consumption modeling: a survey. IEEE Commun. Surv. Tutor. **18**(1), 732–794 (2016)
2. Durao, F., Carvalho, J.F.S., Fonseka, A., Garcia, V.C.: A systematic review on cloud computing. J. Supercomput. **68**, 1321–1346 (2014). Springer
3. Google Apps: Energy Efficiency in the Cloud, Google White Paper (2012)
4. Esfandiarpoor, S., Pahlavan, A., Goudarzi, M.: Structure-aware online virtual machine consolidation for datacenter energy improvement in cloud computing. Comput. Electr. Eng. **42**, 74–89 (2015). Elsevier
5. Whitney, J., Delforge, P.: Data Center Efficiency Assessment. National Resources Defense Council, New York (2014). Issue Paper
6. Lama, P., Guo, Y., Jiang, C., Zhou, X.: Autonomic performance and power control for co-located web applications in virtualized datacenters. IEEE Trans. Parallel Distrib. Syst. **27** (5), 1289–1302 (2016)
7. Beloglazov, A., Abawajy, J., Buyya, R.: Energy-aware resource allocation heuristics for efficient management of data centers for cloud computing. Future Gener. Comput. Syst. **28**, 755–768 (2012). Elsevier

8. Nathani, A., Chaudhary, S., Somani, G.: Policy based resource allocation in IaaS cloud. Future Gener. Comput. Syst. **28**, 94–103 (2012). Elsevier

9. Zhang, S., Qian, Z., Luo, Z., Wu, J., Lu, S.: Burstiness-aware resource reservation for server consolidation in computing clouds. IEEE Trans. Parallel Distrib. Syst. **27**(4), 964–977 (2016)

10. Lin, C., Liu, P., Wu, J.: Energy-aware virtual machine dynamic provision and scheduling for cloud computing. In: 4th International Conference on Cloud Computing, pp. 736–737. IEEE (2011)

11. Song, W., Xiao, Z., Chen, Q., Luo, H.: Adaptive resource provisioning for the cloud using online bin packing. IEEE Trans. Comput. **63**(11), 2647–2660 (2014)

12. Ahmad, R.W., Gani, A., Hamid, S.H.A., Shiraz, M., Yousafzai, A., Xia, F.: A survey on virtual machine migration and server consolidation frameworks for cloud data centers. J. Netw. Comput. Appl. **52**, 11–25 (2015). Elsevier

13. Trivella, A., Pisinger, D.: The load-balanced multi-dimensional bin-packing problem. Comput. Oper. Res. **74**, 152–164 (2016). Elsevier

14. Kusic, D., Kephart, J.O., Hanson, J.E., Kandasamy, N.: Power and performance management of virtualized computing environments via lookahead control. In: International Conference on Autonomic Computing, pp. 3–12. IEEE (2008)

Access Control

An Efficient Framework for Verifiable Access Control Based Dynamic Data Updates in Public Cloud

S. Sabitha[1]([⊠]) and M.S. Rajasree[2]

[1] College of Engineering, Trivandrum, India
ssabithasureshkumar@gmail.com
[2] IIITM-K, Trivandrum, India

Abstract. Attribute-based encryption enables the users to get the data only if attributes of the users are satisfied with the access policy embedded in the ciphertext. Whenever it is used in a collaborative environment, user's claim policy has to be verified before permitting them to update the data. In the existing system, it is verified by the computationally expensive attribute-based signature. We are proposing an efficient method to compute the signature of the encrypted message and claim policy, which enables claim policy verification and thereby allow the users to modify the data. In this system, public cloud server (PCS) permits the users to modify the outsourced data in the cloud after verifying the user's claim policy signature. It does not disclose the claim policy to the cloud service provider, PCS, and unauthorized users. Data owner is able to verify the integrity of the outsourced data set to ensure that the data is always intact with him. He can also validate the updated data by incorporating the signature. The proposed scheme is privacy preserving and avoids insider attack.

Keywords: Cloud computing · Ciphertext-policy attribute-based encryption · Remote data integrity · Verification · Authenticity

1 Introduction

Cloud computing is extensively used for data storage and sharing. In order to overcome challenges associated with the cloud and ensure the security, it is necessary to encrypt the data and then outsource to the cloud. But encryption cannot ensure the access control on outsourced data. Attribute-based encryption (ABE) is a promising cryptographic solution to ensure access control. It can selectively share the data among the users. It provides not only fine-grained access control but also hides data from the CSP and unauthorized users [4]. In attribute-based encryption, owners decide access policy to encrypt the data, which in turn determines the attributes that users should possess to decrypt the data. Multiple key distribution centers (KDC) act as attribute authorities to distribute the attributes and keys to the users. It has disjoint set of attributes

© Springer International Publishing AG 2017
P. Krishnan et al. (Eds.): ICDCIT 2017, LNCS 10109, pp. 147–158, 2017.
DOI: 10.1007/978-3-319-50472-8_12

which is distributed to authorized users by verifying their identity. KDCs distribute secret keys to the users based on attributes possessed by each user [13]. Users are able to decrypt the data only if attributes of the users are satisfied with the access policy embedded in the ciphertext.

Whenever the users want to modify the data in a cloud based collaborative environment, they send a claim policy signature to the PCS. Upon receiving the claim policy signature, cloud verifies the claim to prove the authenticity of the writer and thereby allows them to update the data. In the existing system, authenticity verification of claim policy is done by the attribute-based signature [8], it is a computationally expensive operation [9,11]. Integrity and authenticity verification of the attribute-based encrypted data has not been addressed [11]. We are proposing a novel idea to verify the claim policy to allow the authorized users for data modification. The scheme also supports remote data integrity and authenticity verification of the outsourced data. It resolves the possibility of insider attack emerges due to the unauthorized data modification.

The paper is organized as follows. Related work is described in Sect. 2. Mathematical background and attribute-based encryption is presented in Sect. 3. The proposed scheme and system model is detailed in Sect. 4. Implementation and comparison is reviewed in Sect. 5. The security is analyzed in Sects. 6 and 7 concludes the work.

2   Related Works

Chase et al. [1,2] proposed a multi-authority ABE scheme; several KDCs distribute attributes and secret keys to users. Ruj et al. [10] proposed a distributed access control for data storage in the cloud. The scheme is collusion-secure and redistribution of keys is not needed while user revoked from the system. Lewko et al. [6] proposed a fully decentralized ABE with multiple KDCs; which do not require a trusted server, users can get any number of attributes from any KDC. KDCs have a disjoint set of attributes. But decryption at the user side needs more computation, so mobile phone users are facing some problems while accessing the information. To overcome this problem, outsourcing the decryption of ABE has been proposed by Green et al. [3]. The presence of one KDC and one proxy make it less robust than other decentralized approaches. Yang et al. [16] proposed an anonymous authentication of users while accessing the cloud. It is a privacy-preserving scheme.

Centralized access control scheme proposed by Maji et al. [8] ensure anonymous user authentication. Later they proposed a decentralized approach [9], which provides authentication without disclosing the identity of users. But it is prone to replay attack. Hierarchical attribute based encryption [12] proposed by Wang et al. relies on CP-ABE and hierarchical IBE. It is based on trusted authority.

A decentralized access control with anonymous authentication of data storage in the cloud is proposed by Ruj et al. [11]. It supports authenticity verification of users by cloud without disclosing the identity of user, but user's attributes get disclosed. So the scheme is able to preserve privacy to some extent by keeping the user identity as anonymous. It is also able to prevent the replay attack, supports data dynamics and user revocation. The scheme is robust and performance is comparable as that of centralized access control mechanisms. One of the limitations of the scheme is that it cannot hide the attributes of access policy and user's claim policy. None of these schemes consider the integrity and authenticity verification of access control based shared data. Claim policy signature verification without directly disclosing the claim policy has not been addressed in any of the previous schemes.

3   Preliminaries

3.1   Bilinear Maps

Attribute-based encryption is based on the bilinear map. In this section, we present some facts about bilinear maps. Let G_0 and G_1 be two multiplicative cyclic groups of prime order P and g be a generator of G_0. A bilinear map $e : G_0 \times G_0 \to G_1$ is symmetric [17]. The bilinear map e is an injective function with the following properties [5]:

1. **Bilinearity:** $\forall u, v \in G_0$ and $a, b \in Z_p$, we have $e(u^a, v^b) = e(u, v)^{ab}$.
2. **Non-Degeneracy:** There exists $g \in G_0$ with $e(g, g) \neq 1$, map does not send all pairs in $G_0 \times G_0$ to the identity in G_1.
3. **Computability:** There is an efficient algorithm to compute $e(u, v)$, $\forall u, v \in G_0$.

3.2   Attribute-Based Encryption

Attribute-based encryption with multiple KDCs proposed by Lewko and Waters [6] is a decentralized attribute-based encryption. Users will get the attributes and keys from multiple KDCs which prevent the drawbacks due to centralized attribute-based encryption [11]. The scheme includes the following algorithms:

1. Global Setup(λ) $\to GP$
   Let G_0 and G_T be bilinear groups of prime order p with generator g, $e : G_0 \times G_0 \to G_T$ denote bilinear map and hash function $H : (0, 1)^* \to G_0$ maps the identities of users to the elements of G_0.
2. KDCSetup(GP) $\to (PK, SK)$
   Each KDC $k_j \in K$ has a set of disjoint attributes a_j where $a_i \cap a_j = \phi$ for $i \neq j$. Each KDC chooses two random exponents $\alpha_i, \beta_i \in Z_p$. Secret key and public key of KDC k_j is

$$SK[j] = \{\alpha_i, \beta_i, \forall i \in a_j\}; \quad PK[j] = \{e(g, g)^{\alpha_i}, g^{\beta_i}, \forall i \in a_j\} \quad (1)$$

3. KeyGen(SK,i,GP,u) $\to sk_{i,u}$
   Each KDC distributes attributes and corresponding keys to all the users by verifying the identity of users who are requesting the attributes and secret

key. Then KDC k_j gives a set of attributes A[j,u] and secret key $sk_{i,u}$ corresponding to each $i \in A[j,u]$ to user U_u.

$$sk_{i,u} = g^{\alpha_i} H(u)^{\beta_i} \tag{2}$$

4. Encrypt($M, (L, \rho), GP, PK) \to CT$
   Encrypt the message M using the access policy L decided by the data owner. Access policy determines who can decrypt the ciphertext. Access policy is represented by LSSS scheme [11] which is represented as $n \times l$ access matrix L with ρ mapping its rows to attributes. $\rho(x)$ is the mapping from L_x to the attribute i that is located at the corresponding leaf of the access tree.

$$Ciphertext \quad CT = (L, \rho, ct_0, \{ct_{1,x}, ct_{2,x}, ct_{3,x}\} \forall_x) \tag{3}$$

5. Decrypt(CT,$\{sk_{i,u}\}$, GP) $\to M$
   If the user has the secret key corresponding to the access policy in the ciphertext, then he will be able to decrypt the ciphertext and get the original message M. Authorized user's attributes will be satisfied with the access policy embedded in the ciphertext.

3.3 Integrity Verification

Public auditability [15] of the outsourced data in the cloud is done in 5 phases as follows:

1. SetUp(1^k) $\to (pk, sk)$
   Data owner generates public and private key required for tag generation.
2. TagGen(pk, sk, m) $\to D_m$
   Data owner computes the block tag of each outsourced data block.
3. Challenge(pk, D_m) $\to chal$
   Verifier generates a challenge and sends it towards cloud server for integrity verification.
4. GenProof($pk, D_m, m, chal$) $\to R$
   Cloud server receives the challenge and calculates the block tag of each outsourced data block. Then send it to the verifier.
5. CheckProof($pk, D_m, chal, R$) $\to \{T, F\}$
   Verifier receives the cloud server's response, then compare it with self-computed block tag.

4 Proposed Privacy Preserving Verifiable Authenticated Data Updates in ABE

In this section, we are proposing a privacy preserved remote data integrity verification and dynamic data updates on attribute-based encrypted data. It is a decentralized access control mechanism. In the proposed system, data owner computes the signature (σ) and encrypts the data using attribute-based encryption with the help of access policy, then outsourced to the cloud and share it with the requested users. The system allows the authorized users to update the outsourced data after verifying their claim policy. Authorized users are able to verify the signature and thereby ensure the authenticity and freshness of the data. The format of the outsourced data and system model is shown in Figs. 1 and 2 respectively.

In order to enable the users to update the data, data owner securely sent claim policy signature (σ_0) [14] to the cloud through SSH. Whenever the users want to modify the data, they send their claim policy signature (σ_u) along with the request to the cloud. Cloud verifies the signature and grant permission to modify the data only if user's claim policy signature is satisfied with the claim policy signature securely stored in the cloud. Otherwise, users will not be able to modify the data. Users can decrypt the ciphertext using the secret key obtained from KDCs only if the user's attributes are satisfied with the access policy embedded in the ciphertext. Even though the claim policy of outsourced data is not directly disclosed to the PCS and users, the cloud can verify the user's claim policy signature (σ_u) with the claim policy signature (σ_0) securely stored in the cloud.

Fig. 1. Outsourced data format

Consider a real life situation in which, head of the institution wants to share some documents with his subordinates and selected students. But he has to restrict some recipients to modify the shared data so that he decides the access policy and claim policy required for the purpose. Let the access policy L be ((Instn.X AND (HOD AND Dept.CS)) OR (Instn.X AND (Dean.PG OR Dean.Research)) OR (Instn.X AND Student.Research AND (Dept.CS OR Dept. EC))) and claim policy τ be (Instn.X AND (Dean.PG OR Dean.Research)). Figure 3 represents the corresponding access tree used to encrypt the data and claim policy for valid writers. The proposed scheme supports the following operations.

4.1   Creating and Outsourcing Encrypted Data to the Cloud

Data owner computes the signature (σ) of the data, encrypts the data using ABE and calculates the DataTag (D_i) of the encrypted data. Then outsource the encrypted data and signature to the cloud and keep the DataTag in its local storage. Whenever the user updates the data, data owner recalculates the signature and upload it to the cloud to ensure the authenticity and freshness of the data. PCS can also compute the updated DataTag, but it cannot regenerate the signature since it contains data owner's secret key.

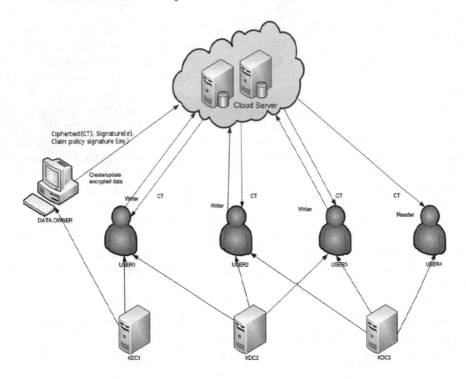

Fig. 2. System model for verifiable decentralized ABE

Data owner determines the claim policy (τ) required to allow the authorized users to modify the data in attribute-based encryption. PCS can verify the user's claim policy request against the claim policy signature (σ_o) securely stored in the cloud. Claim policy is a monotonic boolean expression. Data owner is only able to modify the signature and claim policy signature since it contains data owner's secret key. The encryption and signature computation are as follows:

1. **Encryption.** The access policy needed to encrypt the data is represented as $n \times l$ access matrix L with ρ mapping its rows to attributes. $\rho(x)$ is the mapping from L_x to the attribute i that is located at the corresponding leaf of the access tree [6]. Choose random number $s \in Z_n$, random vector $v \in Z_n^l$ with s as the first entry and random vector $w \in Z_n^l$ with 0 as the first entry. Then

$$\lambda_x = L_x.v; \quad \omega_x = L_x.w \tag{4}$$

Where L_x is the row x of L.
For each row L_x choose random $r_x \in Z_n$

$$ct_0 = M.e(g,g)^s; \quad ct_{1,x} = e(g,g)^{\lambda_x}.e(g,g)^{\alpha_{\rho(x)}.r_x} \forall_x \tag{5}$$

$$ct_{2,x} = g^{r_x} \forall_x; \quad ct_{3,x} = g^{\beta_{\rho(x)}.r_x}.g^{\omega_x} \forall_x \tag{6}$$

$$Ciphertext \quad CT = (L, \rho, ct_0, \{ct_{1,x}, ct_{2,x}, ct_{3,x}\} \forall_x) \tag{7}$$

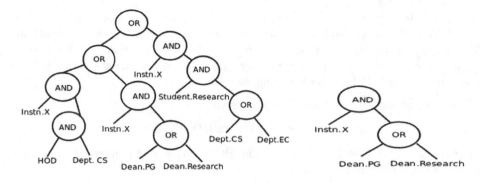

(a) Access policy   (b) Claim policy

Fig. 3. Access tree representations

2. **DataTag.** $D_i = g^{H(CT_i)} mod N$; where $N = pq$; p, q large primes
3. **Signature.** $\sigma = H(M_i)^x, \quad x \in Z_p$
4. **Claim Policy Signature.** $\sigma_o = r_o + x.H(\tau, R_o) mod q$; where *secret key* $x \in Z_p, random\ r_o \in Z_p, R_o = g^{r_o}, q - prime$

4.2   Reading Data from the Cloud

Whenever the user requests ciphertext, cloud server releases the ciphertext (CT). User can decrypt the ciphertext using secret key (SK) obtained from KDC, only if the user's attributes are satisfied with the access policy embedded in the ciphertext. That means, $ABE.Decrypt(CT, \{sk_{i,u}\}, GP) \to M$

$$dec(x) = \frac{ct_{1,x}.e(H(u), ct_{3,x})}{e(sk_{\rho(x),u}, ct_{2,x})} = e(g,g)^{\lambda_x}.e(H(u),g)^{\omega_x} \tag{8}$$

Choose $c_x \in Z_N$ *such that* $\sum_x c_x.Lx = \{1, 0, 0, ...0\}$ *then computes*

$$\prod_x (e(g,g)^{\lambda_x}.e(H(u),g)^{\omega_x})^{c_x} = e(g,g)^s \tag{9}$$

$$M = ct_0/dec(x) = \frac{M.e(g,g)^s}{e(g,g)^s} \tag{10}$$

4.3   Writing to the Cloud

Whenever the data owner decides to allow a particular user in a collaborative environment to modify the data, data owner securely sent claim policy (τ) and claim policy signature (σ_o) to the respective user through SSH. Upon receiving claim policy signature, the user requests PCS to modify the data by sending the user's claim policy signature (σ_u). The PCS verifies the user's claim policy signature and grants permission to modify the data depends on the verification. The colluding attack is not possible in the scheme since user's claim policy signature contains the secret key of user and data owner. User's claim policy signature is computed by the following procedure:

Choose secret key $r_u \in Z_p$; public key $R_u = g^{r_u}$

$$Signature \quad \sigma_u = r_u + \sigma_o.H(\tau, R_u) mod q \tag{11}$$

User sends ($\sigma_u, H(\tau, R_u)$) to the PCS. The PCS verifies σ_u to ensure the authenticity of the writer by the following procedure.

$$g^{\sigma_u} =^? R_u.(R_o.Y^{H(\tau,R_o)})^{H(\tau,R_u)} \tag{12}$$

Where $Y = g^x$; data owner's public key. Claim policy is not directly disclosed so it cannot be misused by the cloud and users.

4.4   Remote Data Integrity and Authenticity Verification

All the users are able to verify the authenticity and freshness of the outsourced data using signature verification. Whenever the data has been modified, the data owner recomputes the signature and upload to the cloud to ensure the authenticity of the outsourced data. All the users as well as data owner is able to perform the integrity verification of a set of outsourced data. Remote data integrity and authenticity verification are done by the following algorithms.

Authenticity Verification

1. BLS.Sign $(M_i, x) \rightarrow \sigma$
   Data owner computes the signature by hashes the message to some element in group G_o, $\sigma = H(M_i)^x$; $x \in Z_p$ then attach the signature along with the ciphertext.
2. BLS.Verify $(\sigma, g^x, g) \rightarrow \{T, F\}$
   Each data owner publishes their public key. All the users can verify the authenticity of the outsourced data using the corresponding signature and data owner's public key. Algorithm returns true if the verification is successful otherwise, returns false. The user verifies the signature of the outsourced data as follows:

$$e(\sigma, g) =^? e(H(M_i), g^x) \tag{13}$$
$$e(H(M_i)^x, g) =^? e(H(M_i), g^x) \tag{14}$$

Remote Data Integrity Verification

1. SetUp(1^k) $\rightarrow (pk, sk)$
   Data owner generates public and private parameters based on the security parameter 1^k. Let $N = pq$, where p and q are large primes and $p = 2p'+1, q = 2q'+1$ where p', q' are primes. Let g be a generator of G_0. $pk = (N, g)$, $sk = (p, q)$. pk is released to the public and sk is kept as secret.

2. DataTagGen$(pk, sk, CT_i) \rightarrow D_i$

   Generate the metadata corresponding to the outsourced data for integrity verification. For each outsourced data $CT_i, i \in [1, n]$ data owner computes the DataTag $D_i = g^{H(CT_i)} mod N$. Whenever the authorized user modifies the data, PCS and data owner can recalculate the DataTag and store it in the local storage for remote data integrity verification.

3. Challenge$(pk) \rightarrow chal$

   In order to verify the integrity of a set of ciphertexts CT_i, verifier generates a random key $r \in [1, 2^k - 1]$ and a random group element $s \in Z_n$ then computes $g_s = g^s mod N$ and sends $chal = < r, g_s, CT_{i \in (1..n)} >$ to the cloud server.

4. GenProof$(pk, chal) \rightarrow R$

   Upon receiving the challenge $chal = < r, g_s, CT_{i \in (1..n)} >$, cloud server generates a sequence of ciphertext indices $a_1, a_2, ..., a_n$ using the function $f_r(i), i \in [1, n]$, which is shared between cloud server and users. Then server computes $R = g_s^{\sum_{i=1}^{n} a_i H(CT_i)} mod N$ and send it to the verifier.

5. CheckProof$(pk, D_i, chal, R) \rightarrow \{T, F\}$

   The verifier receives R from the server and computes the index $\{a_i\}_{i=1..n}$ using the function $f_r(i)$. Then verifier computes P and R'. Compare the R' with received R for integrity verification. It returns T if the verification succeeds otherwise returns F. Whenever the privileged user modifies the data, DataTag is recomputed.

$$P = \prod_{i=1}^{n} (D_i^{a_i} mod N) \qquad (15)$$

$$R' = P^s mod N \qquad (16)$$

5 Implementation and Comparison

All the experiments were done on a 2.2 GHz intel core-i7 processor with 8GB of RAM running 32-bit Linux Kernel version 3.2.0. Proposed scheme implemented using PBC library [7]. All pairing operations were done by the PBC library. The implementation used a 160-bit elliptic curve group based on the supersingular curve $y^2 = x^3 + x$ over a 512-bit finite field.

Table 1. Comparison with other access control schemes

Schemes	Centralized/ decentralized	Access policy	Read/write	Access control	Integrity verification	Claim policy verification	Data authenticity
Yu [17]	Centralized	Any monotonic boolean fn.	1-W-M-R	ABE	No	No	No
DACC [10]	Decentralized	Any monotonic boolean fn.	1-W-M-R	ABE	No	No	No
Ruj [11]	Decentralized	Any monotonic boolean fn.	M-W-M-R	ABE	No	Yes	No
Our scheme	Decentralized	Any monotonic boolean fn.	M-W-M-R	ABE	Yes	Yes	Yes

5.1 Comparison

We have compared our scheme with other existing access control mechanisms, it is described in Table 1. The comparison reveals that the proposed protocol behaves well as that of the existing schemes with additional security features.

6 Security of the System

KDCs distribute attributes to the users by verifying the user's authenticity. The proposed scheme is secure due to the following reasons:

Theorem 1. *Our access control scheme allows access only to the authorized users. Neither unauthorized insider/outsider nor cloud/KDC can decrypt the ciphertext.*

Proof. Initially we are proving that no unauthorized user can access data. Authorized users with relevant secret keys are required for decrypting the ciphertext.

- *Let X be the set of rows of access matrix L. User U_u calculates the set of attributes which are common to itself and access matrix by using $\{\rho(x) : x \in X\} \cap I_u$*
- *For each attribute check whether there is a subset X' of rows of L such that the vector $(1, 0, 0, ...0)$ is their linear combination.*
  - *If not, decryption not possible.*
  - *If yes, calculate constants $c_x \in Z_p$ s.t $\sum_{x \in X'} c_x L_x = (1, 0, 0...0)$*

For each $x \in X'$

$$dec(x) = \frac{ct_{1,x}.e(H(u), ct_{3,x})}{e(sk_{\rho(x),u}, ct_{2,x})}$$

$$= \frac{e(g,g)^{\lambda_x}.e(g,g)^{\alpha_{\rho(x)}.r_x}.e(H(u), g^{\beta_{\rho(x)}.r_x}.g^{\omega_x})}{e(g^{\alpha_{\rho(x)}}H(u)^{\beta_{\rho(x)}}, g^{r_x})}$$

Since $e(P, R.S) = e(P, R).e(P, S)$

$e(P.Q, R) = e(P, R).e(Q, R)$

$$= \frac{e(g,g)^{\lambda_x}.e(g,g)^{\alpha_{\rho(x)}.r_x}.e(H(u), g^{\beta_{\rho(x)}.r_x}).e(H(u), g^{\omega_x})}{e(g^{\alpha_{\rho(x)}}, g^{r_x}).e(H(u)^{\beta_{\rho(x)}}, g^{r_x})}$$

$$= \frac{e(g,g)^{\lambda_x}.e(g,g)^{\alpha_{\rho(x)}.r_x}.e(H(u), g^{\beta_{\rho(x)}.r_x}).e(H(u), g^{\omega_x})}{e(g,g)^{\alpha_{\rho(x)}.r_x}.e(H(u), g^{\beta_{\rho(x)}.r_x})}$$

$$= e(g,g)^{\lambda_x}.e(H(u), g^{\omega_x})$$

$$= e(g,g)^{\lambda_x}.e(H(u), g)^{\omega_x}$$

Remember $\lambda_x = R_x.v$, $\omega_x = R_x.w$ where $v.(1, 0, 0..0) = s$ and $\omega.(1, 0, 0..0) = 0$

Then $\Pi_x(e(g,g)^{\lambda_x}.e(H(u), g)^{\omega_x})^{c_x} = \Pi_x(e(g,g)^{R_x.v.c_x}.e(H(u), g)^{R_x.w.c_x}) = e(g,g)^s$

$$Therefore \quad M = ct_0/dec(x) = \frac{M.e(g,g)^s}{e(g,g)^s}$$

Next, we prove that cloud cannot get data because secret key is not available with the cloud. It cannot decrypt the ciphertext if it colludes with other users who cannot individually decrypt, since different users have different $e(H(u), g)^{\omega_x c_x}$. KDCs cannot decrypt the ciphertext themselves since the attributes and user's secret keys are contributed by different KDCs.

Theorem 2. *Unauthorized data update can be verified.*

Proof. Unauthorized data update attempt, which leads to the insider attack is verified by the public cloud server by verifying the claim policy signature as follows.

$$g^{\sigma_u} = g^{r_u + \sigma_o . H(\tau, R_u)}$$
$$= g^{r_u} . g^{\sigma_o . H(\tau, R_u)}$$
$$= R_u . g^{(r_o + x . H(\tau, R_o)) H(\tau, R_u)}$$
$$g^{\sigma_u} =^? R_u . (R_o . Y^{H(\tau, R_o)})^{H(\tau, R_u)}$$

Next, we show that data owner can verify the integrity of a set of outsourced data and insider attack. Data update done by the unauthorized insider can be verified during remote integrity verification by the data owner, then $R \neq R'$.

$$Data\ owner\ computes \quad P = \prod_{i=1}^{n} (D_i^{a_i} mod N)$$

$$= \prod_{i=1}^{n} ((g^{H(CT_i)})^{a_i} mod N) mod N$$

$$= \sum_{i=1}^{n} (g^{a_i H(CT_i)} mod N) mod N$$

$$P^s = (g^{s \sum_{i=1}^{n} a_i H(CT_i)} mod N) mod N$$

$$= g^{s \sum_{i=1}^{n} a_i H(CT_i)} mod N = R'$$

$$PCS\ computes \quad g_s^{\sum_{i=1}^{n} a_i H(CT_i)} mod N$$

$$= (g^{s \sum_{i=1}^{n} a_i H(CT_i)} mod N) mod N$$

$$= g^{s \sum_{i=1}^{n} a_i H(CT_i)} mod N = R$$

7   Conclusion

In this paper, we proposed an efficient access control framework for dynamic data updates in attribute-based encryption. We have constructed a verifiable scheme which can identify the insider attack due to the unauthorized modification of data. The scheme ensures the authenticity of the outsourced data and prevents the collusion attack. Security and correctness of the scheme has been proved. The scheme allows only the authorized users to modify the data after the user's claim policy verification done by the PCS. In order to preserve the privacy and security, the scheme does not directly disclose the claim policy to the PCS and users. We have compared the scheme with other existing schemes based on the features of the proposed method.

References

1. Chase, M.: Multi-authority attribute based encryption. In: Vadhan, S.P. (ed.) TCC 2007. LNCS, vol. 4392, pp. 515–534. Springer, Heidelberg (2007). doi:10.1007/978-3-540-70936-7_28
2. Chase, M., Chow, S.S.M.: Improving privacy and security in multi-authority attribute-based encryption. In: Proceedings of the ACM Conference on Computer and Communications Security, pp. 121–130 (2009)
3. Green, M., Hohenberger, S., Waters, B.: Outsourcing the decryption of ABE ciphertexts. In: Proceedings of the USENIX Security Symposium, vol. 3 (2011)
4. Bethencourt, J., Sahai, A., Waters, B.: Ciphertext-policy attribute-based encryption. In: Proceedings of the IEEE Symposium Security and Privacy, pp. 321–334 (2007)
5. Hur, J., Noh, D.K.: Attribute-based access control with efficient revocation in data outsourcing systems. IEEE Trans. Parallel Distrib. Syst. **22**(7), 1214–1221 (2011)
6. Lewko, A., Waters, B.: Decentralizing attribute-based encryption. In: Paterson, K.G. (ed.) EUROCRYPT 2011. LNCS, vol. 6632, pp. 568–588. Springer, Heidelberg (2011). doi:10.1007/978-3-642-20465-4_31
7. Lynn, B.: The pairing-based cryptography (PBC) library (2012). http://crypto.stanford.edu/pbc
8. Maji, H.K., Prabhakaran, M., Rosulek, M.: Attribute-based signatures: achieving attribute-privacy and collusion-resistance. IACR Cryptology ePrint Archive (2008)
9. Maji, H.K., Prabhakaran, M., Rosulek, M.: Attribute-based signatures. In: Kiayias, A. (ed.) CT-RSA 2011. LNCS, vol. 6558, pp. 376–392. Springer, Heidelberg (2011). doi:10.1007/978-3-642-19074-2_24
10. Ruj, S., Nayak, A., Stojmenovic, I.: DACC: distributed access control in clouds. In: IEEE 10th International Conference Trust, Security and Privacy in Computing and Communications (TrustCom), pp. 91–98 (2011)
11. Ruj, S., Stojmenovic, M., Nayak, A.: Decentralized access control with anonymous authentication of data stored in clouds. IEEE Trans. Parallel Distrib. Syst. **25**(2), 384–394 (2014)
12. Wang, G., Liu, Q., Wu, J.: Hierarchical attribute-based encryption for fine-grained access control in cloud storage services. In: 17th ACM Conference Computer and Communications Security, (CCS), pp. 735–737 (2010)
13. Wang, G., Liu, Q., Jie, W.: Achieving fine-grained access control for secure data sharing on cloud servers. Concurr. Comput.: Pract. Exp. **23**(12), 1443–1464 (2011)
14. Wang, H., He, D., Tang, S.: Identity-based proxy-oriented data uploading and remote data integrity checking in public cloud. IEEE Trans. Inf. Forensics Secur. **11**(6), 1165–1176 (2016)
15. Wang, Q., Wang, C., Ren, K., Lou, W., Li, J.: Enabling public auditability and data dynamics for storage security in cloud computing. IEEE Trans. Parallel Distrib. Syst. **22**(5), 847–859 (2011)
16. Yang, K., Jia, X., Ren, K., DAC-MACS: effective data access control for multi-authority cloud storage systems. IACR Cryptology ePrint Archive, pp. 419–429 (2012)
17. Yu, S., Wang, C., Ren, K., Lou, W.: Attribute based data sharing with attribute revocation. In: ACM Symposium on Information, Computer and Communications Security (ASIACCS), pp. 261–270 (2010)

Analyzing Protocol Security Through Information-Flow Control

N.V. Narendra Kumar$^{(\boxtimes)}$ and R.K. Shyamasundar

Department of Computer Science and Engineering,
Indian Institute of Technology Bombay, Mumbai, India
naren.nelabhotla@gmail.com, shyamasundar@gmail.com

Abstract. Security protocols are essential for establishing trust in electronic transactions over open networks. Currently used languages/logics for protocol specifications do not facilitate/force the designer to make explicit goals, intentional assumptions or the preceding history across interactions among the stakeholders. This has resulted in gaps in specifications which in turn have led to problems such as: (i) inefficient/non-optimal protocol designs, (ii) incompatible theoretical attacks discovered by analyzers due to different threat models and (iii) faulty or insecure implementations due to insufficient guidelines for the implementer. We have recently developed the readers-writers flow model (RWFM) that has several benefits, including simple and intuitive labels. In this paper, we demonstrate that the problem of incomplete protocol specification can be overcome by enriching them with labels from RWFM, which make explicit the assumptions and goals at each stage of the protocol. In particular, we use readers and writers as labels for data objects and roles for tracking information flows in a protocol that makes explicit the construction of new messages from components of previous messages and also the knowledge of roles at various stages. We illustrate our approach and demonstrate its advantages in comparison to prominent specification languages in the literature by using the example of Needham-Schroeder public key protocol. Further, we argue how the proposed approach leads to a robust protocol specification language including security/cryptographic protocols that shall be of immense aid to the designer, user and the implementer of protocols.

Keywords: Security protocols · Formal methods · Information-flow security

1 Introduction

There has been a tremendous increase in the development and use of networked and distributed systems in the past three decades. For fully realizing the benefits offered by these systems, it is important to provide necessary functionality

N.V. Narendra Kumar—The work was carried out with support from ISRDC (Information Security Research and Development Center), a project sponsored by MeitY, GoI.

© Springer International Publishing AG 2017
P. Krishnan et al. (Eds.): ICDCIT 2017, LNCS 10109, pp. 159–171, 2017.
DOI: 10.1007/978-3-319-50472-8_13

to the user while efficiently utilizing the resources. Security protocols are small programs that aim at securing communications over a public network like the Internet. Authentication protocols are a class of security protocols that are concerned with authenticity and confidentiality properties and aimed at establishing communication channels that protect the integrity and secrecy of the data sent between the intended protocol participants. Other examples of security protocols include protocols for e-commerce and for electronic voting. The task of designing cryptographic protocols is made particularly challenging by the scale and complexity of modern distributed architectures and the number of security properties that have to be simultaneously fulfilled.

In the literature on security protocol design and analysis, protocols are commonly described using an informal notation that only gives an intended trace involving the honest principals. These protocol descriptions/narrations often leave many properties of a protocol unspecified. In particular, there is no way to determine the initial conditions or assumptions about shared information, nor can we see under what conditions the principals will respond to messages.

Designing cryptographic protocols is tremendously difficult and error-prone. The Needham-Schroeder symmetric key protocol was published in 1978 [16] and became the basis for many similar protocols in later years. In 1981, Denning and Sacco demonstrated that the protocol was flawed and proposed an alternative protocol [12]. In 1994, Abadi demonstrated that the public key protocol of Denning and Sacco was flawed [1]. Seventeen years after its publication, Lowe [14] demonstrated an attack on the Needham-Schroeder public key protocol and also proposed a change to the protocol that prevents the attack. In the intervening years, a whole host of protocols have been specified and found to be flawed.

Considering the increasing complexity of networks and their dependence on security protocols, a high level of assurance is needed in the correctness of such protocols. The development of methods for describing and analyzing security protocols started in the early 1980s [6,8,10,13]. Overall, the use of these formal methods has increased our confidence in some protocols. It has also resulted in the discovery of many protocol limitations and flaws, and in a better understanding of how to design secure protocols. Some general principles for guiding the creation and understanding of protocols are proposed in [1,3,4,20,22]. Such principles serve to simplify protocols and to avoid many mistakes. They also serve to simplify informal reasoning about protocols and their formal analysis.

However, despite all these advances in the specification, modelling and analysis of security protocols, carefully designed de facto standards like SSL [21] and PKCS [5], and even widely deployed products such as Kerberos [9] and EMV [7,15] are being successfully attacked.

The important contributions of this paper are:

– demonstrate that information flow control, in particular, the use of readers-writers labels, can be effectively used to design languages for specifying protocols. These languages cleanly capture the designer's intent and the necessary information that will enable local decisions satisfying the principles advocated by Abadi and Needham, and

– establish the significance of concepts like downgrading in showing the correctness of protocol relative to security and privacy policies.

The paper is organized as follows: the Readers-Writers Flow Model is introduced in Sect. 2. Section 3 presents our approach to protocol specifications and illustrates its advantages with the help of the Needham-Schroeder public key protocol. We place our work in comparison with prominent literature in the field of protocol design in Sect. 4, and present concluding remarks and plans for future work in Sect. 5.

2 Readers-Writers Flow Model (RWFM)

The Readers-Writers Flow Model (RWFM) proposed in [17,18] is a novel model for information flow control. RWFM is obtained by recasting the Denning's label model [11], and has a label structure that: (i) explicitly captures the readers and writers of information, (ii) makes the semantics of labels explicit, and (iii) immediately provides an intuition for its position in the lattice flow policy.

Recasting Procedure. Given a Denning's lattice model $DFM = (S, O, SC, \oplus, \leqslant)$ with flow policy $\lambda : S \cup O \to SC$, we recast the labels in terms of the readers and writers to obtain an equivalent flow policy defined by $DFM_1 = (S, O, SC_1, \oplus_1, \leqslant_1)$ and $\lambda_1 : S \cup O \to SC_1$, where: (i) $SC_1 = 2^S \times 2^S$, (ii) $\oplus_1 = (\cap, \cup)$, (iii) $\leqslant_1 = (\supseteq, \subseteq)$, and (iv) $\lambda_1(e) = (\{s \in S \,|\, \lambda(e) \leqslant \lambda(s)\}, \{s \in S \,|\, \lambda(s) \leqslant \lambda(e)\})$, where e is a subject or object.

RWFM is obtained by generalizing the above recasting procedure, and is defined as follows:

Definition 1 (Readers-Writers Flow Model (RWFM)). *Readers-writers flow model RWFM is defined as the eight tuple* $(S, O, SC, \leqslant, \oplus, \otimes, \top, \bot)$, *where S and O are the set of subjects and objects in the information system,*
$SC = S \times 2^S \times 2^S$ *is the set of labels,*
$\leqslant = (-, \supseteq, \subseteq)$ *is the permissible flows ordering,*
$\oplus = (-, \cap, \cup)$ *and* $\otimes = (-, \cup, \cap)$ *are the join and meet operators respectively, and*
$\top = (-, \emptyset, S)$ *and* $\bot = (-, S, \emptyset)$ *are respectively the maximum and minimum elements in the lattice.*

The first component of a security label in RWFM is to be interpreted as the owner of information, the second component as the set of readers, and the third component as the set of influencers. Note that RWFM is fully defined in terms of S, the set of subjects in the information system.

Note that the first component in the label is introduced only to facilitate limited discretionary flows (downgrades), and has no impact on the permissible information flows, or joins and meets. Therefore, we have abused notation in the above definition for simplicity, by uniformly blanking out the first component of the label.

Notation. $\lambda : S \cup O \to S \times 2^S \times 2^S$ denotes a labelling function. $A_\lambda(e)$, $R_\lambda(e)$ and $W_\lambda(e)$ denote the first (owner/admin), second (readers), and third (writers) components of the security class assigned to an entity (subject or object) e. Further, the subscript λ is omitted when it is clear from the context. Note that $A(s) = s$ always.

Note that in RWFM information flows upwards in the lattice as readers decrease and writers increase.

Theorem 1 (Completeness). *RWFM is a complete model, w.r.t Denning's lattice model, for studying information flows in a system.*

The recasting procedure presented at the beginning of this section actually constructs such an equivalent RWFM policy for a given Denning's policy.

RWFM Semantics of Secure Information Flow. RWFM provides a state transition semantics of secure information flow, which presents significant advantages and preserves useful invariants that aid in establishing that the system is secure or not misusing information. In the following, we present the RWFM semantics.

Let S denote the set of all the subjects in the system. RWFM follows a floating-label approach for subjects, with labels $(s, S, \{s\})$ and $(s, \{s\}, S)$ denoting the "**default label**" - the label below which a subject cannot write, and "**clearance**" - the label above which a subject cannot read, for a subject s respectively. Object labels are fixed and are provided by the desired policy at the time of their creation.

Definition 2 (State of Information System). *State of an information system is defined as the set of current subjects and objects in the system together with their current labels.*

Next, we describe the permissible state transitions of an information system, considering the primitive operations that cause information flows. The operations that are of interest are: (i) subject reads an object, (ii) subject writes an object, (iii) subject downgrades an object, and (iv) subject creates a new object. We believe that these operations are complete for studying information flows in a system. Note that we consider the set of subjects as fixed, and hence no operations for creation of new subjects.

READ Rule. *Subject s with label (s_1, R_1, W_1) requests read access to an object o with label (s_2, R_2, W_2).*
If $(s \in R_2)$ then
    change the label of s to $(s_1, R_1 \cap R_2, W_1 \cup W_2)$
    ALLOW
Else
    DENY

WRITE Rule. *Subject s with label (s_1, R_1, W_1) requests write access to an object o with label (s_2, R_2, W_2).*

If $(s \in W_2 \wedge R_1 \supseteq R_2 \wedge W_1 \subseteq W_2)$ then
>   ALLOW

Else
>   DENY

DOWNGRADE Rule. *Subject s with label (s_1, R_1, W_1) requests to downgrade an object o from its current label (s_2, R_2, W_2) to (s_3, R_3, W_3).*
If $(s \in R_2 \wedge s_1 = s_2 = s_3 \wedge R_1 = R_2 \wedge W_1 = W_2 = W_3 \wedge R_2 \subseteq R_3 \wedge (W_1 = \{s_1\} \vee (R_3 - R_2 \subseteq W_2)))$ then
>   ALLOW

Else
>   DENY

Intuitively, downgrading is allowed only by the owner at the same label as the information being downgraded, and (i) unrestricted addition of readers if he is the only influencer of information, or (ii) additional readers restricted to the set of stakeholders that contributed to the computation.

CREATE Rule. *Subject s labelled (s_1, R_1, W_1) requests to create an object o.*
Create a new object o, label it as (s_1, R_1, W_1) and add it to the set of objects O.

Given an initial set of objects on a lattice, the above transition system accurately computes the labels for the newly created information at various stages of the transaction/workflow.

3   Protocol Specifications Enriched with Information Flow Labels

In this section, we illustrate the Needham-Schroeder public key protocol [16] enriched with RWFM labels described in Sect. 2. Through the illustration we demonstrate the advantages of the information-flow model RWFM for protocol design.

3.1   Needham-Schroeder Public Key Protocol

Simplified Needham-Schroeder protocol, assuming that each principal has cached public keys of all other principals, is as below.

>   1 $A \rightarrow B : \{N_a, A\}_{K_b}$
>   2 $B \rightarrow A : \{N_a, N_b\}_{K_a}$
>   3. $A \rightarrow B : \{N_b\}_{K_b}$

The above specification is intended to convey the following:

- Principal A wishes to communicate with principal B. A creates a fresh nonce N_a, encrypts the nonce together with his identity with the public key of B (K_b), and sends it $(m_1 = \{N_a, A\}_{K_b})$ to B.
- Upon receiving m_1, B decrypts the message with his private key (K_b^{-1}), and understands (by looking at the identity in m_1) that A wishes to have a session with him. B then creates a fresh nonce N_b, encrypts A's nonce (obtained from m_1) together with his nonce with the public key of A (K_a), and sends it $(m_2 = \{N_a, N_b\}_{K_a})$ to A.

- Upon receiving m_2, A decrypts the message with her private key (K_a^{-1}), and understands this as B's reply to her request (due to the presence of N_a). At this stage, A is convinced that the principal at the other end is B, because only B could have decrypted m_1 and no other message contains N_a. A then encrypts B's nonce (obtained from m_2) with the public key of B and sends it ($m_3 = \{N_b\}_{K_b}$) to B.
- Finally B receives m_3, decrypts it and verifies the content to be his nonce, and is convinced that the principal at the other end is indeed A, because m_2 could only have been decrypted by A to know N_b.

3.2   Lowe's Attack and Fix

Several extensions of this protocol were deployed for practical usage over the internet. However, 17 years after the protocol is published, in 1995, Lowe discovered an "attack" [14] on the Needham-Schroeder public key protocol. The attack is an interleaving of two runs of the protocol. In one run, A initiates a session with C. Instead of following the protocol normally, C initiates a session (another protocol run) with B with the objective of making B believe that he is having a session with A and succeeds. We present Lowe's attack below, where $C(A)$ denotes C impersonating as A.

1.1 $A \rightarrow C : \{N_a, A\}_{K_c}$

$\qquad\qquad$ 2.1 $C(A) \rightarrow B : \{N_a, A\}_{K_b}$
$\qquad\qquad$ 2.2 $B \rightarrow C(A) : \{N_a, N_b\}_{K_a}$

1.2 $C \rightarrow A : \{N_a, N_b\}_{K_a}$
1.3 $A \rightarrow B : \{N_b\}_{K_b}$

$\qquad\qquad$ 2.3 $C(A) \rightarrow B : \{N_b\}_{K_b}$

In the same paper, Lowe also suggested a fix to the problem for preventing the attack. Lowe's fix was to replace step 2 in the protocol, 2. $B \rightarrow A : \{N_a, N_b\}_{K_a}$, with 2'. $B \rightarrow A : \{N_a, N_b, B\}_{K_a}$. In the modified protocol the attack depicted above is no longer possible because, if C forwards B's reply (2.2) to A, then upon decrypting it A would understand that this message is coming from B while she is expecting a reply from C. So A would suspect foul play by C and would not reply back and might not have further communications with C. Lowe conjectured that the modified protocol is free from attacks, and indeed no formal analysis tool to-date has been able to find an attack on it.

Our Reflections on Lowe's Attack and His Fix. First, note that in Lowe's attack, it is principal B that is being attacked. Lowe's attack was possible because, B, upon receiving message 2.1, had no way to deduce that it was indeed meant for him. Observing the information content of the message, because A's identity and K_b are both public information, anyone could have prepared the message. Note that Lowe's fix does not address this concern, but, avoids attacks by preventing A from replying if message 2 it receives is not from the expected principal. We argue that, from B's perspective (which is the affected party in the attack), lack of response (message 3) from A does not provide him any information about an attempted attack, because, lack of response could happen due to a variety of failures including connection problems and loss of packets in transmission.

3.3 Needham-Schroeder Protocol in Our Approach

From the discussion above, it is clear that the specification at the beginning of this section leaves a lot of assumptions unspecified/implicit about the protocol designer's intentions. In the following, we present our description of the Needham-Schroeder public key protocol in our approach. First we provide an informal interpretation of the protocol before interpreting it as complete information flow of the messages among the stakeholders.

The complete information flow of the Needham-Schroeder public key protocol is given in Fig. 1.

1. **Initial State**: two subjects $A^{(A,\{A,B\},\emptyset)}$ and $B^{(B,\{A,B\},\emptyset)}$, and four objects $K_a^{(S_1,*,\{A,S_1\})}$, $K_a^{-1(S_1,\{A\},\{A,S_1\})}$, $K_b^{(S_2,*,\{B,S_2\})}$ and $K_b^{-1(S_2,\{B\},\{B,S_2\})}$. Subjects can be thought of as processes that will handle the protocol session of principals. For simplicity, subject operating on behalf of a principal 'A' shall also be denoted by 'A'. Subject initial labels reflect that (i) (second component) no one other than 'A' and 'B' may access information generated during the interaction, and (ii) (third component) at this point they ('A' and 'B') have not accessed any information. 'A' and 'B's public-private key pairs are the four objects denoted by K_a, K_a^{-1}, K_b and K_b^{-1}. Label of K_a is $(S_1, *, \{A, S_1\})$ and its components convey the following information respectively: (i) S_1 created it (S_1 is a certification authority/key server), (ii) anyone (denoted by $*$) can access (read) it, and (iii) it was created because of an interaction between 'A' and S_1. Label of K_a^{-1} is similar except that it says only 'A' can read K_a^{-1}. Labels of K_b and K_b^{-1} are to be understood in a similar manner. Note that, we allow the possibility that 'A' and 'B's certification authorities/key servers may be different.

   ADVANTAGE 1: Note how our approach already provides better information than existing systems. In most specification languages, it will be said that: (i) everyone knows everyone else's public key, or (ii) only 'A' knows 'A's private key. Compare it with the information conveyed by labels of K_a and K_a^{-1}.

2. 'A' creates two objects: (i) nonce N_a, and (ii) his identity 'A' (we use 'A' to denote the object corresponding to the identity of principal 'A', to avoid confusion between subjects and objects). Both N_a and 'A' will be labelled $(A, \{A, B\}, \{A\})$, denoting that 'A' owns them, they are readable by 'A' and 'B', and only the information of 'A' is involved in creating them.

3. 'A' then reads N_a, 'A' and K_b. This is permitted after 'A's label is changed to $(A, \{A, B\}, \{A, B, S_2\})$ to reflect that 'A' accessed information accessible by 'A' and 'B', and influenced by 'A', 'B' and S_2.

4. 'A' creates $m_1 = \{N_a, a\}_{K_b}$ and sends it to 'B'. m_1 will be labelled $(A, \{A, B\}, \{A, B, S_2\})$.

5. 'B' receives m_1, checks its label and understands the following: 'A' has prepared it (first component) for a session with 'B' (second component) using the information of 'A', 'B' and S_2.

   INTERPRETATION 1: At this stage, 'B' must make sure that other than 'B' and 'B''s key server (S_2), there is only one other principal that influenced m_1 ('A' in this case), and that principal is also the preparer of the message and the only one (other than 'B') who is entitled to read it. *If any of the above checks fail, 'B' should not respond to the message.* Otherwise, 'B' reads m_1 and K_b^{-1}, which is allowed after 'B''s label is changed to $(B, \{B\}, \{A, B, S_2\})$ (note that K_b^{-1} is accessible only to 'B'), and decrypts m_1 to recover N_a and 'A'.

   INTERPRETATION 2: 'B' must check that the second object denotes the identity of the preparer of m_1, and that the labels of the two objects have the form $(X, \{X, B\}, \{X\})$, where X denotes the preparer of m_1 obtained above. *If any of the above checks fail, 'B' should not respond to the message.* Otherwise,

6. 'B' creates an object: nonce N_b, which will have label $(B, \{B\}, \{A, B, S_2\})$. Note that, with this label 'A' will not be able to read N_b which is crucial for further operation/function of the protocol.

7. 'B' downgrades N_b to $(B, \{A, B\}, \{A, B, S_2\})$, thereby enabling '$A$' to access this information.

   ADVANTAGE 2: From an information flow perspective, any information created by 'B' after accessing his private key might *leak* some information about it. This is acknowledged explicitly in our approach by 'B' having to downgrade N_b for the progress of the interaction. To the best of our knowledge, this important aspect is neither recognized nor acknowledged in any other specification language.

8. 'B' reads N_a, N_b and K_a for preparing the response. 'B''s label is changed to $(B, \{B\}, \{A, B, S_1, S_2\})$ to enable the reading.

9. 'B' creates the response $m_2 = \{N_a, N_b\}_{K_a}$ to be sent to 'A'. m_2 will be labelled $(B, \{B\}, \{A, B, S_1, S_2\})$. Note again that without downgrading, 'A' would not be able to read this message.

10. 'B' downgrades m_2 to $(B, \{A, B\}, \{A, B, S_1, S_2\})$ so as to enable 'A' to read it and sends it to 'A'.

11. 'A', who has been waiting for a response to his message, receives m_2.

    INTERPRETATION 3: 'A' must check m_2's label to ensure that it is created by the only other principal in his readers label ('B' in this case). Further, m_2's readers must be the same as 'A''s readers at this instance, and that 'A''s key server (S_1) is the only additional principal to have influenced m_2. *If any of the above checks fail, 'A' should not respond to the message.* Otherwise, 'A' reads m_2 and K_a^{-1}, which is allowed after 'A''s label is changed to $(A, \{A\}, \{A, B, S_1, S_2\})$ (note that K_a^{-1} is accessible only to 'A'), and decrypts m_2 to recover N_a and N_b.

    INTERPRETATION 4: 'A' must check that the first object recovered from m_2 exactly matches the first object he has created (N_a) for this interaction, including the labels. Further, 'A' must check that the label of the second object recovered from m_2 is $(B, \{A, B\}, X)$ where $X =$ principals that influenced 'A' at this instance - 'A's key server i.e., $X = \{A, B, S_1, S_2\} - \{S_1\} = \{A, B, S_2\}$ in this case. *If any of the above checks fail, 'B' should not respond to the message.* Otherwise,

12. 'A' reads N_b and K_b. No label changes are required.
13. 'A' creates $m_3 = \{N_b\}_{K_b}$ labelled $(A, \{A\}, \{A, B, S_1, S_2\})$. Note again that without downgrading, 'B' would not be able to read this message.
14. 'A' downgrades m_3 to $(A, \{A, B\}, \{A, B, S_1, S_2\})$ and sends it to 'B'.
15. 'B' receives the response m_3.

   INTERPRETATION 5: 'B' must check the label of m_3 to ensure that it has been created by 'A', accessible only to 'A' and 'B', and has been influenced by exactly same principals as himself at this instance. *If any of the above checks fail, 'B' should not respond to the message.* Otherwise, 'B' reads m_3 and K_b^{-1}. No label changes are required.
16. 'B' decrypts m_3 to recover N_b.

   INTERPRETATION 6: 'B' must check that the object recovered from m_3 exactly matches the first object he has created (N_b) for this interaction, including the labels. *If any of the above checks fail, 'B' should not continue the interaction.*

Having discussed the information flow between stakeholders, let us take interpretation in a consolidated manner starting from the IFD shown in Fig. 1.

Figure 1 depicts the global view of state transitions of the information system depicting a run of the Needham-Schoreder protocol. In the figure, states are represented by boxes and transitions are depicted by arrows labelled with operations responsible for the transition. Interpretation of the initial state (top left in figure) is simple and follows directly from item 1 of the protocol description in our approach given above. Note that, we only present the possible changes to state, and not the full state, resulting from transitions. For example, second state in the system resulting from the transition labelled "A creates N_a, a" is to be understood as adding objects N_a and a, both labelled $(A, \{A, B\}, \{A\})$, to

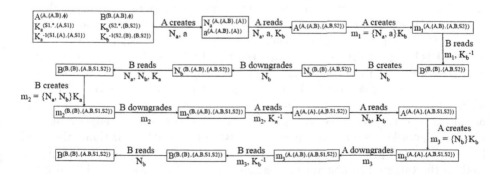

Fig. 1. Expected information flows in a successful honest run of the Needham-Schroeder public key protocol

the system. A subject or object that is already a part of the system may appear after a transition, subject due to read request and object due to downgrading, in which case this denotes label change only and not a new subject/object. This is the case, for example, at state 3 resulting from transition "A reads N_a, a and K_b" and at state 7 resulting from transition "B downgrades N_b".

We refer to the diagram in Fig. 1 as "information flow diagram". Information flow diagrams (IFD) would be of great help to the designers, analyzers and the implementers alike.

The functional requirements and security requirements of applications are often at odds with one another, and it is important to strike a fine balance between the two: a secure system that does not achieve the desired functionality is useless. Secure system design, thus, asks "what is the tightest/best security that one can achieve while being able to realize the desired functionality". From a designer's perspective, IFD could be used to refine the design: start with a basic design, typically using the most permissive labels that enable the functional requirements to be satisfied, and adding security requirements by making the labels more and more restrictive, until a point where further restricting the labels would compromise the functionality.

From an analyzers perspective, IFD can aid in the development of model checking algorithms for establishing that the proposed system provides the guaranteed security in theory/symbolic executions. In our opinion, with a little effort, the IFD could be extended with assertions/checks needed for the transitions to succeed thereby turning it into a security automata framework (or some close relative of it). From an implementer's perspective, these automata will help him arrive at a suitable enforcement mechanism that safeguards/guarantees the desired security during actual runs of the system.

3.4   Resilience of Our Approach to Lowe's Attack

Let us consider Lowe's attack in a setting where our approach is used for protocol specification. Message m_1 from A to C would be labelled $(A, \{A, C\}, \{A, C, S\})$, where S is C's key server. C would first have to decrypt m_1 making his label $(C, \{C\}, \{A, C, S\})$. Now, when he tries to encrypt the contents of m_1 with B's public key, it would result in message m_1' whose label after downgrading would be $(C, \{B, C\}, \{A, B, C, S, S_2\})$. When B receives m_1' and performs the checks in **INTERPRETATION** 1, m_1' fails the test because, there are three principals that influenced m_1' other than B and his key server. Even if one assumes $S = S_2$, there are two principals that influenced m_1' other than B and his key server, leading B to recognize this as an attempted attack. Further, from the perspective of forensics, decrypting m_1' and inspecting its contents would pin point the attacker. Thus, our approach resists Lowe's attack without the need for changing the protocol as opposed to Lowe's fix. Further, our approach also enables the targeted principal to recognize that he is under attack. The key factor here is that in RWFM, although there are rules that allow subjects to change readers in a limited way, there is no way to change the writers.

Threat modelling for security analysis is planned future work. However, we firmly believe that our approach resists most forms of attacks in the literature including the frequent man-in-the-middle attack.

4   Related Work

In [22], Woo and Lam propose the *Principle of Full Information* which says that:

> Authentication protocols should be designed in such a way that its participants include in every outgoing encrypted message all of the information they have gathered so far in the authentication exchange.

Further, they note that strict adherence to this principle could have eliminated many of the flaws in published protocols including their own protocol.

In our approach, label of a message conveys the information accessed by the preparer of the message till the time of preparing the message. Thus, specifications using our approach are closer to satisfying the principle of full information.

In [19], Roscoe observes that attacks generally result not from the overall protocol runs proceeding as intended, but from various nodes believing a run has been completed when it has not. Based on this observation, they define *Canonical Intensional Specifications* as:

> No participant can believe a protocol run has completed unless a correct series of messages has occurred (consistent as to all the various parameters) up to and including the last message the given participant communicates.

Enriching protocol specifications with information flow labels in our approach makes it a canonical intensional specification.

In [2], Abadi notes that the informal description of a protocol as a sequence of messages is incomplete and needs to be complemented with explanations of other forms. He advocates that protocol narrations must provide the following explanations:

- A specification should say which pieces of data are known to principals in advance and which are freshly generated.
- A specification should say how principals check the messages they receive, before responding to them.
- A specification should make explicit any permissible concurrency in message emissions.
- A complete specification should not rely on unclear, implicit conventions about concurrency and roles.

Note that, our narration of the Needham-Schoreder protocol in Sect. 3.3 provides information regarding the first two points above. In particular, the very first step in our narration makes explicit the initial state as consisting of two principals and their public-private key pairs. **INTERPRETATION**s 1 to 6 provide checks to be performed by the message recipients for responding to them.

5   Conclusions and Future Work

In this paper, we have shown that the RWFM based on the information flow principle can be used as a basis for protocol specification. Further, we have illustrated how the model that nicely integrates MAC and DAC satisfies the "principle of full information put forward by Woo and Lam; in a sense, it captures the needed history in a succinct manner to infer the underlying measures of confidentiality and integrity relative to the underlying information flow lattice. The underlying information also clearly keeps track of the downgrading of information when the message gets tainted by the most private information like private key etc. so that full information serves the purpose for which the protocol was designed. In our analysis done so far, we are of the opinion that specifying the protocols using the RWFM shall aid to choose possible choices for secure communication between stakeholders to assure security relative to a given threat model; this shall also aid in preserving performance of the underlying protocol. We are working towards a method to harness such a power in designing or adapting cryptographic protocols relative to different threat models. We are also working on showing how the IFD enables: (i) formal proof of correctness of protocols and also as to how it can be effectively used for checking protocols for compliance with respect to given policies, and (ii) to show that the envisaged model is capable of assessing practical privacy concerns like "only-for" and "not-for" in the context of operations in protocols.

References

1. Abadi, M., Needham, R.: Prudent engineering practice for cryptographic protocols. IEEE Trans. Softw. Eng. **22**(1), 6–15 (1996). http://dx.doi.org/10.1109/32.481513
2. Abadi, M.: Security protocols and their properties. In: Foundations of Secure Computation, NATO Science Series, pp. 39–60. IOS Press (2000)
3. Anderson, R., Needham, R.: Robustness principles for public key protocols. In: Coppersmith, D. (ed.) CRYPTO 1995. LNCS, vol. 963, pp. 236–247. Springer, Heidelberg (1995). doi:10.1007/3-540-44750-4_19. http://dl.acm.org/citation.cfm?id=646760.706015
4. Aura, T.: Strategies against replay attacks. In: Proceedings of the 10th Computer Security Foundations Workshop, 1997, pp. 59–68, June 1997
5. Bleichenbacher, D.: Chosen ciphertext attacks against protocols based on the RSA encryption standard PKCS #1. In: Krawczyk, H. (ed.) CRYPTO 1998. LNCS, vol. 1462, pp. 1–12. Springer, Heidelberg (1998). doi:10.1007/BFb0055716. http://dl.acm.org/citation.cfm?id=646763.706320
6. Blum, M., Micali, S.: How to generate cryptographically strong sequences of pseudo-random bits. SIAM J. Comput. **13**(4), 850–864 (1984). http://dx.doi.org/10.1137/0213053
7. Bond, M., Choudary, O., Murdoch, S.J., Skorobogatov, S.P., Anderson, R.J.: Chip and skim: cloning EMV cards with the pre-play attack. CoRR abs/1209.2531 (2012)
8. Burrows, M., Abadi, M., Needham, R.: A logic of authentication. ACM Trans. Comput. Syst. **8**(1), 18–36 (1990). http://doi.acm.org/10.1145/77648.77649

9. Butler, F., Cervesato, I., Jaggard, A.D., Scedrov, A., Walstad, C.: Formalanalysis of Kerberos 5. Theor. Comput. Sci. **367**(12), 57–87 (2006). http://www.sciencedirect.com/science/article/pii/S0304397506005743, Automated Reasoning for Security Protocol Analysis

10. DeMillo, R.A., Lynch, N.A., Merritt, M.J.: Cryptographic protocols. In: Proceedings of the Fourteenth Annual ACM Symposium on Theory of Computing, STOC 1982, pp. 383–400. ACM, New York (1982) http://doi.acm.org/10.1145/800070.802214

11. Denning, D.E.: A lattice model of secure information flow. Commun. ACM **19**(5), 236–243 (1976)

12. Denning, D.E., Sacco, G.M.: Timestamps in key distribution protocols. Commun. ACM **24**(8), 533–536 (1981). http://doi.acm.org/10.1145/358722.358740

13. Dolev, D., Yao, A.C.: On the security of public key protocols. IEEE Trans. Inf. Theory **29**(2), 198–208 (1983)

14. Lowe, G.: An attack on the Needham-Schroeder public-key authentication protocol. Inf. Process. Lett. **56**(3), 131–133 (1995). http://dx.doi.org/10.1016/0020-0190(95)00144-2

15. Murdoch, S., Drimer, S., Anderson, R., Bond, M.: Chip and pin is broken. In: 2010 IEEE Symposium on Security and Privacy (SP), pp. 433–446, May 2010

16. Needham, R.M., Schroeder, M.D.: Using encryption for authentication in large networks of computers. Commun. ACM **21**(12), 993–999 (1978). http://doi.acm.org/10.1145/359657.359659

17. Narendra Kumar, N.V., Shyamasundar, R.K.: Realizing purpose-based privacy policies succinctly via information-flow labels. In: 4th IEEE BDCloud, pp. 753–760. IEEE (2014)

18. Narendra Kumar, N.V., Shyamasundar, R.K.: POSTER: dynamic labelling for analyzing security protocols. In: 22nd ACM CCS, pp. 1665–1667 (2015)

19. Roscoe, A.W.: Intensional specifications of security protocols. In: Proceedings of the 9th IEEE Computer Security Foundations Workshop, 1996, pp. 28–38, June 1996

20. Syverson, P.: Limitations on design principles for public key protocols. In: Proceedings of the 1996 IEEE Symposium on Security and Privacy, 1996, pp. 62–72, May 1996

21. Wagner, D., Schneier, B.: Analysis of the SSL 3.0 protocol. In: Proceedings of the 2nd Conference on Proceedings of the Second USENIX Workshop on Electronic Commerce, vol. 2. WOEC 1996 (1996)

22. Woo, T.Y.C., Lam, S.S.: A lesson on authentication protocol design. SIGOPS Oper. Syst. Rev. **28**(3), 24–37 (1994). http://doi.acm.org/10.1145/182110.182113

Efficient Image Authentication Scheme Using Genetic Algorithms

Arjun Londhey and Manik Lal Das[✉]

DA-IICT, Gandhinagar, India
maniklal_das@daiict.ac.in

Abstract. We present an efficient image authentication scheme using Genetic algorithm (GA). Using the crossover and mutation process of GA the original image is randomized into a binary string. A pairing function is then used as a checksum function that converts the binary string to a fixed length digest of the original image. A random permutation is used as the secret parameter between the authenticator generator and verifier. The scheme provides a non-reversible compression and collision resistance property, and is secure against chosen plaintext attacks. The experimental results show that the proposed scheme is efficient in comparisons to standard cryptographic authentication algorithms.

Keywords: Image authentication · Genetic algorithm · Multimedia security · Content protection

1 Introduction

With the widespread use of image editing software, altering/tampering multimedia content for own business interest or blackmailing a target entity has become a challenging issue for digital content protection. A malicious party can alter image for target intention such as medical expense claim from insurance company based on forged medical reports, criminal evidence creation and so on. Statistical primitives [1] have been used considerably for digital content analysis. Least Significant Bit (LSB) matching [2], [3], [4], image hashing [5], [6], perturbation [7], [8], chaotic map [9], [10] have been introduced as useful features for watermark, content protection and copyright [11], [12]. Cryptographic primitives such as hash function, message authentication code (MAC) and digital signatures [13] have been used for image authentication [14]. However, image authentication by digital signature takes more cost in comparison to MAC-based image authentication techniques, as the data size of image may be large. A MAC algorithm (*a.k.a.* keyed hash function) accepts as input a secret key and an arbitrary-length message to be authenticated, and outputs a MAC (*a.k.a.* authentication tag). The MAC value provides both integrity and authenticity of the message.

Genetic algorithm (GA) [15] is a classical method used for solving optimization problems based on a natural selection, crossover and mutation process that mimics biological evolution. GA has found enormous applications in diverse fields

© Springer International Publishing AG 2017
P. Krishnan et al. (Eds.): ICDCIT 2017, LNCS 10109, pp. 172–180, 2017.
DOI: 10.1007/978-3-319-50472-8_14

such as image analysis, clustering, and scheduling in the search for optimal states of systems or functions. In general, GA is comprised with the main three operations: (i) Reproduction (current genes) (ii) Crossover (assembles existing genes into new combinations), and (iii) Mutation (produces new genes). The crossover and mutation operations offer interesting properties like confusion and diffusion used in cryptographic primitives like encryption.

In this paper, we present a scheme for image authentication using the features of GA and a paring function. The original image is employed as the initial population for starting the genetic algorithm, which is then iterated such that the resultant image with lowest correlation coefficient among the adjacent pixels is produced. A pairing function is used as a checksum function that converts the intermediate binary string (output of the mutation process) into a fixed length digest. A random permutation is used as the secret parameter between the authenticator generator and verifier. The proposed scheme provides non-reversible compression and collision resistance property, and is secure against chosen plaintext attacks. The experimental results show that the proposed scheme is efficient in comparisons to standard cryptographic authentication algorithms.

The remainder of this paper is organized as follows. In Sect. 2, we provide some preliminaries. In Sect. 3, we present the proposed scheme. In Sect. 4, we analyze the security of the scheme and provide the performance analysis in Sect. 5. We conclude the paper with Sect. 6.

2   Preliminaries

Hash Function. A cryptographic hash function is a function that maps an arbitrary length of binary strings to a fixed length of binary strings, defined as $h : \{0,1\}^* \rightarrow \{0,1\}^n$. The input binary strings is often called the message and the output strings is called the message digest or simply the digest. A hash function is cryptographically secure if is satisfies the following properties

- Pre-image resistance: Given a hash value $h(m)$, it is difficult to deduce any information of the message m. Function that lacks this property is vulnerable to pre-image attacks.
- Second pre-image resistance: Given an input $m1$ it is difficult to find another input $m2$ such that $h(m1) = h(m2)$. Function that lacks this property is vulnerable to second pre-image attacks.
- Collision resistance: It is difficult to find two different messages $m1$ and $m2$ such that $h(m1) = h(m2)$.

Cryptographic hash functions have important applications in achieving message authentication and integrity in various applications.

Correlation Coefficient. The correlation coefficient is defined as

$$r_{xy} = \frac{|cov(x,y)|}{\sqrt{D(x) * D(y)}},$$ where x and y are the gray levels in two adjacent pixels

of the image, and $cov(x,y) = 1/n\Sigma(x_i - E(x))(y_i - E(y))$ is the covariance, $E(x) = 1/n\Sigma_{i=1}^{n}x_i$ is the mean and $D(x) = 1/n\Sigma_{i=1}^{n}(x_i - E(x))^2$ is the variance.

3   The Proposed Scheme

The scheme consists of four algorithms defined as

- Determine the representation scheme.
- Determine the fitness measure.
- Determine the parameters.
- Determine the terminating condition.

In order to form the initial population from the image, the image is divided to a set of N vectors of length L. Then the vectors are employed to the crossover process in which two random values are selected from a vector and the swapping of the pixel value at these two locations is decided by the fitness measure. The crossover process is repeated M number of times for each vector. After applying Crossover process to each vector, the N vectors are imposed to Mutation process in which a random number is selected from each vector and one-bit mutation on the pixel location is performed. The fitness measure is the correlation coefficient of the adjacent pixels of the image. The process is repeated till a minimum fitness value is reached or the sufficient number of repetitions are reached.

3.1   Determine the Representation Scheme

Consider an image $I(W*H)$ such that W and H are the number of rows and columns of the image I. Split the image into set of N vectors each of length L. After that, take an integer array of size $256*256$ as the key set of the algorithm. For each vector N, select two values from key set as $R1$ and $R2$ and set the parameters CrossoverIndex $= R1$, CrossoverIteration $= V(R1)$, MutationIndex $= R2$, and MutationIteration $= V(R2)$. Here, $V(t)$ is the pixel value at index t.

3.2   Determine the Fitness Measure

Fitness value is determined as the minimum correlation coefficient of the adjacent pixel of the image. Until the desired fitness is achieved the crossover and mutation operations will be repeated. Once the desired fitness is achieved, the terminating condition is checked as explained in Subsect. 3.4.

Algorithm 1. Crossover Operation

1: **FOR** $j = 1$ to $CrossoverIteration$
2:     Select two number from key-set
3:     Generate the two offsprings
4:     Swap last four bits of one parent with first four bit of other parent
5:     **IF** fitness(offspring)$>$ fitness(parent) **THEN**
6:         Swap(parent pixel, offspring pixel)
7:     **ELSE**
8:         Parent pixel remains same
9:     **ENDIF**
10: **ENDFOR**
11: Fitness is the correlation coefficient of adjacent pixels

---

3.3   Determine the Parameters

The algorithm consists of two sub-algorithms: Crossover and Mutation. For $i = 0, 1, \cdots, N-1$, perform the following algorithms for each vector Vi from the set of N vectors.

Crossover Algorithm. From j from 0 to CrossoverIteration of vector $V(i)$, select two numbers from the key set. These numbers are considered as the indices of the vector. Then, the pixel values corresponding to these indices are selected. The crossover operation is performed on these pixel values by swapping the last four bits of one pixel with the first four bits of another pixel and vice-versa. After performing the crossover, two new pixel values corresponding to initial pixels are obtained as follows: *IF(fitness(new) > fitness(old))* THEN swap(new with old); ELSE keep original pixels unchanged. The process is repeated for $V(R1)$ times for each vector V.

Mutation Algorithm. From j from 1 to MutationIteration of vector $V(i)$, select a number from the key set R. The most significant bit (MSB) of $V(R)$ is mutated, that is,0 changed from zero to one and vice-versa. After mutation, a mutated pixel value is obtained. The mutation process is repeated for $V(i)$ times for each vector V.

Algorithm 2. Mutation Operation

1: **FOR** $j = 1$ to $MutationIteration$
2:     Select a number from key-set
3:     Generate an offspring
4:     Swap the MSB bit of parent from one to zero or zero to one
5:     **IF** fitness(offspring)> fitness(parent) **THEN**
6:        Swap(parent pixel, offspring pixel)
7:     **ELSE**
8:        Parent pixel remains same
9:     **ENDIF**
10: **ENDFOR**
11: Fitness is the correlation coefficient of adjacent pixels

---

3.4   Determine the Terminating Condition

The *Determine of parameters* algorithm is repeated till a fitness value is reached or the sufficient number of repetitions are reached. The image after passing through the genetic algorithm is finally passed through a pairing function π which is defined as $\pi(k_1, k_2) = \frac{1}{2}(k_1 + k_2)(k_1 + k_2 + 1) + k_2$, where k_1, k_2 are two positive integers. The image digest is calculated by using a modulo operator defined as $b = a \mod m$, where a is the dividend and m is the divisor chosen as 2^{100} to convert the image into 100 bits output.

4   Security Analysis

Theorem 1. The proposed scheme provides preimage resistance property.

Proof. The GA operation starts with taking two random number for choosing the number of crossover and mutation operations on each row of image. These random numbers are secret between the authenticator generator and verifier. For an attacker to get back to original image, the attacker has to guess the correct random numbers, where probability (P) of guessing random numbers is $P(\text{guessing } R_1) = \frac{1}{256}$ and $P(\text{guessing } R_2) = \frac{1}{256}$. Therefore, the combined effort required to obtain the correct pixel values at R_1 and R_2 is $P(\text{guessing } (V(R_1)$ and $V(R_2))|R_1, R_2) = \frac{1}{256^2}$. This implies that $P(\text{guessing correct crossover and mutation}) = \frac{1}{256^2} * \frac{1}{256} * \frac{1}{256} = \frac{1}{256^4} = \frac{1}{2^{32}}$.

It is noted that the number of crossover and mutations that can be performed on the image ranges from 1 to 256. Each Crossover operation changes 2 pixel value and thus producing 4 possible outcomes and Mutation operation changes 1 pixel value and producing 2 possible outcomes, which gives a total 1 out of 8 possible combination. Therefore, $P(\text{guessing correct pixel values}) = \frac{1}{2^3}$ and $P(\text{getting valid pixel in one iteration}) = \frac{1}{2^{32}} * \frac{1}{2^3}$. If we consider only one crossover and one mutation operation in each iteration and the minimum number of iterations to be performed is four, then $P(\text{getting valid pixel in four iteration}) = (\frac{1}{2^{32}} * \frac{1}{2^3})^4 = (\frac{1}{2^{35}})^4$. Therefore, the complexity of getting a valid pixel is 2^{140}, which is a difficult task for an attacker.   □

Theorem 2. The proposed scheme provides collision resistance property.

Proof. The scheme works with applying the input image to GA operation and the output of GA operation is passed through the modular function to generate the digest output as shown in Fig. 1, where P_1 and P_2 are collision probability in the GA operation and the modular operation, respectively.

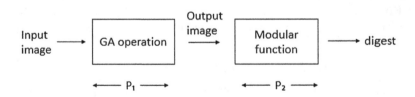

Fig. 1. Collision probability in the scheme

Collision Probability P_1. Consider two different inputs producing the same output in GA operation. The two different images will produce same output after mutation operation when,

- Input of Mutation operation is same.
- Input of Mutation operation is compliment to each other.

Case 1: It is possible when input to crossover operation is same for which the images have to be same.

Case 2: The output of mutation operation will be same only when either output of crossover is same or output is compliment to each other.

For each pixel we have two possible outputs which are compliment to each other. For 256 pixels in the image, possibility of producing same value at output is 2^{256}. The total possible output combination is 256^{256}, as each pixel contains 256 different values.

Therefore, the probability of producing a collision $P_{1(collision)} = \dfrac{2^{256}}{256^{256}} = \dfrac{1}{2^{1800}}$

Collision Probability P_2. The output of GA operation is applied to modular function which converts output into 256 bits. The two inputs will produce the same output when 256 bits are changed and thus the probability of two different input producing the same output $P_{2(collision)} = \dfrac{1}{2^{256}}$ because the output is repeated only after 256 bits of the input are changed. The overall probability of the scheme $P_{collision} = P_1 + (1 - P_1) * P_2 \approx \dfrac{1}{2^{256}}$.   □

Theorem 3. The scheme is secure against chosen plaintext attacks.

Proof. The GA operation starts with taking a random number R for each vector set, where the random number ranges from $\{1, 256\}$ different values which will give 2^8 different possible outcomes. The original image is divided into n vector sets where each vector set has a random number R. Choosing a different random number R produces a different output as number of crossover and mutation operation is dependent on the random number. If an image consists of 10 random numbers for 10 vector sets, then any input produces $2^8 * 2^8 * \cdots$ (10 times) $= 2^{80}$ different possible outcomes. If an attacker wants to guess the correct the output (digest of image) from given two images I_1 and I_2, then he can do so with probability $\dfrac{1}{2^{80}}$. The probability can be further negligible by choosing a large number of vector set for an image. Therefore, the attacker cannot distinguish a digest with non-negligible probability, which ensures the scheme's security strength against chosen plaintext attacks.   □

5   Experimental Results

We have implemented the proposed scheme on the gray scale (8-bit) bit mapped (bmp) images with 256 gray values. All experiments were done on Intel core i5 processor with MATLAB coding on Windows platform.

We have used 100 different images of varying sizes for experimenting the proposed algorithm. From the results (Figs. 2, 3, 4, 5 and Table 1), it is seen that the adjacent correlation between the pair of pixels are significantly reduced, and the adjacency correlation image shows that the adjacent pixels are scattered throughout the image. Table 2 shows the running time of the proposed

Fig. 2. Original image

Fig. 3. Randomized (GA) Image

Fig. 4. High correlation image

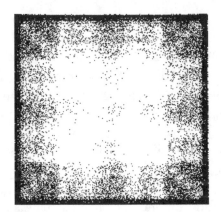

Fig. 5. Image GA operations

Table 1. Correlation coefficient of image

Image	Horizontal correlation	Vertical correlation	Average
Original	0.9478	0.9482	0.948
Randomized (GA)	0.0356	0.0267	0.0271

Table 2. Running time (msec)

Algorithm	512 * 512	768 * 768	1024 * 1024	2048 * 2048
MD5	3912.29	5361.03	7101.34	12116.76
SHA-1	4122.40	5534.19	8279.91	14346.91
SHA-2	4191.62	5661.72	8428.32	15397.19
SHA-3	4017.34	5455.67	7217.16	13218.28
HMAC	5419.18	6521.01	9516.47	16226.14
CBC-MAC	5619.14	6921.01	9726.47	17126.13
Proposed (GA)	4010.63	5305.19	7112.18	13174.38

Fig. 6. Original image   **Fig. 7.** GA using original key

scheme (GA) in comparison with the standard symmetric key based authentication algorithms. It is observed from Table 2 that the proposed scheme (GA approach) takes less time than other algorithms (except MD5). We note that the time taken by the proposed scheme is substantially reduced in comparison to cryptographic algorithms when the image size is increased.

To test the sensitivity of the key in the method used, first the Lena image (Fig. 6) is encrypted using the proposed algorithm (Fig. 7) and the original key, and later the same image is encrypted once again using the proposed algorithm with the difference that during the stage of producing initial population one bit of the key of the member is changed and the population is formed. After this new population is formed, the rest of the proposed algorithm is executed and in the end the results, shown in Fig. 8, is obtained. Figure 9 shows the similarity of the encrypted images (the white points are the common points of the two encrypted images). It is clear that the two images are about 98.18% different.

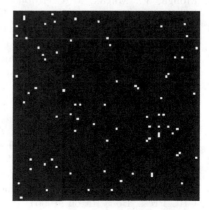

Fig. 8. GA using one-bit change in key   **Fig. 9.** Common points between images

6   Conclusions

We proposed an image authentication scheme using Genetic algorithm and a pairing function. Using the crossover and mutation features of GA the original image is randomized into a binary string. A pairing function is then used to convert the binary strings to a fixed length digest value of the original image. A random permutation is used as the secret parameter between authenticator generator and verifier. The scheme is secure with respect to pre-image resistance, collision resistance, and provides indistinguishability property. We have shown the experimental results of the proposed scheme, which is efficient in comparisons to standard cryptographic authentication algorithms. The proposed scheme can also be used for anti-piracy, ownership control and copyright of digital images.

References

1. Furht, B., Kirovski, D.: Multimedia Security Handbook. CRC Press, Boca Raton (2004)
2. Wan, R.Z., Lin, C.F., Lin, J.C.: Image hiding by optimal LSB substitution and genetic algorithm. Pattern Recogn. **34**(3), 671–683 (2001)
3. Afarin, R., Mozaffari, S.: Image encryption using genetic algorithm. In: proceedings of the Conference of Machine Vision and Image Processing, pp. 441–445 (2013)
4. Khodaei, M., Faez, K.: Image hiding by using genetic algorithm and LSB substitution. In: Elmoataz, A., Lezoray, O., Nouboud, F., Mammass, D., Meunier, J. (eds.) ICISP 2010. LNCS, vol. 6134, pp. 404–411. Springer, Heidelberg (2010). doi:10.1007/978-3-642-13681-8_47
5. Wang, X., Pang, K., Zhou, X., Zhou, Y.: A visual model-based perceptual image hash for content authentication. IEEE Trans. Inf. Forensics Secur. **10**(7), 1336–1349 (2014)
6. Liu, F., Wang, H., Cheng, L.-M., Ho, A.T.S., Li, S.: Enhanced perceptual image authentication with tamper localization and self-restoration. In proceedings of IEEE International Conference on Multimedia and Expo, pp. 1–6 (2014)
7. Monga, V., Mhcak, M.K.: Robust and secure image hashing via non-negative matrix factorizations. IEEE Trans. Inf. Forensics Secur. **2**(3), 376–390 (2007)
8. Swaminathan, A., Mao, Y., Wu, M.: Robust and secure image hashing. IEEE Trans. Inf. Forensics Secur. **1**(2), 215–230 (2006)
9. Enayatifar, R., Abdullah,A.H.: Image security via genetic algorithm. In: proceedings of International Conference on Computer and Software Modeling, pp. 198–203 (2011)
10. Ismail, I.A., Amin, M., Diab, H.: A digital image encryption algorithm based a composition of two chaotic logistic maps. Int. J. Netw. Secur. **11**(1), 1–10 (2010)
11. Chang, C.C., Hu, Y.S., Lu, T.C.: A watermarking-based image ownership and tampering authentication scheme. Pattern Recogn. Lett. **27**(5), 439–446 (2006)
12. Ahmed, F., Siyal, M.Y., Abbas, V.U.: A secure and robust hash-based scheme for image authentication. J. Signal Process. **90**(5), 1456–1470 (2010)
13. Vanstone, S., van Oorschot, P., Menezes, A.: Handbook of Applied Cryptography. CRC Press, Boca Raton (1996)
14. Tang, Y.L., Hwang, M.S., Yang, C.R.: An image authentication scheme based on digital signatures. Pak. J. Appl. Sci. **2**(5), 553–557 (2002)
15. Holland, J.H.: Genetic algorithms. Sci. Am., 66–72 (1992)

Security and Privacy

Dynamic Labelling to Enforce Conformance of Cross Domain Security/Privacy Policies

N.V. Narendra Kumar[(✉)] and R.K. Shyamasundar

Department of Computer Science and Engineering,
Indian Institute of Technology Bombay, Mumbai, India
naren.nelabhotla@gmail.com, shyamasundar@gmail.com

Abstract. Conformance of declared security policies while traversing different sites has been a challenge for realizing work-flows on clouds that need to move from one cloud domain to another domain from the perspective of optimization of utilization. Such a possibility will enable optimization of communication and thereby realize the tenet of Utility Computing or Cloud computing. In this paper, we show how dynamic relabelling realized through the Readers-Writers Flow Model (RWFM) enables us to realize such an important property. We shall illustrate the modelling through an example wherein the privacy policies of two domains that permit each other have different security policies and show how, it is possible to realize a joint policy that is in conformance with both the domains. This enables us to inform the user when the privacy policy for which he has signed differs from the cross-site traversal and thereby assure him that his main privacy policy is preserved. If not, he can provide an explicit endorsement as long as that will not compromise the security policy of the main domain for which he has signed.

Keywords: Privacy · Information flow · Conformance

1 Introduction

Current web applications often present a single visualization of resources accessed from multiple domains. This is enabled by mashups using the technology of cross-origin resource sharing (CORS). While this presents a large potential for business development, it also brings with it serious security challenges. In this context, it becomes imperative to have strong access controls to prevent devastating attacks including cross-site request forgery (CSRF) and cross-site scripting (XSS) which have been consistently featuring in the OWASP top 10 list of web vulnerabilities. In particular, even accidental disclosure of private data (data consisting of personal identifiable information) could lead to a crippling/life-altering effect on the user whose privacy has been compromised.

N.V. Narendra Kumar—The work was carried out with support from ISRDC (Information Security Research and Development Center), a project sponsored by MeitY, GoI.

© Springer International Publishing AG 2017
P. Krishnan et al. (Eds.): ICDCIT 2017, LNCS 10109, pp. 183–195, 2017.
DOI: 10.1007/978-3-319-50472-8_15

Privacy is quite a complicated notion in this digital world. In general terms, privacy has been defined to be the ability of an individual or group to seclude themselves, or information about themselves, and thereby express themselves selectively. Formalization of privacy has gained significant importance in the context of querying big data, health information systems, electronic patient records, etc. [2]. Consider the classic example of interactions between a patient and a physician discussed in [2]:

- A patient goes to a hospital and provides medical information to a physician.
- The physician needs help and passes some of this information to a nurse.
- The nurse then turns around and sells the information to a drug company that uses it for marketing.

Since some patients object to such uses of their health information and the society, wants to encourage open communication between patients and their physicians, countries like USA have adopted privacy policies, such as HIPAA, that prohibit such uses of patient information without their consent. To ensure that employees comply with these policies, hospitals employ auditors who examine accesses to and transmissions of protected information looking for actions that violate the privacy policies in place.

In view of this, a new research area of formalizing privacy policies has emerged [2] with the following two broad objectives:

1. Formalize Privacy Policies: Arrive at precise semantics of privacy concepts,
2. Enforce Privacy Policies for purposes like:
   - Audit: Detect violations of policy, and
   - Accountability: Identify agents to blame for policy violations and punish to deter policy violations.

One of the widely used strategies [2] is to formalize the notion of *purpose* in privacy policies. For instance,

- Yahoo!s privacy policy governing its email service says that it "will not use the contents of emails for marketing purposes".
- The social security administrations privacy policy says it "will use information collected only for the purposes for which it was collected".

Possible interpretation of the above examples are as envisaged in [2]:

- Yahoo!'s practice is not to use the content of messages [...] for marketing purposes. That is: Yahoo!s policy is an example of an *"not-for"* restriction,
- By providing your personal information, you give [Social Security Administration] consent to use the information only for the purpose for which it was collected. This will be an example of *"only-for"* restriction

Purpose restrictions are widely used in specifying privacy policies. Some of the prominent ones are mentioned below:

- OECDs Privacy Guidelines,
- US Privacy Laws such as HIPAA, GLBA, FERPA, COPPA ...
- EU Privacy Directive
- Enterprise Privacy Policies Google, Facebook, Yahoo ...

In this paper we demonstrate that "not-for" and "only-for" purpose restrictions can be succinctly captured through the dynamic labelling of RWFM discussed in Sect. 2 and further, the RWFM model permits a wide range of specifications.

The rest of the paper is organized as follows: a brief introduction to our Readers-Writers Flow Model is presented in Sect. 2, and its application to verifying and enforcing compliance of privacy policies across multiple interacting domains is described and illustrated with an example in Sect. 3. Section 4 discusses the application of our technique for protecting hybrid cloud environments, and Sect. 5 provides comparison with related work and concluding remarks.

2 Readers-Writers Flow Model (RWFM)

The Readers-Writers Flow Model (RWFM) proposed in [4,5] is a novel model for information flow control. RWFM is obtained by recasting the Denning's label model [3], and has a label structure that: (i) explicitly captures the readers and writers of information, (ii) makes the semantics of labels explicit, and (iii) immediately provides an intuition for its position in the lattice flow policy.

Recasting Procedure. Given a Denning's lattice model $DFM = (S, O, SC, \oplus, \leqslant)$ with flow policy $\lambda : S \cup O \rightarrow SC$, we recast the labels in terms of the readers and writers to obtain an equivalent flow policy defined by $DFM_1 = (S, O, SC_1, \oplus_1, \leqslant_1)$ and $\lambda_1 : S \cup O \rightarrow SC_1$, where:

(i) $SC_1 = 2^S \times 2^S$,
(ii) $\oplus_1 = (\cap, \cup)$,
(iii) $\leqslant_1 = (\supseteq, \subseteq)$, and
(iv) $\lambda_1(e) = (\{s \in S \mid \lambda(e) \leqslant \lambda(s)\}, \{s \in S \mid \lambda(s) \leqslant \lambda(e)\})$, where e is a subject or object.

RWFM is obtained by generalizing the above recasting procedure, and is defined as follows:

Definition 1 (Readers-Writers Flow Model (RWFM)). *Readers-writers flow model RWFM is defined as the 8-tuple* $(S, O, SC, \leqslant, \oplus, \otimes, \top, \bot)$*, where*

S and O are the set of subjects and objects in the information system,
$SC = S \times 2^S \times 2^S$ is the set of labels,
$\leqslant = (-, \supseteq, \subseteq)$ is the permissible flows ordering,
$\oplus = (-, \cap, \cup)$ and $\otimes = (-, \cup, \cap)$ are the join and meet operators respectively, and
$\top = (-, \emptyset, S)$ and $\bot = (-, S, \emptyset)$ are respectively the maximum and minimum elements in the lattice.

The first component of a security label in RWFM is to be interpreted as the owner of information, the second component as the set of readers, and the third component as the set of influencers. Note that RWFM is fully defined in terms of S, the set of subjects in the information system.

Note that the first component in the label is introduced only to facilitate limited discretionary flows (downgrades), and has no impact on the permissible information flows, or joins and meets. Therefore, we have abused notation in the above definition for simplicity, by uniformly blanking out the first component of the label.

Notation $\lambda : S \cup O \rightarrow S \times 2^S \times 2^S$ denotes a labelling function. $A_\lambda(e)$, $R_\lambda(e)$ and $W_\lambda(e)$ denote the first (owner/admin), second (readers), and third (writers) components of the security class assigned to an entity (subject or object) e. Further, the subscript λ is omitted when it is clear from the context. Note that $A(s) = s$ always.

Note that in RWFM information flows upwards in the lattice as readers decrease and writers increase.

Theorem 1 (Completeness). *RWFM is a complete model, w.r.t Denning's lattice model, for studying information flows in a system.*

The recasting procedure presented at the beginning of this section actually constructs such an equivalent RWFM policy for a given Denning's policy.

RWFM Semantics of Secure Information Flow RWFM provides a state transition semantics of secure information flow, which presents significant advantages and preserves useful invariants that aid in establishing that the system is secure or not misusing information. In the following, we present the RWFM semantics.

Let S denote the set of all the subjects in the system. RWFM follows a floating-label approach for subjects, with labels $(s, S, \{s\})$ and $(s, \{s\}, S)$ denoting the "**default label**" - the label below which a subject cannot write, and "**clearance**" - the label above which a subject cannot read, for a subject s respectively. Object labels are fixed and are provided by the desired policy at the time of their creation.

Definition 2 (State of Information System). *State of an information system is defined as the set of current subjects and objects in the system together with their current labels.*

Next, we describe the permissible state transitions of an information system, considering the primitive operations that cause information flows. The operations that are of interest are: (i) subject reads an object, (ii) subject writes an object, (iii) subject downgrades an object, and (iv) subject creates a new object. We believe that these operations are complete for studying information flows in a system. Note that we consider the set of subjects as fixed, and hence no operations for creation of new subjects.

For each of the above operations, we describe the conditions under which it is safe (causes only permissible information flows) and hence can be permitted. Note that when a subject s requests a new session, system assigns $(s, S, \{s\})$ as its current label.

READ Rule. *Subject s with label (s_1, R_1, W_1) requests read access to an object o with label (s_2, R_2, W_2).*
If $(s \in R_2)$ then
    change the label of s to $(s_1, R_1 \cap R_2, W_1 \cup W_2)$
    ALLOW
Else
    DENY

WRITE Rule. *Subject s with label (s_1, R_1, W_1) requests write access to an object o with label (s_2, R_2, W_2).*
If $(s \in W_2 \wedge R_1 \supseteq R_2 \wedge W_1 \subseteq W_2)$ then
    ALLOW
Else
    DENY

CREATE Rule. *Subject s labelled (s_1, R_1, W_1) requests to create an object o.*
Create a new object o, label it as (s_1, R_1, W_1) and add it to the set of objects O.

DOWNGRADE Rule. *Subject s with label (s_1, R_1, W_1) requests to downgrade an object o from its current label (s_2, R_2, W_2) to (s_3, R_3, W_3).*
If $(s \in R_2 \wedge s_1 = s_2 = s_3 \wedge R_1 = R_2 \wedge W_1 = W_2 = W_3 \wedge R_2 \subseteq R_3 \wedge (W_1 = \{s_1\}$
$\vee (R_3 - R_2 \subseteq W_2)))$ then
    ALLOW
Else
    DENY

Intuitively, downgrading is allowed only by the owner at the same label as the information being downgraded, and (i) unrestricted addition of readers if he is the only influencer of information, or (ii) additional readers restricted to the set of stakeholders that contributed to the computation.

Given an initial set of objects on a lattice, the above transition system accurately computes the labels for the newly created information at various stages of the transaction/workflow.

The transition system above satisfies the following invariants that are handy to establish flow security:

1. subject and object labels float upwards only,
2. for a subject s, $A(s) = s$, $s \in R(s)$, and $s \in W(s)$,
3. the set of writers of information is always accurately maintained (exactly the set of subjects that influenced the information content), this plays a vital role in forensics and audit,
4. label of newly created objects precisely reflects the circumstances under which they are created,

5. downgrade rule is within the boundaries of the flows permissible under a given transaction, and
6. multiple sessions of the same subject are handled cleanly.

3 Formalizing and Analyzing Privacy Policies in RWFM

Information system is a collection of subjects and objects, where subjects are the users of the system and objects denote the information stored in the system.

Definition 3 (Data Usage/Privacy Policy). *Data usage or privacy policy of an information system* (S, O), *is defined as a function* $\lambda : O \rightarrow S \times 2^S \times 2^S$ *that assigns* RWFM *labels to the objects in the system.*

Given the intuitive nature of RWFM labels and their explicit use of readers and writers to encode the policy, we firmly believe that converting natural language descriptions of typical privacy policies - use terms like transfer, permit, prohibit, use, collect etc. - to RWFM labels should be much simpler than other languages and logics developed for this purpose.

Recall that, given two RWFM labels $L_1 = (s_1, R_1, W_1)$ and $L_2 = (s_2, R_2, W_2)$, we say that L_1 can-flow-to L_2 denoted by $L_1 \leqslant L_2$, if and only if $R_1 \supseteq R_2$ and $W_1 \subseteq W_2$ i.e., L_1 has more readers and fewer influencers compared to L_2.

Definition 4 (Policy Comparison ($\sqsubseteq$)). *Given an information system* (S, O), *and two policies* λ_1 *and* λ_2, *we say that:*

- λ_1 *is* **weaker** *than* λ_2, *written* $\lambda_1 \sqsubseteq \lambda_2$, *if and only if* $\forall o \in O, \lambda_1(o) \leqslant \lambda_2(o)$,
- λ_1 *is* **stronger** *than* λ_2, *written* $\lambda_1 \sqsupseteq \lambda_2$, *if and only if* $\lambda_2 \sqsubseteq \lambda_1$, *and*
- λ_1 *and* λ_2 *are* **incomparable**, *if and only if* $\lambda_1 \not\sqsupseteq \lambda_2$ *and* $\lambda_2 \not\sqsupseteq \lambda_1$.

Intuitively, a weaker policy allows more readers for objects because of the superset ordering on the corresponding RWFM labels. Note that the relation $\sqsubseteq$ amongst policies is a partial-order.

Recall that, given two RWFM labels $L_1 = (s_1, R_1, W_1)$ and $L_2 = (s_2, R_2, W_2)$, we obtain label L on the combined information of the labels L_1 and L_2 denoted by $L_1 \oplus L_2$, as $(s, R_1 \cap R_2, W_1 \cup W_2)$.

Definition 5 (Policy Combination ($\boxplus$)). *Given an information system* (S, O), *and two policies* λ_1 *and* λ_2, *their combined policy* λ *denoted* $\lambda_1 \boxplus \lambda_2$, *is defined as follows:* $\forall o \in O, \lambda(o) = \lambda_1(o) \oplus \lambda_2(o)$.

Intuitively, the readers of an object in a combined policy are obtained by intersecting the readers of both the component policies. Note that the combined policy defined above is the weakest policy stronger than both the component policies.

Definition 6 (Policy Lattice). *The set of all possible policies of an information system* (S, O), *denoted by* Λ, *forms a lattice* $(\Lambda, \sqsubseteq, \boxplus, \lambda_\perp)$, *where* $\lambda_\perp$ *defined as* $\forall o \in O, \lambda_\perp(o) = (s, S, \{\})$ *denotes the weakest policy.*

3.1   Checking Policy Conformance in Federated Information Systems Through RWFM

Often two (or more) information systems fuse to form a federated system for advancing their business goals through sharing/exchanging data. A major concern in such systems is the security of data sharing i.e., compatibility of the data usage/privacy policies of the systems involved. In this section, we shall demonstrate how this can be effectively addressed through RWFM.

Definition 7 (Secure Information Sharing). *Consider information systems* $IS_1 = (S_1, O_1)$ *and* $IS_2 = (S_2, O_2)$ *with policies* λ_1 *and* λ_2 *respectively. We say that it is safe for* IS_1 *to share data* o_1 *with* IS_2 *if and only if,* $\lambda_1(o_1) \leqslant \lambda_2(o_1)$. *In this case, we also say that* IS_2 **conforms** *to* IS_1'*s policy on* o_1.

Intuitively, the above definition says that if the data receiver's policy allows fewer readers than the data owner's policy, then it is safe for the owner to share the data. Note that the asymmetry in the above definition captures the directionality of data movement.

Example 1. *Facebook's policy* (λ_1) *prohibits transfer of its user data* (o_1) *to advertising partners* (ad) *while it permits the use of this data by platform content providers like Zynga - in terms of* RWFM *labels this means* $ad \notin R(\lambda_1(o_1))$. *Zyngas policy* (λ_2) *permits transfer of user-id* (o_1) *to advertisers* (ad) *for preventing fraud - in terms of* RWFM *labels this means* $ad \in R(\lambda_2(o_1))$. *Facebook sharing user data with Zynga is insecure because* $\lambda_1(o_1) \not\leqslant \lambda_2(o_1)$, *because* $R(\lambda_1(o_1)) \not\supseteq R(\lambda_2(o_1))$, *because* $ad \notin R(\lambda_1(o_1))$ *but* $ad \in R(\lambda_2(o_1))$ *- a clear case of Zynga's non-conformance to Facebook's policy i.e., policy conflict.*

When multiple systems are combined to form a federated system, the set of subjects (objects) in the federated system is the union of the subjects (objects) of the component systems. While some objects in the federated system are exclusive to one component system, other objects - the objects that are agreed to be shared - may belong to multiple systems. However, note that there is exactly one component system that owns a shared object, and as far as the usage of that data is concerned the policy of the owner component must be the final word. Based on these intuitions, we now define a federated system of two component systems - can be generalized easily to $n > 2$ systems - as follows:

Definition 8 (Federated Information System). *The federated system of two information systems* $IS_1 = (S_1, O_1)$ *and* $IS_2 = (S_2, O_2)$ *with policies* λ_1 *and* λ_2, *is defined as a system* $FS = (S, O)$ *with policy* λ, *where* $S = S_1 \cup S_2$, $O = O_1 \cup O_2$, *and* $\forall o \in (O_{11} \cup O_{12}), \lambda(o) = \lambda_1(o)$, $\forall o \in (O_{22} \cup O_{21}), \lambda(o) = \lambda_2(o)$, *where*
$O_{11} = O_1 - O_2$ *Objects exclusive to* IS_1
$O_{22} = O_2 - O_1$ *Objects exclusive to* IS_2
$O_{12} \subseteq (O_1 \cap O_2)$ *Objects owned by* IS_1 *shared with* IS_2
$O_{21} \subseteq (O_1 \cap O_2)$ *Objects owned by* IS_2 *shared with* IS_1

Note that $(O_{12} \cap O_{21}) = \emptyset$, and $(O_{12} \cup O_{21}) = (O_1 \cap O_2)$.

Example 2. *Consider the scenario of Example 1. Assuming Facebook owns the user data o_1, in a federated system consisting of Facebook and Zynga, the policy on o_1 should be that of Facebook's i.e., $\lambda_1(o_1)$.*

Note how our definition of a federated system forces conformance to data owner's policy on its usage. As desired, the above definition reflects that in a federated system "owner of the data controls its usage", alternatively "in case of a conflict, the owners policy always wins".

Theorem 2. *Data sharing in a federated information system constructed per Definition 8 is secure.*

3.2 Enforcing Policy Conformance Through RWFM Dynamic Labelling

In the previous section, we have demonstrated how secure data sharing among multiple systems be achieved by combining them to form a federated system. Although conceptually simple, in practice it is not possible to achieve such a combined system due to a variety of reasons, and the systems have to operate from their individual domains. In this section, we shall show how even in this case RWFM dynamic labelling can achieve the desired security when sharing information that crosses domains.

Example 3. *Continuing the scenario in Examples 1 and 2, Facebook labels the user personal details (o_1) as $\lambda_1(o_1) = (F, \{F, Z, U\}, \{F, U\})$, where F, Z and U denote Facebook, Zynga and user respectively. If Z tries to read o_1 at a stage where Z's label is (Z, R_1, W_1), as per the READ rule of RWFM, it will be allowed because $Z \in R(\lambda_1(o_1))$, however Z's label will be changed to $(Z, R_1 \cap \{F, Z, U\}, W_1 \cup \{F, U\})$. As per the RWFM dynamic labelling rules, any object o that Z creates/writes after this step will have to satisfy $R(\lambda_2(o)) \subseteq (R_1 \cap \{F, Z, U\})$, which in turn implies $R(\lambda_2(o)) \subseteq \{F, Z, U\}$, which automatically enforces conformance with Facebook's policy.*

The example above demonstrates that dynamic labelling in RWFM i.e., semantics of operations **read**, **write**, and **create** in RWFM ensure that even if the receivers policy on data usage is in conflict with the owners policy, it is the owners policy that will be respected, alternatively, the receivers policy cannot override the owners policy. However, it is possible that the receivers policy is stronger than the owners policy, in which case the receivers policy already conforms to the owners policy and will be enforced.

The reason for such a result is the following: when an object o is fetched from a domain with policy $\lambda_1(o)$ into a domain with policy $\lambda_2(o)$, RWFM dynamic labelling rules ensure that the effective policy for o in the second domain would be $\lambda_1(o) \oplus \lambda_2(o)$, which is stronger than $\lambda_1(o)$ by definition and hence also conforms to $\lambda_1(o)$. The advantage of using RWFM is that this holds transitively i.e., even when the object crosses multiple domains.

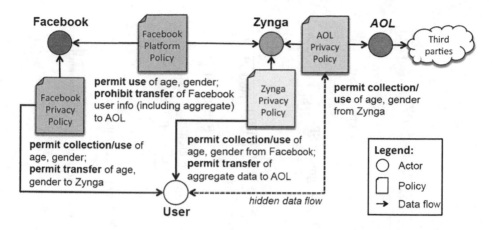

Fig. 1. Interaction of Facebook and Zynga privacy policies

Theorem 3. *Information systems implementing* RWFM *dynamic labelling can* **freely share data** *(labelled objects) amongst themselves - even through multiple hops - without the fear of compromising security, and worrying about the compatibility/conformance of the receivers policy.*

Illustrative End-to-End Example. Consider Facebook-Zynga policy in Fig. 1.

RWFM dynamic labelling for a typical usage scenario where a user logs in to his Facebook page, checks his messages, and plays a Zynga provided game, is depicted in Fig. 2. In the figure, states are represented by boxes and transitions are depicted by arrows labelled with operations responsible for the transition.

In the initial state, there are three subjects: F denoting Facebook, Z denoting Zynga, and U denoting the user, and three objects: CDb denoting the credential database of Facebook accounts, DZ denoting the default content provided by Zynga that is presented on the welcome page of the user, and UD denoting the contact details of the user. CDb is labelled $(F, \{F\}, \{F, U\})$, denoting that F is the owner, F is the only permissible reader, and F and U are the influencers - indeed password has to be provided by the user and hence his influence. DZ is labelled $(Z, \{F\}, \{Z\})$, denoting that Z is the owner and the only influencer, and F is the only permissible reader. UD is labelled $(F, \{F, U\}, \{F, U\})$, denoting that F owns it, F and U are the only influencers who are also the only permissible readers. Note that the label on UD can be automatically set based on the user's sharing preferences.

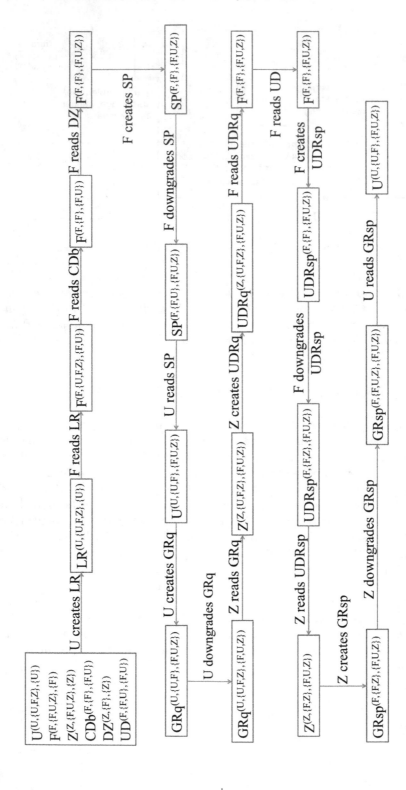

Fig. 2. IFD for a typical usage scenario. NOTE: for lack of space, we have depicted only the changes to the state and not the entire state after a transition.

Given the initial state and the operations performed by the user, observe how RWFM is able to automatically label all the subjects and new objects. Interpretation of the objects in the figure and are as follows:

LR - loginRequest   SP - startupPage
UD - userDetails   CDb - credentialDatabase
GRq - gameRequest   UDRsp - userDetailsResponse
DZ - defaultZyngaContent   UDRq - userDetailsRequest
GRsp - gameResponse

Note that, in the figure, we present only the changes to state, and not the full state, resulting from transitions. For example, second state in the system resulting from the transition labelled "U creates LR" is to be understood as adding the object LR, labelled $(U, \{U, F, Z\}, \{U\})$, to the system. A subject or object that is already a part of the system may also appear after a transition, subject due to read request and object due to downgrading, in which case this denotes label change only and not a new subject/object. This is the case, for example, at state 3 resulting from transition "F reads LR" and at state 7 resulting from transition "F downgrades SP".

From the figure, note that when F first creates the startup page (SP), F is its only permitted reader because before creation of SP, F had accessed the credential database which is sensitive and can only be accessed by F. However, because the startup page is prepared for the user, F downgrades it by adding U as a reader. In RWFM, this downgrading is allowed because SP has been created only upon the request from U and therefore influenced by him.

In Fig. 2, note that Facebook's response to Zynga's request for providing user details, denoted by UDRsp, is labelled (after downgrading) as $(F, \{F, Z\}, \{F, U, Z\})$. This guarantees that this information is not accessible by anyone other than Facebook and Zynga, thus, automatically forcing conformance on Zynga.

Further, note that the final labels of the three subjects are $F^{(F, \{F\}, \{U, F, Z\})}$, $U^{(U, \{U, F\}, \{U, F, Z\})}$, and $Z^{(Z, \{F, Z\}, \{U, F, Z\})}$. From this we can derive that as far as this transaction is concerned, F dominates both U and Z in the hierarchy (because the readers of F is a subset of the readers of both U and Z). Intuitively, this says that U and Z could connect and interact only via F. This hierarchy inferred by our approach is depicted in Fig. 3.

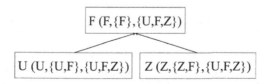

Fig. 3. Hierarchy of the subjects inferred by RWFM for the Facebook-Zynga example.

4   Application to Hybrid Cloud Security

ICT infrastructure requirements of organizations have grown several fold to meet the needs of its users, and has resulted in increasingly costly infrastructure proliferation. This increase in cost hindered organization's (particularly large heterogenous organizations) ability to modernise and fully exploit recent ICT developments.

Cloud computing is a way to access and use ICT services in a flexible and agile fashion, buying (hiring) only the services needed when they are needed. Cloud computing can be deployed through primarily four different models - private, public, hybrid and community. While the public cloud will offer substantial cost savings and increased flexibility for many ICT services and service users, data and privacy restrictions prevent some services from being hosted or provided through such means. The problem is particularly acute in the case of Government clouds. In these cases, a hybrid cloud service model can be used where the private cloud (managed in-house) provides the necessary security assurance to hold and process personal or restricted data.

Note that a hybrid cloud is a federated system, and that even in this case it is important to safeguard the data shared between the various clouds. Using the techniques sketched in the preceding section, we are working towards developing methods for data security and privacy from various perspectives in a hybrid cloud.

From a top-level view, the first step would be to secure the interactions between the clouds. This can be done at the level of a cloud manager, that is responsible for ensuring the authenticity of the stakeholders involved. Once this is achieved, then the next step would be to safeguard the privacy and security within a cloud when the computation is taking place. Towards achieving this, we are working on integrating an RWFM monitor with the map-reduce framework and the storage aspects including HDFS.

5   Comparison and Conclusions

In [1], authors encode data requirements from natural language privacy policies in Description Logic (DL), and analyse data flows within policies for detecting conflicts. Drawbacks of this approach compared to our approach are as follows: (i) DL is much harder to use compared to the intuitive nature of RWFM labels, (ii) no clear enforcement mechanism, and (iii) no remedies suggested for conflict resolution.

In [6], authors developed a system for automatic privacy compliance checking in big data systems and demonstrated its application to Bing. Drawbacks of this approach compared to our approach are as follows: (i) greater manual effort involved, (ii) works only for a centrally managed system, and (iii) does not control data propagation once released.

In this paper, we have demonstrated that: (i) RWFM labels provide a formalization for privacy policies in an intuitive way, (ii) RWFM labels provide an algorithm for checking policy conformance and/or resolving policy conflicts, and (iii) the dynamic labelling approach of RWFM forces policy conformance in a distributed manner as data moves across multiple domains.

References

1. Breaux, T.D., Hibshi, H., Rao, A.: Eddy, a formal language for specifying and analyzing data flow specifications for conflicting privacy requirements. Requirements Eng. **19**(3), 281–307 (2014)
2. Datta, A.: Privacy, audit and accountability. In: 22nd IFIP WCC 2012. http://www.wcc2012.org/pdfs/AData.pdf. Accessed 15 Aug 2016
3. Denning, D.E.: A lattice model of secure information flow. Comm. ACM **19**(5), 236–243 (1976)
4. Narendra Kumar, N.V., Shyamasundar, R.K.: Realizing purpose-based privacy policies succinctly via information-flow labels. In: 4th IEEE BDCloud, pp. 753–760. IEEE (2014)
5. Narendra Kumar, N.V., Shyamasundar, R.K.: POSTER: dynamic labelling for analyzing security protocols. In: 22nd ACM CCS, pp. 1665–1667 (2015)
6. Sen, S., Guha, S., Datta, A., Rajamani, S.K., Tsai, J.Y., Wing, J.M.: Bootstrapping privacy compliance in big data systems. In: IEEE SP, pp. 327–342 (2014)

Privacy Preserving Signcryption Scheme

Payal Chaudhari$^{(\boxtimes)}$ and Manik Lal Das

DA-IICT, Gandhinagar, India
payal.ldrp@gmail.com, maniklal_das@daiict.ac.in

Abstract. Signcryption is a public-key cryptographic primitive that is a synthesis of encryption and digital signature schemes. We present a signcryption scheme using anonymous attribute based encryption. The scheme uses the notion of identity-based digital signature on the message encrypted under the attribute based encryption scheme. The scheme provides both sender and receiver anonymity, in particular, only the legitimate receiver can identify the sender after the successful decryption operation. We show that the scheme is secure against adaptive chosen ciphertext attack and chosen message attack.

Keywords: Signcryption · Attribute based encryption · Identity based signature · Anonymity

1 Introduction

Attribute Based Encryption (ABE) is an interesting crypto primitive that supports fine-grained access control and message confidentiality. There are two variants of ABE: Key - Policy Attribute Based Encryption (KP-ABE) and Ciphertext - Policy Attribute Based Encryption (CP-ABE). Goyal *et al.* first introduced the KP-ABE scheme in [1], where user access rights are embedded in his secret key and the list of attributes are involved in ciphertext. Later Sahai and Waters proposed the first CP-ABE construction in [2], where the access control policy is attached with ciphertext and attribute values are included in user's key. Subsequently, many CP-ABE schemes have been proposed in literature [3–9], where ciphertext carries the access structure in clear form. As the access structure provides the information of which attribute(s) is/are required to decrypt the ciphertext, it discloses information about the intended recipients of the ciphertext from the ciphertext message. To overcome this problem, receiver anonymity is introduced in ABE schemes [10–13] known as Anonymous Attribute Based Encryption(AABE), which hides the access structure inside the ciphertext. As AABE hides legitimate receiver's identity, every user who receives a ciphertext may attempt to decrypt it believing that he is the intended recipient of the ciphertext. Therefore, the decryption operation in AABE scheme should have some novelty such that a recipient should not spend a significant cost for the decryption operation. In other words, the detection of wrong-person in wrong-ciphertext should be done with minimum use of computing resources.

© Springer International Publishing AG 2017
P. Krishnan et al. (Eds.): ICDCIT 2017, LNCS 10109, pp. 196–209, 2017.
DOI: 10.1007/978-3-319-50472-8_16

The schemes [11–13] suffers from performance bottleneck on receiver side because the receiver is enforced to perform decryption operation that involves a number of bilinear pairing operations for every ciphertext he receives, whether or not he is the intended recipient. To address this problem, Zhang *et al.* [14] proposed an approach called *Match-then-Decrypt*, where a receiver performs a matching operation on the received ciphertext using his key. If the match function succeeds, then the decryption function is performed, else not. In [15], it has been shown that Zhang *et al.*'s scheme suffers from some security flaws. In [16], the receiver's anonymity is supported with constant size ciphertexts, but the access structure used in [16] does not support multiple values for an attribute in a single ciphertext. In this work we present a scheme that includes least costly decryption operation and least size of ciphertext when compared with existing AABE schemes.

Although, ABE supports message confidentiality, there are some applications (e.g., healthcare, e-commerce) where message authenticity is another important requirement that the receiver wants to be assured about. Suppose that a doctor gets his patient's medical report in encrypted format from the hospital's laboratory. The doctor wants to verify whether the report is sent by the laboratory. For those applications, encryption can ensure confidentiality and signature can ensure message authenticity. Signcryption [17] is another interesting crypto primitive that performs signature and encryption operations simultaneously. It carries less computational cost in comparison to signature-then-encrypt operations. Identity Based Signcryption (IDSC) and Attribute Based Signcryption (ABSC) schemes are two different implementation flavors in the domain of signcryption.

The IDSC is the combination of Identity Based Encryption and Identity Based Signature techniques. Over the years, many IDSC schemes [18–22] have been proposed, which work for a single sender and a single receiver scenario. Subsequently, single sender and multiple receiver IDSC schemes [23–25] have been constructed. The major limitation of the multi-receiver IDSC schemes is the inclusion of receiver identities in the ciphertext, as it makes the ciphertext size long. In such schemes the ciphertext length increases as the number of recipient increases. ABSC schemes [26–28] can be an alternative to address this issue. An ABSC scheme is the result of merging Attribute Based Encryption technique with Attribute Based Signature. However, ABSC schemes fail when sender's and receiver's privacy is a need.

In this paper we present an anonymous Signcryption scheme that provides sender and receiver anonymity. The scheme uses AABE scheme with "AND gate on multivalued attributes" access structure and identity-based signature as the building blocks. In the scheme, if a receiver is not able to decrypt the message because of insufficient access privileges, then he will not be able to determine who is the sender. At the same time, when an authorized recipient decrypts a ciphertext, then he will be able to learn and verify who is the sender. The proposed construction is the first which provides both sender and receiver anonymity in Attribute Based Signcryption area with least costly unsigncryption cost

(decryption operation is part of the unsigncryption algorithm). The characteristics of the proposed scheme are as follows:

- The user key size is constant irrespective to the number of attributes in the
  system.
- Along with access control, message confidentiality, integrity and authenticity,
  the scheme provides sender and receiver anonymity.
- The scheme is existential unforgeable in adaptive-predicate chosen message
  attack (AP-EUF-CMA) and secure in indistinguishability in selective ciphertext policy and adaptively chosen ciphertext attack (IND-sCP-CCA2).
- The decryption operation of our scheme is efficient and least costly in comparison to existing AABE schemes. Therefore the unsigncryption operation
  also becomes cost-effective, because the decryption operation is part of an
  unsigncryption operation.

The remainder of the paper is organized as follows. Section 2 discusses some
preliminaries. Section 3 presents the proposed scheme. Section 4 provides the
security analysis of the scheme followed by the performance analysis in Sect. 5.
We conclude the paper in Sect. 6.

2   Preliminaries

2.1   Bilinear Mapping

Let G_0 and G_1 be two multiplicative cyclic groups of prime order p. Let g be
a generator of G_0 and e be a bilinear map, $e: G_0 \times G_0 \to G_1$ satisfying the
following properties:

- Bilinearity: $e(g^a, g^b) = e(g, g)^{ab}$ for all $a, b \in Z_p$.
- Non-degeneracy: There exists $g_1, g_2 \in G_0$ such that $e(g_1, g_2) \neq 1$.
- There exists an efficient computable algorithm to compute $e(g_1, g_2)$ for all g_1,
  $g_2 \in G_0$.

We say that G_0 is a bilinear group if it satisfies all above properties.

2.2   Access Structure

Like the schemes presented in [12–14], our scheme also uses the access structure
built upon the policy of "Single AND gate on Multivalued Attributes".

Here in proposed scheme we use the following notations. Let there be n
attribute in the universe and the attributes are denoted using the notation
$\{A_1, A_2, \cdots, A_n\}$. In subsequent discussion we use just i to indicate the attribute
$A_i(1 \leq i \leq n)$. Each value set $V_i = \{v_{i,1}, v_{i,2}, \cdots, v_{i,m_i}\}$ is the set of possible
values for an attribute i and m_i is the size of set V_i. A ciphertext policy T is
defined as $T = [T_1, T_2, \cdots, T_n]$. Here each T_i represents the set of permissible
values of an attribute i in order to decrypt the ciphertext. $T_i \subseteq V_i$. Each user
possesses an attribute value list $L = [L_1, L_2, \cdots, L_n]$, where each L_i represents
one value from the value set $V_i(L_i \in V_i)$. An attribute list L satisfies an access
structure T, if $L_i \in T_i$ for all $1 \leq i \leq n$. We define a binary relationship $F(L, T)$,
which gives output 1 if L satisfies an access structure T; else, it outputs 0.

2.3   Discrete Logarithm Assumption

Let $a \in \mathbb{Z}_p$ be chosen at random and g be a generator of G_0. We say that the Discrete logarithm assumption holds in G_0 if no probabilistic polynomial-time algorithm $\mathcal{P}$ can compute the value of a from the values of g and g^a with non-negligible advantage ϵ_{dl}. The advantage of $\mathcal{P}$ is $\Pr[\mathcal{P}(g, g^a) = a] = \epsilon_{dl}$.

2.4   Decisional Linear (D-Linear) Assumption

Let $z_1, z_2, z_3, z_4, z \in \mathbb{Z}_p$ be chosen at random and g be a generator of G_0. We say that the D-Linear assumption holds in G_0 if no probabilistic polynomial-time algorithm $\mathcal{P}$ can distinguish the tuple $(g, Z_1 = g^{z_1}, Z_2 = g^{z_2}, Z_3 = g^{z_1 z_3}, Z_4 = g^{z_2 z_4}, Z = g^{z_3 + z_4})$ from the tuple $(g, Z_1 = g^{z_1}, Z_2 = g^{z_2}, Z_3 = g^{z_1 z_3}, Z_4 = g^{z_2 z_4}, Z = g^z)$ with non-negligible advantage ϵ_{dli}. The advantage of $\mathcal{P}$ is $\Pr[\mathcal{P}(Z_1, Z_2, Z_3, Z_4, g^{z_3 + z_4}) = 0] - Pr[\mathcal{P}(Z_1, Z_2, Z_3, Z_4, g^z) = 0] = \epsilon_{dli}$.

3   The Proposed Scheme

3.1   System Model

The system comprises the following entities:

- Attribute Center(AC): It is a trusted third party. It is responsible for generating system parameters and issuing secret keys to users.
- Users: Data senders are the users who signcrypt and send the data. Data receivers are the users who receive the encrypted data, decrypt them using their secret key and on successful decryption they verify the sender identity.

3.2   Design Goals and Assumptions

The design goals and assumptions of the proposed scheme are as follows.

- A user can not generate a valid signcryption of a message with a false identity.
- A receiver whose secret key satisfies the access policy of the ciphertext can decrypt the ciphertext and learn the sender identity.
- After the successful decryption of a ciphertext the receiver will be able to verify the signature.
- Even the authorized receiver of a ciphertext cannot gain the details about the ciphertext policy more than the information that his attributes satisfy the access policy.
- The AC who issues keys to users is assumed to be a trusted authority.

3.3   Scheme Definition

The scheme is defined with a 4-tuple (Setup, KeyGen, Signcrypt, Unsigncrypt) as follows.

Setup (1^l): The AC inputs a security parameter l and outputs the master private key MK and public parameters PK.

KeyGen (MK, ID, L): It is a randomized algorithm run by AC, that takes as input the master key MK along with user's unique identity ID and a set of attributes L of the user. It outputs two secret keys SK_s and SK_d. SK_s is generated from ID and used for signcryption operation of data. SK_d comprises all attributes in L and used for unsigncryption operation of the received ciphertext.

Signcrypt (PK, M, T, ID, SK_s): Signcrypt is a randomized algorithm run by the sender. It takes as input the system's public parameters PK, the message M to be encrypted, the access structure T, the sender's identity ID and the sender's secret key for signature SK_s. The output is a signed ciphertext CT.

Unsigncrypt (PK, CT, SK_d): Unsigncrypt is a deterministic algorithm, where the user first performs the decryption operation on the ciphertext CT using his secret key SK_d and then performs verification procedure to check authenticity of message and sender identity.

3.4   Detailed Construction of the Scheme

Setup (1^l): The AC selects two groups G_0 and G_1 of prime order p whose bit-length is l and a bilinear mapping function $e : G_0 \times G_0 \to G_1$. The AC chooses two random generators g_1 and g_2 from group G_0 and a secure hash function $H:\{0,1\}^* \to G_0$. The master secret key MK is chosen as $\langle \alpha, \beta \in_R \mathbb{Z}_p \rangle$. The corresponding set of public parameters also known as public key $PK = \left\langle g_1, g_2, g_1^\alpha, g_2^\beta \right\rangle$ is published.

KeyGen (MK, ID, L): Every user in the system gets two secret keys - SK_s for signcryption and SK_d for unsigncryption.

- The SK_s is computed as $\langle\ S = H(0\|ID)^\alpha,\ \bar{S} = H(0\|ID)^{\frac{1}{\alpha}}\ \rangle$, where $H(.)$ is a cryptographic hash function.
- Let $L = [L_1, L_2, \cdots, L_n] = [v_{1,j_1}, v_{2,j_2}, \cdots, v_{n,j_n}]$ be the attribute list for the user who requires a secret key. The AC picks a random value ρ and generates a user's secret key SK_d as follows.
  $D = (g_2 \prod_{i=1}^n H(1\|i\|v_{i,j_i}))^\alpha \cdot g_2^\rho$, where $L_i = v_{i,j_i}$.
  $\bar{D} = g_1^{\frac{\rho}{\beta}}$.
  The user gets the unsigncryption key SK_d as $\langle D, \bar{D} \rangle$.

The user also calculates $\prod_{i=1}^n H(1\|i\|v_{i,j_i})$, which will be used in the unsigncryption algorithm.

Signcrypt (PK, M, T, ID, SK_s): To signcrypt a message M, the sender selects five random numbers r, s, t, s' and t' from $\mathbb{Z}_p$. Now, the sender makes the n

portions of r as r_i for $1 \leq i \leq n$ such that $\sum_{i=1}^{n} r_i = r$ and the n portions of t as t_i and s' as s'_i such that $\sum_{i=1}^{n} t_i = t$ and $\sum_{i=1}^{n} s'_i = s'$. Then, the sender computes two cipher components as

- $C_{s1} = e(g_1^{\alpha}, g_2)^{(s-1)t} = e(g_1, g_2)^{\alpha(s-1)t}$
- $C_{s2} = g_1^{\alpha s'}$.

The message M is wrapped with the sender identity ID and the two cipher components. The wrapped message is computed as $M' = M\|ID\|C_{s1}\|C_{s2}$. Now, the remaining cipher components are computed as follows:

- $\check{C} = M' e(g_1, g_2)^{\alpha(s-1)t} e(g_1^{\alpha}, H(0\|ID) \cdot H(M)^{s'})$
- $C_{sign} = H(0\|ID)^{\frac{\alpha+r}{st}}$
- $\hat{C} = g_1^{st}$
- $\bar{C} = g_2^{st\beta}$
- $C' = g_1^{t'\alpha}$
- For all attribute values from each set T_i, the cipher components $\{\tilde{C}_{i,j}\}_{1 \leq j \leq m_i}$ are generated as follows.
  - If $v_{i,j} \in T_i$ then
    $\tilde{C}_{i,j} = H(M)^{-s'_i} g_2^{t_i} H(1\|i\|v_{i,j})^{st+t'} H(0\|ID)^{\frac{r_i}{\alpha}}$
  - If $v_{i,j} \notin T_i$ then $\tilde{C}_{i,j}$ is a random value.

The final ciphertext is $CT = \langle\ \check{C},\ C_{sign},\ \hat{C},\ \bar{C},\ C',\ \{\{\tilde{C}_{i,j}\}_{1 \leq j \leq m_i}\}_{1 \leq i \leq n}\ \rangle$

Unsigncrypt (PK, CT, SK_d): The Unsigncrypt algorithm consists of two procedures - *Decryption of ciphertext* and *Verification of sender identity*. The decryption procedure works as follows.

$$C_v = \frac{e(\hat{C}, D \cdot C_{sign}) e(C', \prod_{i=1}^{n} H(1\|i\|v_{i,j}))}{e(\prod_{i=1}^{n} \tilde{C}_{i,j}, g_1^{\alpha}) e(\bar{C}, \bar{D})}$$
$$= e(g_1, g_2)^{\alpha(s-1)t} e(g_1, H(0\|ID))^{\alpha} e(g_1, H(M))^{\alpha s'}$$

$$\check{C}/C_v = \frac{M' \cdot e(g_1, g_2)^{\alpha(s-1)t} e(g_1, H(0\|ID))^{\alpha} e(g_1, H(M))^{\alpha s'}}{e(g_1, g_2)^{(\alpha(s-1))t} e(g_1, H(0\|ID))^{\alpha} e(g_1, H(M))^{\alpha s'}}$$
$$= M'$$

The receiver extracts the cipher components $C_{s1} = e(g_1, g_2)^{\alpha(s-1)t}$, $C_{s2} = g_1^{\alpha s'}$, and ID from M'. The receiver now starts the Verification procedure as follows.

$$R_1 = \frac{C_v}{C_{s1}}$$
$$= \frac{e(g_1, g_2)^{\alpha(s-1)t} \cdot e(g_1, H(0\|ID)^{\alpha}) \cdot e(g_1, H(M))^{\alpha s'}}{e(g_1, g_2)^{\alpha(s-1)t}}$$
$$= e(g_1, H(0\|ID))^{\alpha} e(g_1, H(M))^{\alpha s'}$$
$$R_2 = e(g_1^{\alpha}, H(0\|ID)) \cdot e(C_{s2}, H(M))$$
$$= e(g_1, H(0\|ID))^{\alpha} \cdot e(g_1, H(M))^{\alpha s'}$$

If R_1 and R_2 are equal then the verification succeeds and the sender identity is known to the receiver; else, it returns $\perp$.

4   Security Analysis

Indistinguishability against chosen ciphertext attack in selective ciphertext-policy (IND-sCP-CCA2). We consider this security model to prove that the proposed scheme provides message (and sender ID) confidentiality and receiver anonymity.

Our first theorem is to prove our claim that unless a valid decryption key is available, the adversary can not decrypt the ciphertext nor he can learn the access policy or sender information.

Theorem 1. *The proposed scheme is IND-sCP-CCA2 secure under the D-Linear assumption.*

Proof. We consider a challenger $\mathcal{C}$, a simulator $\mathcal{S}$ and a polynomial-time adversary $\mathcal{A}$. Suppose that $\mathcal{A}$ is able to distinguish a valid ciphertext from a random element with advantage $\epsilon_{dli}(l)$. We build $\mathcal{S}$ that can play the D-Linear game with advantage $\frac{\epsilon_{dli}(l)}{2}$. In the proof we are using a variant of D-Linear assumption which is equivalent to that defined in Sect. 2.4 and used in [12,13]. The simulation proceeds as follows.

Let $\mathcal{C}$ set the groups G_0 and G_1 with an efficient bilinear map e and generator g. The $\mathcal{C}$ flips a fair binary coin μ, outside of $\mathcal{S}$'s view. If $\mu = 0$, then $\mathcal{C}$ sets $(g, Z_1, Z_2, Z_3, Z_4, Z) = (g, g^{z_1}, g^{z_2}, g^{z_2 z_4}, g^{z_3+z_4}, g^{z_1 z_3})$, otherwise it sets $(g, Z_1, Z_2, Z_3, Z_4, Z) = (g, g^{z_1}, g^{z_2}, g^{z_2 z_4}, g^{z_3+z_4}, g^z)$ for values z_1, z_2, z_3, z_4 and z chosen randomly from $\mathbb{Z}_p$.

Init: $\mathcal{S}$ runs $\mathcal{A}$. $\mathcal{A}$ commits two access policies T_0^* and T_1^* for which he wishes to be challenged upon.

Setup: $\mathcal{S}$ takes the following values: $g_1 = g^{z_1}, g_2 = g^{z_2}, g_2^\beta = g^{\beta' z_1}$, where $\beta = \frac{\beta' z_1}{z_2}$ for some randomly chosen value β' from $\mathbb{Z}_p$. With the selection of random value α from $\mathbb{Z}_p$, g_1^α is calculated as $g^{z_1 \alpha}$. $H(x)$ is computed as $g^{z_1(1+H'(x))} = Z_1^{(1+H'(x))}$. H' is defined to map any random string from $\{0,1\}^*$ to an element of $\mathbb{Z}_p$. $\mathcal{S}$ announces the public key as $g_1 = Z_1, g_2 = g^{z_2}, g_1^\alpha = Z_1^\alpha, g_2^\beta = Z_1^{\beta'}$.

Phase 1: $\mathcal{A}$ issues a polynomially bounded number of queries to $\mathcal{S}$ and collects the following results in response of his queries.

– Whenever $\mathcal{A}$ makes its kth key generation query for the set L_k of attributes such that $F(L_k, T_0^*) = F(L_k, T_1^*) = 0$. $\mathcal{S}$ picks a random value $\rho \in \mathbb{Z}_p$ and calculates the key components as.

$$D = (g_2 \prod_{i=1}^{n} H(1\|i\|v_{i,j_i}))^\alpha \cdot g_2^\rho$$

$$= g^{z_2\alpha} \cdot g^{z_1\alpha(n+\sum_{i=1}^{n}(H'(1\|i\|v_{i,j_i})))}$$

$$= Z_2^\alpha \cdot Z_1^{\alpha(n+\sum_{i=1}^{n}(H'(1\|i\|v_{i,j_i})))}$$

$$\bar{D} = g_1^{\frac{\rho}{\beta}} = g^{z_1 \frac{\rho z_2}{\beta' z_1}}$$

$$= Z_2^{\frac{\rho}{\beta'}}$$

- In the result of query for signature key with respect to ID, $\mathcal{S}$ submits $H(0\|ID)^\alpha = Z_1^{(1+H'(0\|ID))\alpha}$ and $H(0\|ID)^{1/\alpha} = Z_1^{\frac{(1+H'(0\|ID))}{\alpha}}$.
- In response to the query for signcryption of messages M as per the access policies T (where $T \neq T_0^* \neq T_1^*$) and sender identity ID submitted by $\mathcal{A}$, $\mathcal{S}$ computes the ciphertext with the selection of the random numbers s, t, s' and r from $\mathbb{Z}_p$. The cipher components are generated with the public key parameters set up by $\mathcal{S}$.
- In response to the query for unsigncryption of CT with respect to attribute set L, $\mathcal{S}$ generates the secret keys for attributes included in set L. If the unsigncryption is successful, then $\mathcal{S}$ returns the unsigncrypted message M and sender identity ID. Else, $\mathcal{S}$ returns $\perp$ and aborts.

Challenge: Let the two challenge ciphertext policies submitted by the adversary $\mathcal{A}$ are $T_0^* = [T_{0,1}^*, T_{0,2}^*, \cdots, T_{0,n}^*]$ and $T_1^* = [T_{1,1}^*, T_{1,2}^*, \cdots, T_{1,n}^*]$. The $\mathcal{A}$ outputs two message, ID pairs (M_0, ID_0) and (M_1, ID_1), on which he wishes to be challenged upon with respect to the challenge access policy T_0^* and T_1^*. If for any key generated in Phase 1 on an attribute list L, such that $F(L, T_0^*) = F(L, T_1^*) = 1$, then $M_0 = M_1$ and $ID_0 = ID_1$.

Now, $\mathcal{S}$ flips a random coin ν, and signcrypts M_ν as per sender identity ID_ν and access policy T_ν^*. $\mathcal{S}$ assumes $st = z_3$, $t = z_4$, and $t' = \frac{z_3 + z_4}{z_1}$. The value of parameter r is assumed to be as $r'z_3$ - α with a random value r' chosen from $\mathbb{Z}_p$ and partitioned in n portions with each portion denoted as $r_i = (r'z_3 - \alpha)/n$. Similarly, a random value s' is picked up from $\mathbb{Z}_p$ and divided in n portions, where each portion is defined as s_i'. For the values which are included in T_ν^*, $\mathcal{C}$ calculates $\tilde{C}_{i,j} = H(M_\nu)^{-s_i'} g_2^{t_i} H(1\|i\|v_{i,j})^{st+t'} H(0\|ID_\nu)^{\frac{r_i}{\alpha}} = g^{-z_1(1+H'(M_\nu))\frac{s'}{n}} \cdot g^{\frac{z_2 z_4}{n}} \cdot g^{z_1(1+H'(1\|i\|v_{i,j}))(z_3 + \frac{z_3+z_4}{z_1})} \cdot g^{z_1(1+(H'(0\|ID_\nu)))(\frac{r'z_3-\alpha}{n\alpha})}$. This results in $\tilde{C}_{i,j} = Z_1^{(1+H'(M_\nu))(\frac{-s'}{n})} \cdot Z_3^{\frac{1}{n}} \cdot Z^{(1+H'(1\|i\|v_{i,j}))} \cdot Z_4^{(1+H'(1\|i\|v_{i,j}))} \cdot Z^{\frac{r'(1+H'(0\|ID_\nu))}{n\alpha}} \cdot Z_1^{\frac{(1+H'(0\|ID_\nu))}{n}}$. Now, for other attribute values which are not included in T_ν^*, $\tilde{C}_{i,j}$ are random values. The cipher components are computed by $\mathcal{S}$ as $\check{C} = M_\nu' \cdot e(g_1, g_2)^{\alpha(s-1)t} \cdot e(g_1, H(0\|ID_\nu)^\alpha) \cdot e(g_1, H(M_\nu))^{\alpha s'} = M_\nu' \cdot \frac{e(Z, Z_2)^\alpha}{e(Z_1, Z_3)^\alpha} \cdot e(Z_1, Z_1)^{(1+H'(0\|ID_\nu))\alpha} \cdot e(Z_1, Z_1)^{(1+H'(M_\nu))\alpha s'}$, $\hat{C} = g_1^{st} = Z$, $\bar{C} = g_2^{st\beta} = Z^\beta$, $C' = g_1^{t'\alpha} = g^{(z_3+z_4)\alpha} = Z_4^\alpha$ and $C_{Sign} = H(0\|ID_\nu)^{\frac{(\alpha+r)}{st}}$ $= g^{z_1 \frac{(1+H_1'(ID_\nu))(\alpha+r'z_3-\alpha)}{z_3}} = Z_1^{(1+H_1'(ID_\nu))r'}$. Here, $M_\nu' = M_\nu\|C_{s1}\|Z_1^{\alpha s'}\|ID_\nu$ ($C_{s1} = \frac{e(Z, Z_2)^\alpha}{e(Z_1, Z_3)^\alpha}$). The ciphertext is correct if $Z = g^{z_1 z_3}$. Else, it will be a random string. The ciphertext components $\{\{\tilde{C}_{i,j}\}_{1 \leq j \leq m_i}\}_{1 \leq i \leq n}$, $\bar{C}$, $\hat{C}$, C', C_{Sign}, $\check{C}$ are given to $\mathcal{A}$.

Phase 2: $\mathcal{A}$ is allowed to run a polynomially bounded number of queries for secret keys, signcryption and unsigncryption with the same conditions as imposed in the phase 1. One more restriction included here is that $\mathcal{A}$ can not query for unsigncryption of CT_b to $\mathcal{S}$.

Guess: $\mathcal{A}$ submits a guess ν' of ν. If $\nu' = \nu$, then $\mathcal{S}$ outputs $\mu = 1$ to indicate that it was given a valid D-Linear tuple; else, it outputs $\mu = 0$ to indicate that the ciphertext is a random element. Therefore, $\mathcal{A}$ gains no information about ν, in turn, $Pr[\nu \neq \nu' | \mu = 0] = \frac{1}{2}$. As $\mathcal{S}$ guesses $\mu' = 0$ when $\nu \neq \nu'$, $Pr[\mu = \mu' | \mu = 0] = \frac{1}{2}$. If $\mu = 1$, then $\mathcal{A}$ is able to view the valid encryption components with advantage $\epsilon_{dli}(l)$, a negligible quantity in security parameter in l. Therefore, $Pr[\nu = \nu' | \mu = 1] = \frac{1}{2} + \epsilon_{dli}(l)$. Similarly, $\mathcal{S}$ guesses $\mu'=1$ when $\nu = \nu'$, in turn, $Pr[\mu' = \mu | \mu = 1] = \frac{1}{2} + \epsilon_{dli}(l)$. The overall advantage of the $\mathcal{S}$ in D-Linear game is $\frac{1}{2} \times Pr[\mu = \mu' | \mu = 0] + \frac{1}{2} \times Pr[\mu = \mu' | \mu = 1] - \frac{1}{2} = \frac{1}{2} \times \frac{1}{2} + \frac{1}{2} \times (\frac{1}{2} + \epsilon_{dli}(l)) - \frac{1}{2} = \frac{\epsilon_{dli}(l)}{2}$.

Therefore, if $\mathcal{A}$ has a non-negligible advantage $\epsilon_{dli}(l)$ in the above game then we can build a simulator (S) which can break the D-Linear problem with non-negligible quantity $\frac{\epsilon_{dli}(l)}{2}$, which is an intractable problem. Hence, proved.

Our next theorem is to prove that the cipher components provide receiver anonymity. We show that even if an adversary gains a valid decryption key, he can decrypt the message and identify the sender, but can not find out the underlying access policy. This proves that a receiver decrypts the message with his secret key, but he is not able to determine which attribute values other then those possessed by the receiver are included in ciphertext access policy.

Theorem 2. *The proposed scheme provides receiver anonymity in IND-sCP-CCA2 game, if the Discrete Logarithm(DL) assumption holds with a negligible advantage ϵ_{dl} and if the $H(.)$ is a collision resistant hash function.*

Proof. We assume that $\mathcal{A}$ has obtained the hash outputs of every attribute values in the system.

Init: $\mathcal{A}$ commits two access policies T_0^* and T_1^* for which he wishes to be challenged upon. To make the differentiation between two policies let $\mathcal{A}$ has chosen the attribute λ $(1 \leq \lambda \leq n)$. In T_0^* and T_1^* for the attribute λ, $T_{0,\lambda}^* \neq T_{1,\lambda}^*$. There is at least one value $v_{\lambda,r}$ from the value set of attribute λ, such that $v_{\lambda,r} \notin T_{0,\lambda}^*$ and $v_{\lambda,r} \in T_{1,\lambda}^*$. Here, $1 \leq r \leq m_\lambda$. For rest of the attributes we assume that $T_{0,i}^* = T_{1,i}^*$, where $1 \leq i \leq n$ and $i \neq \lambda$.

Setup: $\mathcal{C}$ computes and announces the public keys: g_1, g_2, g_1^α, and g_2^β.

Phase 1: $\mathcal{A}$ issues a polynomially bounded number of queries to $\mathcal{S}$ and collects the following results in response of his queries.

- $\mathcal{A}$ makes its kth key generation query for the set L_k of attributes such that $F(L_k, T_0^*) = F(L_k, T_1^*)$. That is, $\mathcal{A}$ is allowed to issue a valid decryption key which can decrypt the challenge ciphertext, with the restriction that the key should be able to satisfy both the challenge access structure T_0^* and T_1^* or it should satisfy none of the challenge access structure.
- $\mathcal{A}$ also gets response for the query of issuing signature key related to ID, as $\langle\, H(0\|ID)^{\alpha}$ and $H(0\|ID)^{\frac{1}{\alpha}}\, \rangle$.
- In response to the query for signcryption of messages M as per the access policies T (where $T \neq T_0^* \neq T_1^*$) and sender identity ID, submitted by $\mathcal{A}$, $\mathcal{C}$ computes the ciphertext with the selection of random numbers s, t and t' from Z_p.
- In response to the query for unsigncryption of CT with respect to attribute set L, $\mathcal{C}$ generates the secret keys for attributes included in set L. If the decryption and verification are finished successfully, then $\mathcal{C}$ returns the unsigncrypted message M and sender id ID. Else, $\mathcal{C}$ returns $\perp$ and aborts.

Challenge: $\mathcal{A}$ submits two message-ID pairs (M_0, ID_0) and (M_1, ID_1). The $\mathcal{C}$ flips a random coin ν and submits the CT_ν for (M_ν, ID^*, T_ν^*).

- If $\mathcal{A}$ has retrieved a key for any queried $L=[L_1, L_2, \cdots, L_n]$, such that $F(L, T_0^*)$ $= F(L, T_1^*) = 1$, then $M_0 = M_1$ and $ID_0 = ID_1$.
- In case when $M_0 \neq M_1$, then the game is as described in Theorem 1. If M_0 $= M_1$ then only the ciphertext components which makes a differentiation between access policies T_0^* and T_1^* is $\tilde{C}_{\lambda,r}$.
  - If $\nu = 0$ then $\tilde{C}_{\lambda,r}$ is a random value. This is valid because $v_{\lambda,r}$ is not in $T_{0,\lambda}$ as per the definition.
  - If $\nu = 1$ then $\tilde{C}_{\lambda,r}$ is set as $H(M_\nu)^{-s_i'} g_2^{t_i} H(1\|\lambda\|v_{\lambda,r})^{st+t'}$.

$\mathcal{A}$ is given ciphertext $\langle\, \check{C}, C_{sign}, \hat{C}, \bar{C}, C', \{\{\tilde{C}_{i,j}\}_{1 \leq j \leq m_i}\}_{1 \leq i \leq n}\, \rangle$.

Phase 2: $\mathcal{A}$ is allowed to run a polynomially bounded number of queries for secret keys, signcryption and unsigncryption with the same conditions as imposed in the Phase 1. Another restriction is that $\mathcal{A}$ can not issue the unsigncrypt queries for CT_b.

Guess: $\mathcal{A}$ submits a guess ν' of ν. If $\nu' = \nu$, then $\mathcal{A}$ wins the game. To win the game $\mathcal{A}$ needs to discover whether the value of $\tilde{C}_{\lambda,r}$ is a correct ciphertext component or a random element. We will show that the advantage of $\mathcal{A}$ in making this decision is negligible.

To win the game, $\mathcal{A}$ tries to find the value of st and t' from $\hat{C} = g_1^{st}$ (or from $\bar{C} = g_2^{st\beta}$) and $\check{C} = g_1^{t'\alpha}$. ($g_1, g_2^\beta$ and g_1^α are issued as a part of public keys.) The advantage of $\mathcal{A}$ in retrieving the values of st and t' is equivalent to the advantage of breaking the Discrete Logarithm assumption, which is an intractable problem. In an alternative way to win the game, $\mathcal{A}$ tries to find a pair of values from the valueset of an attribute whose hash values of H function collide. $\mathcal{A}$ does so before committing the access policies T_0^* and T_1^*. Suppose that $\mathcal{A}$ has found such a pair of $(v_{\lambda,\eta}, v_{\lambda,r})$, that is, $H(1\|\lambda\|v_{\lambda,\eta}) = H(1\|\lambda\|v_{\lambda,r})$ then he can include the value of $v_{\lambda,\eta}$ for the attribute λ in both the challenge access policies T_0^* and T_1^*, but the value of $v_{\lambda,r}$ is included in only one of the access policies, say in T_1^*. Now at the time of making guess $\mathcal{A}$ compares the value of $\tilde{C}_{\lambda,\eta}$ with $\tilde{C}_{\lambda,r}$. If both are same then $\mathcal{A}$ gives the answer as $\nu' = 1$; else, $\nu' = 0$. The probability of winning the game is equivalent to the probability of finding two different values of one attribute which have the same hash values. Let there are at maximum m values for an attribute. Then the probability that any two values will have the same hash values is $O(\frac{m^2}{p})$. Considering the polynomial space m for an attribute value set and sufficient large size of p, the advantage of $\mathcal{A}$ is negligible. Therefore, the total advantage of $\mathcal{A}$ in this game is $\epsilon \leq \epsilon_{dl} + O(\frac{m^2}{p})$, which is negligible.

Existential Unforgeability. Existential unforgeability ensures that unless a valid signature key is available, an adversary will not be able to calculate a valid signature on a message. Our proposed scheme is existentially unforgeable against chosen message attack in adaptive predicate (AP-EUF-CMA) model.

5   Performance Analysis

We have evaluated our scheme and other AABE schemes [12–14] on a Linux system with Intel core-i3 processor running at 2.30 GHz and 3GB RAM. Bilinear pairings are constructed on the curve $y^2 = x^3 + x$ over the field F_q for some prime $q=3 \bmod 4$. The order p of the groups G_0 and G_1 is a prime number of size 160 bits, where the length of q is 512 bits. The Tables 1 and 2 shows the comparison of our scheme with the other AABE schemes [12–14] having the similar access structure as of our scheme. Because of space limitations, the comparison is shown only between the schemes having the similar access structure of "AND gate on Multivalued Attributes". However when compared the performance of proposed scheme with other existing AABE schemes, the decryption operation of proposed scheme has been found cost-effective. We have also not considered the parameters for the *Matching phase* of [14] while making the comparison, because the Matching phase of [14] suffers from the security flaws [15]. It is easy to see from Table 1 that the computational cost of the decryption operation in our scheme is much less than the schemes [12–14].

Table 1. Comparison of the schemes.(n = Number of attributes in the system, # For our scheme the decryption operation refers to unsigncryption operation)

Parameters		[12]	[13]	[14]	Our scheme
Expressiveness of access policy		AND gate on multivalued attributes			
Receiver anonymity		Yes	Yes	Yes	Yes
No. of decryption operation #	No. of bilinear pairing operation	O(n)	O(n)	O(n)	O(1)
	No. of multiplication operation	O(n)	O(n)	O(n)	O(n)

In Table 2 the comparison of our scheme is made with [12–14] for the ciphertext size and encryption time. Both the ciphertext size and encryption time are affected by the number of attributes (n) and size of valueset for each attribute. Furthermore, we have compared our scheme with some existing multi-receiver IDSC schemes [24,25] and shown the results in Table 3. These two schemes provide the same functionality of single sender and multiple receivers as our scheme does. The scheme of Ming et al. [24] requires 5 pairing operations for unsigncryption of a message. The unsigncryption algorithm of [24] is not affected by number of receivers of a signcrypted text. However, their scheme doesn't provide receiver anonymity. The scheme by Pang et al.[25] provides receiver anonymity. However, in their scheme the cost of unsigncryption operation and ciphertext size linearly depends on the number of receivers of the ciphertext. Our scheme provides receiver anonymity. The unsigncryption operation in our scheme linearly depends on the number of attributes in the system. But the number of attributes are fixed during the setup of the system. This yields that once a system is established, the unsigncryption operation of our scheme requires a constant number of operations.

Table 2. Comparison for ciphertext size and encryption time. (n = No. of attributes, m= Maximum size of valueset for an attribute. *: For our scheme Encryption time refers to Signcryption time.)

n,m	Ciphertext size (kb)				Encryption time* (s)			
	[12]	[13]	[14]	Our scheme	[12]	[13]	[14]	Our scheme
10,10	62	242	62	32	1.63	2.29	1.56	1.07
10,20	123	245	123	62	2.89	5.42	2.78	1.72
15,10	92	244	93	47	2.29	4.18	2.31	1.72
15,20	183	366	184	93	4.2	8.03	4.24	2.72
20,10	122	245	123	62	3.03	5.57	3.06	2.12
20,20	245	489	245	123	5.6	11.06	5.7	3.69

Table 3. Comparison of our scheme with the existing multi-recipient ID-based signcryption schemes (Here P: No. of Pairing Operations; Mu: No. of Multiplication operations; E: Number of Exponentiation Operation; A: No. of Addition Operations; N_r: No. of receivers in ID-based signcryption schemes; n: No. of attributes in our scheme which is fixed during the setup algorithm of the scheme.

Schemes parameters	[24]	[25]	Our scheme
Unsigncryption cost	$5P$	$3P + (N_r + 1)Mu + (N_r - 1)E + (N_r + 2)A$	$6P + (2n + 6)Mu$
Receiver anonymity	No	Yes	Yes
Model	Standard model	Standard model	Standard model

6   Conclusion

We proposed an anonymous attribute based signcryption scheme that provides sender privacy and receiver anonymity. In our scheme, the sender identity can be disclosed and verified only after a successful decryption of the ciphertext. The scheme is found secure in the IND-sCP-CCA2 and AP-EUF-CMA model. The implementation results of our scheme shows that the unsigncryption procedure is efficient in comparison to the decryption procedure of other AABE schemes. Also the scheme is compared with existing multi-receiver IDSC schemes with the similar motive as our scheme has, and found the proposed scheme better than those existing schemes.

References

1. Goyal, V., Pandey, O., Sahai, A., Waters, B.: Attribute-based encryption for fine-grained access control of encrypted data. In: Proceedings of the ACM Conference on Computer and Communications Security, pp. 89–98 (2006)
2. Bethencourt, J., Sahai, A., Waters, B.: Ciphertext-policy attribute-based encryption. In: Proceedings of IEEE Symposium on Security and Privacy, pp. 321–334 (2007)
3. Cheung, L., Newport, C.: Provably secure ciphertext policy ABE. In: Proceedings of the ACM Conference on Computer and Communications Security, pp. 456–465 (2007)
4. Goyal, V., Jain, A., Pandey, O., Sahai, A.: Bounded ciphertext policy attribute based encryption. In: Aceto, L., Damgård, I., Goldberg, L.A., Halldórsson, M.M., Ingólfsdóttir, A., Walukiewicz, I. (eds.) ICALP 2008. LNCS, vol. 5126, pp. 579–591. Springer, Heidelberg (2008). doi:10.1007/978-3-540-70583-3_47
5. Lewko, A., Okamoto, T., Sahai, A., Takashima, K., Waters, B.: Fully Secure functional encryption: attribute-based encryption and (hierarchical) inner product encryption. In: Gilbert, H. (ed.) EUROCRYPT 2010. LNCS, vol. 6110, pp. 62–91. Springer, Heidelberg (2010). doi:10.1007/978-3-642-13190-5_4
6. Okamoto, T., Takashima, K.: Fully secure functional encryption with general relations from the decisional linear assumption. In: Rabin, T. (ed.) CRYPTO 2010. LNCS, vol. 6223, pp. 191–208. Springer, Heidelberg (2010). doi:10.1007/978-3-642-14623-7_11
7. Ostrovsky, R., Sahai, A., Waters, B.: Attribute-based encryption with non-monotonic access structures. In: Proceedings of the ACM Conference on Computer and Communications Security, pp. 195–203 (2007)
8. Waters, B.: Ciphertext-policy attribute-based encryption: an expressive, efficient, and provably secure realization. In: Catalano, D., Fazio, N., Gennaro, R., Nicolosi, A. (eds.) PKC 2011. LNCS, vol. 6571, pp. 53–70. Springer, Heidelberg (2011). doi:10.1007/978-3-642-19379-8_4
9. Yamada, S., Attrapadung, N., Hanaoka, G., Kunihiro, N.: Generic constructions for chosen-ciphertext secure attribute based encryption. In: Catalano, D., Fazio, N., Gennaro, R., Nicolosi, A. (eds.) PKC 2011. LNCS, vol. 6571, pp. 71–89. Springer, Heidelberg (2011). doi:10.1007/978-3-642-19379-8_5
10. Kapadia, A., Tsang, P.P., Smith, S.W.: Attribute-based publishing with hidden credentials and hidden policies. In: Proceedings of Network and Distributed System Security Symposium, vol. 7, pp. 179–192 (2007)
11. Yu, S., Ren, K., Lou, W.: Attribute-based content distribution with hidden policy. In: Proceedings of Workshop on Secure Network Protocols, pp. 39–44. IEEE (2008)
12. Nishide, T., Yoneyama, K., Ohta, K.: Attribute-based encryption with partially hidden encryptor-specified access structures. In: Bellovin, S.M., Gennaro, R., Keromytis, A., Yung, M. (eds.) ACNS 2008. LNCS, vol. 5037, pp. 111–129. Springer, Heidelberg (2008). doi:10.1007/978-3-540-68914-0_7

13. Li, J., Ren, K., Zhu, B., Wan, Z.: Privacy-aware attribute-based encryption with user accountability. In: Samarati, P., Yung, M., Martinelli, F., Ardagna, C.A. (eds.) ISC 2009. LNCS, vol. 5735, pp. 347–362. Springer, Heidelberg (2009). doi:10.1007/978-3-642-04474-8_28

14. Zhang, Y., Chen, X., Li, J., Wong, D.S., Li, H.: Anonymous attribute-based encryption supporting efficient decryption test. In: Proceedings of the ACM SIGSAC Symposium on Information, Computer and Communications Security, pp. 511–516 (2013)

15. Chaudhari, P., Das, M.L., Mathuria, A.: On anonymous attribute based encryption. In: Jajodia, S., Mazumdar, C. (eds.) ICISS 2015. LNCS, vol. 9478, pp. 378–392. Springer, Heidelberg (2015). doi:10.1007/978-3-319-26961-0_23

16. Rao, Y.S., Dutta, R.: Recipient anonymous ciphertext-policy attribute based encryption. In: Bagchi, A., Ray, I. (eds.) ICISS 2013. LNCS, vol. 8303, pp. 329–344. Springer, Heidelberg (2013). doi:10.1007/978-3-642-45204-8_25

17. Zheng, Y.: Digital Signatures or how to achievecost (Signature & Encryption) << Cost (Signature) +Cost(Encryption). In: Kaliski, B.S. (ed.) Advances in Cryptology - CRYPTO. LNCS, vol. 1294, pp. 165–179. Springer, Heidelberg (1997)

18. Malone-Lee, J.: Identity-Based Signcryption. IACR Cryptology eprint Archieve, report 2002/098 (2002)

19. Libert, B., Quisquater, J.J.: New identity based signcryption schemes from pairings. IACR Cryptology ePrint Archive, report 2003/23 (2003)

20. Chen, L., Malone-Lee, J.: Improved identity-based signcryption. In: Vaudenay, S. (ed.) PKC 2005. LNCS, vol. 3386, pp. 362–379. Springer, Heidelberg (2005). doi:10.1007/978-3-540-30580-4_25

21. Barreto, P.S.L.M., Libert, B., McCullagh, N., Quisquater, J.-J.: Efficient and provably-secure identity-based signatures and signcryption from bilinear maps. In: Roy, B. (ed.) ASIACRYPT 2005. LNCS, vol. 3788, pp. 515–532. Springer, Heidelberg (2005). doi:10.1007/11593447_28

22. Boyen, X.: Identity-based signcryption. In: Dent, A.W., Zheng, Y. (eds.) Practical Signcryption. Information Security and Cryptography, pp. 195–216. Springer, Heidelberg (2010)

23. Duan, S., Cao, Z.: Efficient and provably secure multi-receiver identity-based signcryption. In: Batten, L.M., Safavi-Naini, R. (eds.) ACISP 2006. LNCS, vol. 4058, pp. 195–206. Springer, Heidelberg (2006). doi:10.1007/11780656_17

24. Ming, Y., Zhao, X., Wang, Y.: Multi-receiver identity-based signcryption scheme in the standard model. In: Liu, B., Chai, C. (eds.) ICICA 2011. LNCS, vol. 7030, pp. 487–494. Springer, Heidelberg (2011). doi:10.1007/978-3-642-25255-6_62

25. Pang, L., Gao, L., Li, H., Wang, Y.: Anonymous multi-receiver ID-based signcryption scheme. Inf. Secur. IET 9(3), 194–201 (2015)

26. Wang, C., Huang, J.: Attribute-based signcryption with ciphertext-policy and claim-predicate mechanism. In: Proceedings of the International Conference on Computational Intelligence and Security, pp. 905–909. IEEE (2011)

27. Gagné, M., Narayan, S., Safavi-Naini, R.: Threshold attribute-based signcryption. In: Garay, J.A., Prisco, R. (eds.) SCN 2010. LNCS, vol. 6280, pp. 154–171. Springer, Heidelberg (2010). doi:10.1007/978-3-642-15317-4_11

28. Emura, K., Miyaji, A., Rahman, M.S.: Dynamic attribute-based signcryption without random oracles. Int. J. Appl. Cryptogr. 2(3), 199–211 (2012)

MalCrawler: A Crawler for Seeking and Crawling Malicious Websites

A.K. Singh[✉] and Navneet Goyal

Department of Computer Science, BITS-Pilani, Pilani Campus, Pilani, India
aksingh24ll@gmail.com,
goel@pilani.bits-pilani.ac.in

Abstract. Over the years, internet has become the major source of security threat to computer systems. With the number of people browsing internet increasing exponentially in the last couple of years, browser based attacks have become the preferred means of infecting a computer system. These browser based attacks, known as 'Drive-by Download' attacks, inject malicious Java-Script from the server hosting the malicious web application to the browser. Since, the numbers of malicious websites launching such attacks have increased in the past few years; it has become critical to detect them. Typically, search for malicious web pages involves three steps- crawling URLs on the internet, using fast analysis filters to reject benign pages, and then running complex but slow detailed analysis (using Honey Clients) on the filtered list. While effective, these techniques consume substantial time and computing resources. This limitation can be overcome by designing a crawler which can seek more malicious sites than benign sites, thus, increasing the "toxicity" of the URLs collected in the first step. In this paper, we propose a focused web crawler, named "Mal-Crawler", which has been designed to crawl and search malicious websites efficiently. This crawler, when compared to a generic crawler, will not only seek more malicious sites than benign sites, but will also handle cloaking, entanglement and AJAX content in malicious sites. MalCrawler, designed, developed and tested, as part of the scope of this paper, proved to be more efficient than generic crawlers.

Keywords: Cyber security · Focused crawling · Web security · Drive-by download attacks · Malicious web mining

1 Introduction

The Internet has these days become a source of information, entertainment and e-commerce, resulting into its augmented utilization. With this increased use by the users, the reprobaters have also become quite active. The web crawlers, in this context, are helpful in detecting and eliminating the miscreants and their exploits. Focused web crawlers, are being used for variety of purposes to maintain the safety of the Internet now-a-days. They have been used extensively for scientific research, apart from being used for selective search indexing. In this paper, one such focused web crawler has been designed and developed which will help search malicious web pages efficiently and accurately.

© Springer International Publishing AG 2017
P. Krishnan et al. (Eds.): ICDCIT 2017, LNCS 10109, pp. 210–223, 2017.
DOI: 10.1007/978-3-319-50472-8_17

Malicious web sites are now-a-days a major concern in the field of cyber security. As per Annual Internet Threat Report 2016 published by Symantec [1], web attacks using malicious web sites have increased. Out of the billions of URLs present on the internet, one in every 1,126 websites is infected with malware. Drive-by download web attacks by malicious web sites, in which attack malware gets downloaded as the user clicks and browses the web page, are a major threat to internet security [2]. Conventional security measures, such as antivirus based on signature detection have limited success in today's scenario [3]. Drive-by download attacks from malicious web pages that compromise the computer through the browser route have become the major means of spreading infected code [3]. With ever increasing web traffic, the vulnerability from this type of attack is also on the rise. Generally, cyber security agencies and antivirus firms are on the lookout for such malicious sites. These agencies generally maintain a black list of infected web sites and keep updating them by crawling new sites. These agencies also analyze the malwares to develop an antivirus signature or prevention mechanism for the type of attack detected. As it emerges from this discussion, web crawling is the first step towards the detection of such sites. In this paper we propose one such focused crawler named "MalCrawler", which can find these sites efficiently and accurately. Comparing MalCrawler to a normal crawler used for search indexing, the following aspects can be highlighted:

- MalCrawler finds more malicious sites compared to the existing search crawlers. If the probability of encountering malicious sites by a common search crawler is 'x', then the probability of finding a malicious site by this crawler is 'a * x', where a > 1.
- MalCrawler is able to handle cloaking (websites which cloak, show a different webpage to a web crawler and to a user's browser). It uses various tricks to detect whether the HTTP request has come from a web crawler or a web browser. The commonly used trick is to read the User Agent string of the HTTP request. MalCrawler sends multiple HTTP requests to a web site, staggered in time, with different User Agent strings, one being of a popular search bot and other being of common browsers. Thus, it would detect cloaking by comparing the response to these HTTP requests.
- Generally, sites with large content, for example social networking sites, have very complex graph of hyperlinks. Such sites are also targets of cross site scripting attacks by hackers. Thus, these sites may have malicious code implanted by such attacks. Many small and big loops exist in such sites, which can entangle a crawler and leave it stuck for a long time. MalCrawler is designed to avoid such entanglement, while doing a detailed crawl in depth. Therefore, this crawler will be able to handle entanglement [4].
- Now-a-days AJAX has become a very popular web technology. Since, we are looking for malicious sites and malwares in them; we need to dig a little deep and hence cannot avoid AJAX content. MalCrawler is designed to manage websites with AJAX content as well.

To ensure that the crawler spends more time crawling malicious web sites, MalCrawler has an advisory engine, which uses variety of information to advise the crawler. The advisory engine keeps track of the URLs being crawled currently, and if the crawler gets entangled in the site, it helps the crawler to recover from it. The advisory engine also advises the crawler on the breadth and depth of crawl for the web site.

Certain aspects of crawler design were considered by us while designing this focused crawler. Firstly, as the first step, we need to crawl and reach the malicious web pages. Crawling the complete web is difficult. How do we crawl to reach maximum malicious pages in minimum time? Secondly, most of the malicious content is hidden deep into websites and are only accessible through queries to their linked databases. How do we crawl deep to catch malicious code? Thirdly, on many websites, especially social media portals, malicious content is found in dynamic pages that use JavaScript extensively. Social media sites are generally not crawled by commercial search crawlers. These sites are now-a-days used extensively for malicious drive-by-download attacks by injecting malicious JavaScripts. How do we crawl such sites with dynamic content? A general purpose web crawler cannot do these jobs, and thus, we require a specially designed crawler. MalCrawler has the following capabilities:

- Maximizes malicious page seek rate.
- Crawls deep to detect hidden pages.
- Uses anti-cloaking measures.
- Emulates various browsers.
- Emulates a user.
- Crawls AJAX pages up to a desired depth while avoiding entanglement.

1.1 Maximizing Malicious Page Seek Rate

Malicious page seek rate (α) is defined as:

$$\left(\frac{Malicious\ Pages\ Crawled}{Total\ Pages\ Crawled} \right) \times 100 = \alpha$$

The main objective is to maximize α for a crawl. As internet is huge, when we start looking for malicious content, we might end up wasting time in crawling benign sites. Crawling complete web is difficult, and moreover, the crawl cycle takes days. If we take long time looking for malicious websites, the malicious content might get removed in that time frame. So, how do we maximize α? Few strategies used in this paper to maximize α are given below:

- **Starting Crawl with Malicious Seed.** Usually, crawling starts with a seed of URLs. Using the initial seed of URLs, the crawler follows the hyperlinks and crawls further. We can start our crawl from known malicious sites. Since, a malicious site is more likely to host hyperlinks to other malicious sites [5], this approach as compared to random crawling, gives us higher probability of encountering malicious sites.
- **Seeking Dynamic Content.** Dynamic content is more likely to contain malicious code. Dynamic content uses many server side scripts and client side scripts (JavaScripts) to provide interactive high intuitive web experience. While this is

appealing to users, and the web is moving rapidly towards it, it is also vulnerable to hacks like cross-side scripting [4], and thus, ends up hosting malicious drive-by-download JavaScript code. So, if we want to seek more malicious content, we need to crawl sites with dynamic content.

- **Smart Filtering.** With smart filtering techniques, we reduce the number of pages which need to be examined in detail [6]. This fast filter uses static heuristics algorithm, to quickly identify and discard pages that are likely to be benign.

1.2 Crawls Deep to Detect Hidden Pages

Vast amount of web pages are placed deep and are generally difficult to be handled by crawlers. It has been observed that malicious content is found at greater depth, especially in dynamic pages with database related form submission, as they are more vulnerable to cross side scripting [4]. A traditional crawler avoids crawling in depth and will not submit dynamic queries during the crawl. On the contrary, MalCrawler, which has been designed as a deep Web crawler checks for dynamic content and submits queries [7]. It will crawl at greater depths, while taking adequate precautions to avoid getting stuck or entangled.

1.3 Uses Anti-cloaking Measures

Malicious sites have now-a-days become smarter. They sense the user agent trying to send them HTTP request and accordingly guide them to different pages on a site. For example, if the malicious site gets a HTTP request from a 'Mozilla Firefox Browser' then it guides it to a malicious page, and if it gets a HTTP request from Googlebot, it guides it to a different benign page. Basically, they show malicious pages to users (who are targeted victims) and different benign pages to crawlers (of search engines and malware detection firms). Our crawler has capability to detect cloaking and we do this by manipulating the user agent field of the HTTP request.

1.4 Emulates Various Browsers

Some malwares hosted on sites are targeted for particular browser and environment [8]. For example, there might be a targeted malware for 'Internet Explorer 8.0'. The malicious site may not redirect us to the malware location until it is sure that we have 'Internet Explorer 8.0'. Thus, the focused crawler should be able to emulate all browser environments. We have implemented emulation for 'Internet Explorer', 'Mozilla Firefox' and 'Google Chrome'.

1.5 Emulates a User

Crawling speed and pattern should be similar to a user. Patterns available from Web Usage Mining statistics could be emulated. To compensate for slow speed of crawling, parallelization could be adopted and multiple sites could be crawled simultaneously. We have not used parallelization to avoid complicating the design. We have not even slowed the crawling speed. However, we have tried to keep it similar to any user's style of browsing (like opening breadth first links, etc.)

1.6 Crawls AJAX Pages up to a Desired Depth While Avoiding Entanglement

Web 2.0 AJAX concept has made browsing more interactive and integrated to backend databases. A link to a weblog is expected to point to a perennially changing page. Depth of such dynamic sites varies and increases as more links are added by user actions. How deep should a crawler crawl these sites? If the crawler goes too deep, then crawler might get entangled in a host of links. We have used the crawler guidance engine to guide the crawler through such sites and prevent it from getting entangled.

The design of "MalCrawler" has been validated on the internet by implementing it using a Java application. Subsequent sections will provide the Background and Literature Survey, Methodology and Design, Testing, Results and Analysis.

2   Background and Literature Survey

Web crawling for search indexing is an extensively researched field, which has now matured to a certain extent. The search engines like Google, Yahoo, Bing, etc., are a testimonial to this advancement. Web crawling for web content mining of malicious sites is somewhat similar to crawling for search indexing, barring a few differences. These differences, listed below, though few, are important:

- **Importance of Links to Pages.** Forward and back links from a website to certain suspicious sites are indicative of malicious activity.
- **Seed[1] for Crawling.** A good selection of malicious seeds can help us find more malicious sites as has brought out by Invernizzi et al. in their paper on EVILSEED [5].
- **Crawling Dynamic Content.** Dynamic web sites are more prone to cross side scripting and SQL injection attacks [4, 9]. Thus, they become the major source of spread of malware. The depth of crawl in dynamic content also varies. At times, the crawler is expected to increase depth and at times it has to keep it low to avoid getting entangled. The crawler needs to be supported by a smart algorithm which can help it avoid such entanglements and still be effective.
- **Bot Detection by Malicious Web Sites.** Malicious sites increasingly become aware of bots used to crawl them for malware detection. They cloak and provide a different benign page when a bot visits [10]. The crawler needs to crawl in a manner to evade such detection.

The process of finding malicious web pages involves many steps [11]. In the first step, the crawler needs a point to start the search, i.e. seeds. In the second step, the

---

[1] Seed refers to the initial set of URLs from where crawl starts.

initial URLs are crawled, downloaded and parsed to extract the hyperlinks. These hyperlinks can be sorted out and queued in priority based on the crawler design. In the third step, the crawl is expanded to all those queued URLs. While the pages are being queued and crawled, fast filters can tell us whether the crawler is finding more malicious sites or not [6, 12]. For the fourth step, we need detection systems with high accuracy in predicting maliciousness of web pages. For this Honey Clients can be used [13, 14]. Honey Client based systems use browser emulation, client emulation and various other methods to detect malicious code. Such Honey Clients are very accurate, but are slow by magnitudes. Resources for checking malicious web sites are neither free nor infinite. Thus, the number of URLs given to such Honey Clients should be reduced by making our first three steps more efficient. MalCrawler has been designed specifically to meet this requirement.

3   Methodology and Design

In this paper, we have designed, developed and analyzed a web crawler that seeks more malicious web sites efficiently.

3.1   System Architecture

The broad system architecture is shown below (Fig. 1):

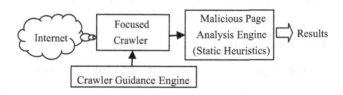

Fig. 1.   Architecture

3.2   Focused Crawler Module

This crawler module is capable of carrying out focused crawling. It has the following sub modules (Fig. 2):

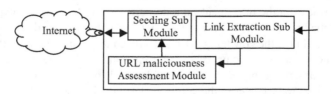

Fig. 2.   Crawler module

- **Seeding Sub Module.** The seeding module provides the initial seed for crawl. In crawlers, the initial seed is the set of links and webpages from which a crawler starts crawling. As it crawls, it extracts links from all pages visited and provides it to a FIFO queue. The crawler, thereafter, keeps picking up URLs from the FIFO queue and keeps crawling. This is how the process of crawl starts and continues. Since, we have made a focused crawler to crawl malicious sites; the initial seed has to be malicious. We have taken the initial seed from website 'Malware Domain List'. Thereafter, the crawl succeeds following the links extracted from the URLs provided in the initial seed. The links extracted are processed, as discussed in the module described later, and the selected malicious URLs are added to the FIFO queue for crawl.
- **Link Extraction Sub Module.** The link extraction sub module is responsible for extraction of URL links from the pages crawled by the crawler. The link extraction sub module extracts all these links and stores them in a linked list for evaluation. Thereafter, the URL maliciousness assessment module works on these links to select the malicious links. Links which are not likely to be malicious are dropped.
- **URL Maliciousness Assessment Module.** The URL maliciousness assessment module is responsible for picking up the URLs and assessing whether they are malicious or not.

The crawler has been written with the help of JSoup [15] Java library. It provides a very convenient API for extracting and manipulating data, using the best of DOM, CSS, and jquery-like methods. Though, we will see later in the software design section, the crawler has been written from scratch in Java, the JSoup library has been used extensively for parsing functions, extractions, etc. MalCrawler requires lot of help in parsing and link extraction, for which we have used this library.

3.3   Crawler Guidance Engine

The crawler guidance engine is the one which controls the crawler. It does the following:

- Keeps track of the URLs crawled and being crawled.
- Keeps track of crawl time.
- Recovers crawler when it gets entangled or stuck.
- It decides the depth and breadth of crawl.

This module works closely with the crawler module. The crawler module updates its state in the guidance engine by using various local and global variables. Every time the crawler sends a HTTP get request, it updates the variable. The crawler module keeps a close watch on the time spent on a domain and on its URL. It keeps checking the depth and the breadth of crawl using the URL separators. If the depth goes beyond the laid down limit or if the crawler is taking too much time, the guidance engine resets the crawler and resumes crawling of a different domain. We have not used parallelization while designing this crawler, to avoid complexity. However, the application is multithreaded, as we see later in the software design, with each module running on a different thread.

3.4 Malicious Page Analysis Engine

The malicious page analysis engine does an analysis of the pages crawled to identify maliciousness. Here, we do analysis of primarily JavaScript based malwares. We use the Rhino Emulation library and the HTML Unit Browser library for doing this. We have used Rhino engine and the HTML Unit emulator to check and analyze the following aspects of JavaScript based malwares. We have extracted features from each of these aspects and have used classification using the WEKA library [16].

Redirection and Cloaking. Most malicious web sites use redirections and cloaking. Redirection is used to guide the browser to a page containing the exploit code. Cloaking is generally used to avoid showing malicious pages to search engine crawlers, or to serve different pages for different vulnerable browser environments (based on browser & OS fingerprinting results). We used the two features, described below, to detect these activities:

Feature 1: Redirections. There are two types of redirections. Firstly, HTTP response status 302 redirection, and secondly, redirection using JavaScript 'document.location' property. We recorded the number of times that these two redirections took place, and, also tracked the targets of each redirection. The HTTP status 302 redirection can be checked by the response received by the browser (in our case the HTML Unit [17] emulated the browser). And, 'document.location' based redirect was picked up by running the script using Rhino JavaScript Engine [18]. Thus, this feature can be picked up as described above, and this feature will have nominal values {Yes, No}.

Feature 2: Cloaking. We detect cloaking by manipulating the user agent field of the HTTP request. We change user agent strings to emulate 'Mozilla Firefox', 'Google Chrome', 'Internet Explorer', 'GoogleBot', etc. If we receive a different response every time, then it indicates cloaking. This feature will be limited to the values {Yes, No}. HTML Unit has been used for detecting cloaking. It has been used to taper the User Agent field in the HTTP request header for depicting various browsers.

De-obfuscation. It has been found that most malicious JavaScript is obfuscated. In obfuscation, the JavaScript is coded to avoid detection by detection engines which work on signatures. The obfuscated code is de-obfuscated only at the run time to avoid detection by anti-malware software [19, 20]. Varieties of obfuscation techniques are used, for example, base64, and also at times encryption algorithms are used. However, no matter how they are coded, they have to be decoded in clear text JavaScript code at runtime to enable running. We have used this runtime catching technique to find analyze the de-obfuscated code. We extract following five features:

Feature 3: String Definitions and Uses in Code. We had measured the number of JavaScript functions used to define new strings (for example substring, from Char-Code), and number of their uses (for example document.write operations and eval () function calls). A large number of definitions of string variables are a good indicator of commonly used de-obfuscation techniques. This can be picked up by running the eval() function in Rhino and analyzing the output with Java code. The feature will have numeric value from 0 to 5.

Feature 4: Number of Dynamic Code Executions. We measured the number of function call runs for dynamic interpretation of JavaScript Code (e.g., DOM changes using document.createElement, document.write, eval and setTimeout) [21]. We checked this by running the code in Rhino [18] sandbox. The results were analyzed with Java code. This feature has a numeric value depicting the number of dynamic code executions.

Feature 5: Length of Dynamically Evaluated Code. We measured the string (dynamic code) length passed on to the eval() function as arguments. The eval() is used for dynamic execution in JavaScript. The length of the dynamic code passed is a good indicator of malicious obfuscated code, as malicious code is several kilobytes long. We pick up the length of dynamically evaluated code using Rhino, by running the code in the Rhino sandbox and checking the dynamic code generated using Java code. This feature has a numeric value depicting the code length.

Feature 6: Bytes Allocated in Memory Space. We monitor at runtime the memory space allocated to string functions like concat(). Heap exploitation techniques generally allocate large memory [20]. For example, heap spraying attacks may allocate up to 100 MB of space. This feature is captured as a numeric value using Rhino sandbox.

Feature 7: Number of Likely Shell Code Strings. Exploits which target memory violation vulnerabilities attempt to execute shell code. Shell code can be statically embedded in the JavaScript, or are dynamically created. For identifying shell code, we parsed the script and extracted Unicode encoded non-printable character strings longer than a certain threshold (we took 128 bytes as the threshold). Rhino [18] with some Java code was used for this. The feature has numeric value 0, 1,..., etc. based on the number of shell code strings found.

Exploitation. The last step of any malware attack is exploitation. We use the following three features for checking exploitation:

Feature 8: Number of Instantiated Browser Components. Browser components (like, plug-ins) are checked for instantiation. Vulnerabilities in such components are generally used by exploits. HTML Unit [16] has been used to emulate the browser environment and the exploitation actions have been picked up using the Java code encapsulating HTML Unit. This feature has a numeric value depicting the number of instantiated components.

Feature 9: Attribute and Parameter Values in Method Calls. Exploits generally use long strings to cause buffer overflow. Thus, we keep track of values passed in method calls, as large string values may be indicative of buffer flow. This has been analyzed using Rhino sandbox and some Java code encapsulating Rhino. The feature is nominal with values {Yes, No} describing presence or absence of such attributes or parameters in method calls.

Feature 10: Sequence of Execution of Method Calls. Sequence of execution of method calls are strong indicators of good or ill intent of the code. Many sequences (like file download followed by execution) are known to indicate malicious intent. This feature has been analyzed by using both Rhino and HTML Unit. The feature is nominal with values {Yes, No} describing presence of such malicious sequence of calls.

3.5   Software Design

The software design of the project is based on the modular architecture described above. The complete application has been designed as a standalone application on Java SE 7. The various modules are running on various threads to improve responsiveness of the application. Postgres SQL server has been for the database in this application. The Java application connects to the Postgres SQL server using JDBC connector. The thread-wise architecture of the application is given below (Fig. 3):

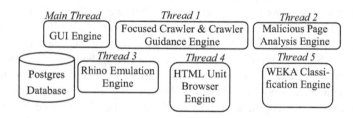

Fig. 3. Thread wise software design

The crawler has been developed on the Java SE platform. The complete architecture is modular and following libraries have been used in the design:

- **JSoup Library** [15]**.** The JSoup library is a Java-based library which has web page parsing capability. We have used this library for parsing web pages and extracting - hyperlinks, document content, and JavaScript tags.
- **Rhino** [18] **JavaScript Emulation Library.** Rhino is also a Java-based library which has capability to run JavaScript. We have used it to run JavaScript in a sandboxed environment to analyze the runtime behavior of JavaScript.
- **HTML Unit** [17] **Browser Emulation Library.** HTML Unit is a browser emulation library based in Java. We have used HTML Unit browser emulation library to emulate a browser session. There are certain features which can be tested only by emulating a browser session, for example, re-direction, cloaking, etc. We have used this for testing such features.

- **WEKA [16] Data Mining Library.** We have used the WEKA Data Mining library for classification of our results. We have used a training set of already know malicious sites. We test the dataset of the URLs collected by our crawler to check the efficacy of our malicious search.

4 Testing of Software

To test the software and the concept of the "MalCrawler", we first need to see as to what we have been trying to achieve. As discussed in preceding sections, we are trying to achieve the following:

- Maximize malicious page seek rate (α).
- Crawl deep to detect hidden pages.
- Use anti-cloaking measures.
- Emulate various browsers.
- Emulate a user.
- Crawl AJAX Web 2.0 pages up to a desired depth.

The main aim is to maximize α in our crawl. Why do we want to do this? Firstly, internet is huge. When we start looking for malicious content we might end up wasting maximum time in crawling benign sites. Crawling complete web is practically impossible. Commercially popular search engines like Google crawl about 60–70% web. So, when we know we can't crawl the complete web, why waste time and effort crawling benign sites. We want to look for malicious sites. Secondly, the crawl cycle takes months. If we delay looking for malicious sites, the content might get removed in that time frame. So, it is pointless wasting time crawling benign sites when we are seeking malwares. We may run out of time to detect a new malware. This is the aim of our focused crawler, to crawl maximum malicious sites in the minimum amount of time. We have used our judgment of malicious sites and cross checked it with Google safe browsing API [22]. This gives us a score of whether our judgment was right or wrong. The other capabilities, viz., crawling deep, using anti-cloaking measures, browser emulation, user emulation and crawling AJAX sites to adequate depth without entanglement, make the crawler fully capable of searching and crawling malicious web sites. Without these features, the "MalCrawler" will be incapable of meeting its aim. We used the above mentioned parameters for testing the crawler application on the internet. The results of the crawl and its analysis are given in succeeding sections.

5 Results

The results are presented for the parameters mentioned in the previous section. The Java application was hosted on the internet for crawling. The application log, which is collected in the log file and the Postgres database, where all data gets collected, was analyzed. Summary of results obtained is given below (Table 1, Fig. 4):

Table 1. Summary of results

Parameter	Result
Results with Focused Crawling Off	
Websites Crawled with focused crawling off	567898*
Malicious sites visited with focused crawling off	702
Malicious Page Seek Rate (α) with focused crawling off	0.123%
Results with Focused Crawling Turned On	
Websites Crawled with focused crawling on	567544*
Malicious sites visited with focused crawling on	1978
Malicious Page Seek Rate (α) with focused crawling on	0.348%
Results of Entanglement Avoidance	
Entanglement with crawl depth set to 3	4
Entanglement with crawl depth set to 5	17
Entanglement with crawl depth set to 8	56
Results of Anti-cloaking	
No of websites where cloaking detected	93
Results of User Emulation	
Browsers Emulated	Mozilla, Chrome and Internet Explorer.
Regulating crawling speed	Speed regulated by guidance engine.
Results of Handling AJAX Sites	
AJAX sites handled	7866
Depth to which handled with 0% entanglement	3
Depth to which handled with 50% entanglement	8

*Note: Due to limited computing resources available for this test, crawl had to be stopped at about 0.57 million records.

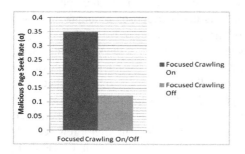 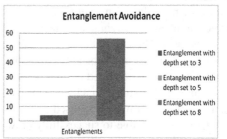

Fig. 4. Malicious Page Seek Rate and Entangle Avoidance

6 Analysis

The malicious page seek rate was better with focused crawling turned on. Thus, this focused crawler is able to seek more malicious sites than benign sites. The focused crawler exhibited good entanglement avoidance. The Crawler Guidance Engine was able to pull it out successfully in most situations. We saw the log of the crawler and found that at times the entanglement was only for few seconds, and thereafter, it extracted itself successfully and continued crawling. The crawler detected cloaking successfully on most sites which exhibited it. The overall detection rate exhibited by the anti-cloaking engine was good (better than 98%). The crawler could emulate both the user environment and his browsing behavior successfully. Various browsers like Mozilla, Chrome and Internet Explorer were emulated. The crawling behavior was also kept close to know human style. AJAX content was handled well by the crawler. After analyzing the crawler logs, it was found that the entanglements were few while crawling AJAX sites. The crawler could send and handle XMLHTTPRequests (XHR) the way it is done while opening an AJAX site in a browser, thereby, emulating human behavior while opening an AJAX site.

Evasion. To escape detection by MalCrawler, the intruder can manipulate some of its features by detecting the crawler's visits. Also, the IP address of the crawler can be tracked by the cyber attackers. To mitigate the risk of evasion from detection by the attackers, the crawl can be done from various IP addresses or using multiple proxies.

Comparison with EVILSEED Crawler. An approach of improving the effectiveness of searching malicious web pages was proposed by Invernizzi et al. [5], where the researchers use a set of malicious seeds and gadgets. Using this information, the researchers utilized the infrastructure of a search engine to retrieve URLs and also used the Google's blacklist for URL selection. On the other hand, Malcrawler, is not dependent on an external search engine or black list. Further, MalCrawler has certain additional capabilities not seen in EVILSEED approach, viz., its ability to detect and handle cloaking, handle AJAX content, crawl deep and emulate various browsers.

7 Conclusion

MalCrawler crawls web to detect web pages that are malicious in nature and are well aware of how they can exploit a user (host). This paper proposes a unique approach which aims at improving the effectiveness of the search process for malicious pages over the web. The aim of designing MalCrawler, as brought out at the start of the paper, has been achieved and substantiated by the tests carried out on the internet. MalCrawler can be used for specialized requirements where malicious sites are to be searched or to be avoided. The study concludes that the page seek rate for the malicious pages was better with MalCrawler's focused crawling. Regarding the entanglement of the crawler, MalCrawler was able to successfully draw out of the entanglement after a few seconds and the cloaking was detected quite easily as depicted by the result of cloaking detection being higher than 98%. Thus, the crawler logs suggest that MalCrawler can be used by search engines to make search experience safer, or, it can be used by internet security agencies and firms to discover new malwares.

References

1. Symantec Corporation: Internet Security Threat Report 2016. Symantec (2016). http://www.symantec.com
2. Jayasinghe, G.K., Culpepper, J.S., Bertok, P.: Efficient and effective realtime prediction of drive-by download attacks. J. Netw. Comput. Appl. **38**, 135–149 (2014)
3. Cao, Y., Pan, X., Chen, Y., Zhuge, J.: JShield: towards real-time and vulnerability-based detection of polluted drive-by download attacks. In: Proceedings of the 30th Annual Computer Security Applications Conference, pp. 466–475 (2014)
4. Sarwade, S., Patil, P.D.D.: Document-based and URL-based features for automatic classification of cross-site scripting in web pages. IOSR J. Eng. **3**, 1–10 (2013)
5. Invernizzi, L., Benvenuti, S., Cova, M., Kruegel, C., Vigna, G.: EVILSEED : a guided approach to finding malicious web pages. In: IEEE Symposium on Security and Privacy (SP), pp. 428–442 (2012)
6. Canali, D., Vigna, G., Kruegel, C.: Prophiler : a fast filter for the large-scale detection of malicious web pages. In: Proceeding of 20th International Conference on World Wide Web, pp. 197–206 (2011)
7. Rohit, P.S., Krishnaveni, R.: Deep malicious website detection. Int. J. Comput. Sci. Mob. Comput. **2**(4), 517–522 (2013)
8. Provos, N., Mavrommatis, P., Rajab, M.A., Monrose, F.: All your iFRAMEs point to us. In: USENIX Security Symposium (2008)
9. Hou, Y.-T., Chang, Y., Chen, T., Laih, C.-S., Chen, C.-M.: Malicious web content detection by machine learning. Expert Syst. Appl. **37**(1), 55–60 (2010)
10. Pham, K., Santos, A., Freire, J.: Understanding website behavior based on user agent. In: Proceedings of the 39th International ACM SIGIR Conference on Research and Development in Information Retrieval. ACM (2016)
11. Likarish, P., Jung, E.: A targeted web crawling for building malicious javascript collection. In: Proceeding of the ACM DSMM, vol. 21, issue 4, pp. 23–26 (2009)
12. Jo, H.Y.I., Jung, E.: Interactive website filter for safe web browsing. J. Inf. Sci. **131**, 115–131 (2013)
13. Qassrawi, M.T., Zhang, H.: Detecting malicious web servers with honeyclients. Directory Open Access J. (DOAJ) **6**(1), 145–152 (2011)
14. Ikinci, A., Holz, T., Freiling, F.C.: Monkey-spider: detecting malicious websites with low-interaction honeyclients. Sicherheit, vol. 8 (2008)
15. JSoup- JSoup Java Library. http://www.jsoup.org
16. N.Z. Univeristy of Waikato, WEKA. http://www.cs.waikato.ac.nz/ml/weka
17. HtmlUnit. http://htmlunit.sourceforge.net/
18. Rhino-Mozilla. https://developer.mozilla.org/docs/Mozilla/Projects/Rhino
19. Karbalaie, F., Sami, A., Ahmadi, M.: Semantic malware detection by deploying graph mining. Int. J. Comput. Sci. Issues (IJCSI) **9**(1), 373–379 (2012)
20. Kaplan, S., Siefert, C., Livshits, B., Zorn, B., Curtsinger, C.: NoFus : automatically detecting obfuscated javascript code (2011)
21. Pintol, B.S., Barnete, R.: A novel algorithm for obfuscated code analysis. In: 2011 IEEE International Workshop of Information Forensics and Security (WIFS), pp. 1–5 (2011)
22. Safe Browsing API. https://developers.google.com/safe-browsing

Poster Papers

Spying Mobrob
Innovative Mobile Number Tracking System

Sayar Kumar Dey[1]([✉]), Prerna Choudhary[1], and Günter Fahrnberger[2]

[1] KIIT University, Bhubaneswar, Odisha, India
sayarkumardey@gmail.com, prernasoni.choudhary@gmail.com
[2] University of Hagen, Hagen, North Rhine-Westphalia, Germany
guenter.fahrnberger@studium.fernuni-hagen.de

Abstract. According to the Varanasi edition of *The Times of India*, dated July 3, 2013, only 2% of the lost or stolen mobile phones in India are recovered [1]. This motivated the authors of this scholarly piece to work in this field and come up with Spying Mobrob – a solution that can improve the recovery success rate of stolen mobile phones. Spying Mobrob does not only help to recover stolen mobile phones but also to capture their thieves. In the present scenario, whenever a mobile phone is stolen, Spying Mobrob tries to track down the mobile number of its thief by dint of signaling data from mobile network operators. The innovation here is that Spying Mobrob does not trace the stolen mobile phone. Rather it tracks down the mobile phone of the thief and traces down the network of thieves involved in the process. For example, if X's phone is stolen and Y is the thief, then Y's phone will be tracked rather than X's phone.

Keywords: Cellphone · Cellular phone · Mobile phone · Recovery · Theft · Thievery · Tracking

1 Architecture

The architecture of Spying Mobrob can be divided into three blocks in accordance with Fig. 1. The input block describes the generation of the input data, i.e. of the call logs. The data processing block embraces the processing of the input data to a suspect list. The output block depicts how the previously generated suspect list is finally stored for further refinement and display purposes.

The input block mainly comprises of various components of cellular radio technology that are necessary for the generation of the call log data [2].

In the data processing block, different operations are carried out in order to get appropriate output. The call log L generated by the input block is loaded into the HDFS (Hadoop Distributed File System). Consecutively, an authority executes a prepared Apache Pig script.

First, the records of L are sifted according to t_{loc} and t_{time}. Then, the operation to find the callers is carried out. Thereby, it is checked whether they have

© Springer International Publishing AG 2017
P. Krishnan et al. (Eds.): ICDCIT 2017, LNCS 10109, pp. 227–230, 2017.
DOI: 10.1007/978-3-319-50472-8_18

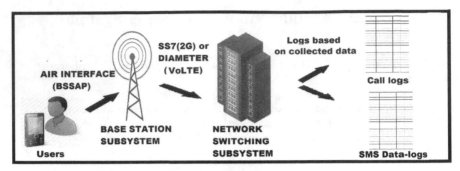

INPUT BLOCK

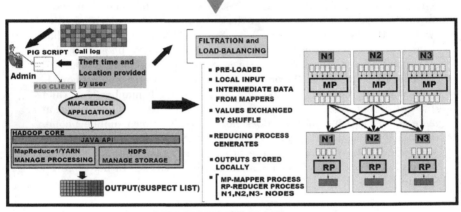

DATA-PROCESSING BLOCK

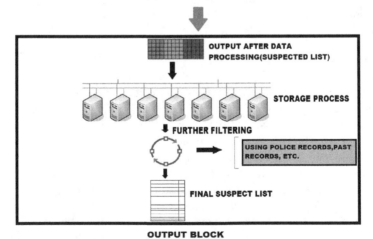

OUTPUT BLOCK

Fig. 1. Architecture of Spying Mobrob

a call duration equal or longer than the minimum duration ϵ_{length}, based on the fact that a conversation cannot be completed in a shorter period. Additionally, every MOC (Mobile Originated Call) record without a corresponding MTC (Mobile Terminated Call) record respectively every MTC record without an associated MOC record becomes ignored. All these filter criteria together entail the output list L_0. In the next step the datasets with MSISDNs (Mobile Station Integrated Services Digital Network Numbers), which appear together with multiple IMEIs (International Mobile Equipment Identities), are filtered out of L_0 to L_1. Vice versa, a subset L_2 of L_0 is created that merely comprises of data records with IMEIs which occur together with multiple MSISDNs. Afterwards, a list R is generated that stores all occurring called identities in L_1 and L_2. Another step outputs the intermediate list L_3 by extracting those call records of L_0 whose calling identities can be found in R. The next operation matches the receivers in L_3 with the callers in L_1 and L_2 to detect a chain or cycle and stores the output in L_4. If L_4 is empty, then a while-loop iterates with the receivers of L_3 as R until a cycle is found.

The main purpose of this block is to get a list of mobile thief suspects by analyzing their behavior. Generally, a thief who has stolen a mobile phone will have a tendency to make many calls as well as SIM (Subscriber Identity Module) changes. On this account, an attempt is made to trace this behavior and also to check whether the end level receiver calls back to the suspects in the first stage. Finally, after execution of the algorithm, the list L_4 is the final output having all the possible theft suspects.

The assignment of the output block is to store the suspect list from the data-processing block in the HDFS architecture for further processing.

2   Performance Analysis

Due to the huge main memory consumption of Hadoop, the prototype of Spying Mobrob was merely fed with 30 out of 600,000 available input records during the conducted experiment. The MSISDNs and the call durations of three called parties were manually manipulated to let Spying Mobrob detect a level-2-chain (loop with two different parties). That happens whenever a person A calls a person B, and B in turn calls back A. Then, a level-2-chain with person A as the parent and person B as the last layer has emerged. The algorithm must detect the loop and identify A and B as suspects. Spying Mobrob fulfilled this expectation and, on these grounds, successfully disclosed both *culprits*. Ten records were retrieved as the expected output.

Table 1 shows how an increasing number of Hadoop-cluster nodes reduces the time taken for execution. The execution time is sublinearly reduced by linearly increasing the number of slave nodes. This happens because work gets shared by all the nodes, i.e. they all work simultaneously to produce the result. Hence, the execution time decreases.

Table 1. Statistical performance of Spying Mobrob

Statistical indicator	1-node-cluster	2-node-cluster	3-node-cluster
Sample size	100	100	100
Minimum	75.03 s	70.13 s	61.01 s
Median	80.63 s	71.00 s	65.58 s
Mean	82.38 s	71.95 s	63.97 s
Maximum	99.40 s	104.76 s	67.55 s
Standard deviation	8.78 s	3.98 s	2.36 s

The descriptive statistics were drawn by means of a laptop with limited computing power. It goes without saying that much better processing times can be expected by employing clouds or commercial server products for running the prototype.

3   Conclusion

Implementations that are capable of doing the same thing that this paper intends to do were searched, but until now no such system exists to track down a thief's phone instead of the lost mobile.

The experiment was first tried with all available 600,000 input records, but it was impossible to complete as the memory consumption exceeded the available 500 GB. Thence, the complete processing of all input records would require a distributed architecture and multi-node processing.

It was successfully proved that a linearly increasing number of nodes sublinearly decreases the processing time. The accuracy of the results also depends on the accuracy of the data. The experiment was conducted on a five minute long call log of a single base station by the Indian mobile network operator Bharti Airtel. Additional sources for personal data (such as police records and official documents) can be used to further improve the accuracy of the output.

Acknowledgments. Many thanks to Krittika Choudhary, Kushagra Desai, and Abhishek Ray from the KIIT University for contributing to Spying Mobrob! Many thanks to Bettina Baumgartner from the University of Vienna for proofreading this paper!

References

1. Dikshit, R.: Only 2% of lost or stolen mobile phones recovered, July 2013. http://timesofindia.indiatimes.com/city/varanasi/Only-2-of-lost-or-stolen-mobile-phones-recovered/articleshow/20889356.cms
2. Sauer, M.: From GSM to LTE-Advanced: An Introduction to Mobile Networks and Mobile Broadband. Wiley, Hobken (2014)

A Domain Specific Language for Clustering

Saiyedul Islam$^{(\boxtimes)}$, Sundar Balasubramaniam, Poonam Goyal,
Mohit Sati, and Navneet Goyal

Advanced Data Analytics and Parallel Technologies Laboratory,
Department of Computer Science and Information Systems,
Birla Institute of Technology and Science, Pilani, India
{sislam,sundarb,poonam,
mohit.sati,goel}@pilani.bits-pilani.ac.in

Abstract. Clustering of large volumes of data is a complex problem which requires use of sophisticated algorithms as well as High Performance Computing hardware like a cluster of computers. It is highly desirable that data mining experts have a solution which on one hand provides a simple interface for ex-pressing their algorithms in terms of domain specific idioms and on the other hand automatically generates parallel code that can run on a cluster of multicore nodes. The proposed Domain Specific Language (DSL) along with its parallelizing compiler attempts to provide a solution. In this paper, we give the design of the DSL, called DWARF. Various language constructs have been described along with the rationale behind their inclusion in the language. A qualitative comparison of abstraction provided by DWARF is compared with MapReduce, Spark, and other MPI-based implementations to establish the usefulness of the proposed clustering DSL.

Keywords: Clustering · Domain specific language · High performance computing · Big data

1 Introduction

Data clustering is complex process having wide range of application areas, including bioinformatics, information retrieval, geographical information systems, medical imaging, social network analysis, etc. With tremendous increase in volume, velocity, variety, and veracity of data, more complex algorithms are being designed for clustering. It is well understood that parallel/distributed processing on High Performance Computing (HPC) hardware is the only way to process Big Data in reasonable time.

The software interface provided by typical HPC systems usually prefers flexibility of choice for optimally exploiting the system, than a simple interface which requires minimum user intervention. As a result, the expertise required to write parallel code for HPC systems is quite different from the expertise possessed by data mining researchers. Even the simplest implementation of distributed memory version of Kmeans clustering algorithm [1] by a data scientist using Message Passing Interface (MPI) will expect an understanding of message passing, process communicators, blocking and non-blocking calls, inter-process synchronization, etc. Similarly, it will be challenging for a pure HPC expert to design and understand a state-of-the-art clustering algorithm. This problem

© Springer International Publishing AG 2017
P. Krishnan et al. (Eds.): ICDCIT 2017, LNCS 10109, pp. 231–234, 2017.
DOI: 10.1007/978-3-319-50472-8_19

seriously limits the productivity of data mining researchers. We believe that it can be broken down into two parts, as in a serial Domain Specific Language (DSL) for Clustering and an automatic parallelizing compiler. The DSL should be able to provide clustering specific idioms and the compiler should be able to parallelize the code for a cluster of commodity computers, giving a satisfactory speedup.

2 Requirement Analysis

The proposed work targets a data mining researcher who designs new algorithms, as well as, sometimes, use the existing algorithms for clustering. We assume that this researcher possess basic programming skills but is not familiar with any parallel programming concepts. We also assume that the researcher is more interested in quick prototyping of his/her ideas instead of long term maintainability. These assumptions require that the DSL is serial in nature so that user explicitly need not to specify any kind of parallelism. We chose to design an external DSL [2] so that we have freedom to introduce domain specific abstraction at all levels of design i.e. from operator level to construct level.

3 Domain Definition

We have considered Partitioning based (Kmeans, Kmedoid, CLARANS, etc.), Density based (DBSCAN, DENCLUE, OPTICS, etc.), and, Hierarchal Agglomerative algorithms (Single link, CURE, etc.), as the preliminary domain. Algorithms in each category exhibit a similar pattern of processing steps and use similar data structures. We tend to exploit this through the parallelizing compiler.

4 Programming Style

Literature of clustering algorithm suggests that experts writing pseudo code of these algorithms tends to repeatedly use notion of multi-sets, like in representing collection of points, collection of clusters, collection of points belonging to a cluster, etc. By definition, a multi-set is a set with multiple similar values (similar points in space). We have provided multisets as the primary representation of a collection of any kind of data. This representation has been named as List to keep it more intuitive to the user.

The proposed DSL supports minimal object oriented features, to be specific, only inheritance, operator and method over-loading, and method over riding. Inheritance is always public. The language has been intentionally kept weakly object-oriented, so that the user has freedom to use OOP features, or not. DSL also supports a minimal functional style by allowing functions to be passed as argument to another functions. The design decision to support all these three separate styles in one language was driven by the target to provide most intuitive way of expressing clustering algorithms.

5 DWARF Language Description

We now present the description of the proposed DSL.

5.1 Data Types

DSL supports primitive numeric data types like Integer, Float, and Double, as well as non-numeric primitive types as that of String, Boolean, and Enumeration. Classes, Points, Lists, and Clusters form the set of complex type supported by language. Enumeration type is provided to support the representation of categorical (nominal and ordinal) data. Integer, Float, Double, String, and, Boolean types have their usual meanings.

Point Type. A point in clustering is a D-dimensional representation of a tuple with D attributes. DWARF supports a generic definition of point, where it is a heterogeneous collection of D-values of primitive type. Each of these values can belong to a different primitive data type. If all values of a point are numeric then it is internally represented as a Numeric Point Type. Operators (+, −, and, *) are applied over each corresponding dimension of two points when applied over points of compatible numeric types.

List Type. List Type implements the concept of multisets. It is defined as a homogeneous and indexable collection of values of any type, including another list. A list can be either created by giving lower and upper limits for a continuous numeric lists, or through List Comprehension [3]. The operator "+" works as List Union, while the operator "−" works as List Difference operator. Type of list is identified by the compiler by inferring the type of its elements. List also support List Reduction [3] where a binary associative operator is applied on each element of the list to generate a single output.

Cluster Type. Cluster is represented as a built-in class containing a list of points as member. Sum of Squared Errors (SSE) calculation is provided as method of this class. User can inherit this class to customize the cluster as per his/her requirement.

5.2 Miscellaneous

DSL supports *while loop* as condition based loop, *for loop* as list based loop and *RepeatUntil* [4] as converging loop. It also supports Classes, methods and functions to modularly structure a code. It also supports defining libraries in DWARF (*.dw files), and, in C++ by providing function declarations in DWARF (*.dwh files).

6 Related Work

Here is a brief comparison of our DSL with MapReduce, Spark, and MPI based implementation for clustering domain (Table 1).

Table 1. Comparison with related work

Criteria	MapReduce	Spark	MPI	DWARF
Clustering specific Iterators and Operators	None			RepeatUntil loop and overloaded operators for Points and Lists
I/O Constructs	Yes		Explicitly parsed	Direct function call
Library Support	Mahout [5]	MLlib [6]	Many	Internally supported
User code size	Medium		Large	Small
Code complexity	Fairly Complex		Very complex	Simple
Parallelization	Backend executes special constructs in parallel		Explicitly parallelized	Parallelizing Compiler
Parallel Performance	Good	Better	Best	Best where a pattern is detected, Average otherwise

7 Conclusion and Future Work

In this paper, we present DWARF, a DSL for clustering. The main objective of the DSL is to provide programming abstraction to Data Mining experts to prototype new algorithms quickly and also to implement existing algorithms to leverage a cluster infrastructure. Abstraction is provided through clustering specific constructs. Domain specific patterns are also identified to facilitate automatic parallelization. In this way, parallelization is also completely abstracted from Data Mining experts. The work can be extended to include more categories of clustering algorithms. We also plan extend the framework to work on different parallel architectures.

References

1. Jain, A.K.: Data clustering: 50 years beyond K-means. Pattern Recogn. Lett. **31**, 651–666 (2010)
2. van Deursen, A., Klint, P., Visser, J.: Domain-specific languages: an annotated bibliography. ACM Sigplan Not. **35**, 26–36 (2000)
3. Bird, R., Wadler, P.: An Introduction to Functional Programming. Prentice Hall International (UK) Ltd., London (1988)
4. Brown, K.J., Wu, M., Atreya, A.R., Odersky, M., Sujeeth, A.K., Lee, H., Rompf, T., Chafi, H., Olukotun, K.: OptiML: an implicitly parallel domain-specific language for machine learning. In: Getoor, L., Scheffer, T. (eds.) International Conference on Machine Learning, pp. 609–616. Omnipress, Madison (2011)
5. Apache Software Foundation: Apache Mahout: Scalable machine-learning and data-mining library. http://mahout.apache.org/
6. MLlib | Apache Spark. http://spark.apache.org/mllib/

Designing a Secure Data Retrieval Strategy Using NoSQL Database

Sayantani Saha[1(✉)], Tanusree Parbat[2], and Sarmistha Neogy[2]

[1] School of Mobile Computing and Communication,
Jadavpur University, Kolkata, India
sayantanircc@gmail.com
[2] Department of Computer Science and Engineering,
Jadavpur University, Kolkata, India
tanusree.parbat@gmail.com,
sarmisthaneogy@gmail.com

Abstract. Data collection from distributed cloud storage through SaaS application requires efficient execution of the overall process. This type of cloud computing mechanism can be furnished through shared resources, improved service levels and minimal management effort. Data retrieval from cloud storage by different users through shared resources environment may blend data from different data requests in a single place. Here lies the need of efficient data retrieval strategy among different users that will help in secure data retrieval. When sensitive information is transmitted over the Internet there is high chance of information leakage. So, to prevent security attack like interference attack during query execution becomes a big challenge. This work explores a novel data retrieval strategy in extremely robust and linearly scalable high performance NoSQL database like Cassandra and presents a brief security analysis while retrieving stored data in shared environment.

Keywords: Data retrieval security · Flow control · Information leakage · NoSQL database

1 Introduction

Cloud storage system may store different types of data, some of which are sensitive while some are general. But, a secure data retrieval mechanism must be able to share data only to the authorized users. Therefore, there is a demand for proper data handling as these data-centric applications share the same data in different applications and might cause information leakage.

In a typical data retrieval service, the client process will issue data request through user interface. This type of request also performs security checks like authentication, authorization and access control to validate secure data passing. In cloud environment when different users with different authorization permissions, request data from the shared cloud storage, the data requests are handled through some data retrieval services. The resources for storage, computation are shared among different users all the while without compromising security. Efficient data retrieval technique needs sharing

© Springer International Publishing AG 2017
P. Krishnan et al. (Eds.): ICDCIT 2017, LNCS 10109, pp. 235–238, 2017.
DOI: 10.1007/978-3-319-50472-8_20

of resources for amortizing cost and utilization. More the sharing higher the information leakage. So, the motivation of the present work is to achieve higher sharability
in presence of security. Common security practices like data confidentiality using any
cryptosystem or any fine grained access control mechanism enforcement is not sufficient to provide information security – the flow control of different application execution in the shared environment must be handled wisely for a better secure data
communication.

For the secure data flow different literature [3, 4] discussed about the Information
Flow Control (IFC) technique for a secure information flow. The authors in [1] have
shown how an isolated user request can be served in the shared environment. The
authors in [2] present their work with markov chain based task scheduling concept.
They also measure the performance of the overall system based on the task completion
probability. However, they have mainly stressed on the drop out tasks. The authors in
[5] have showed how IFC can be integrated in the cloud environment but did not show
any end-to-end design architecture.

This is the motivation of our work. We have used the concept of information flow
to propose a data retrieval strategy that logically isolates user requests in the shared
environment.

In the next section we have discussed about the proposed work and different
technical details of the proposed work. The paper is concluded in Sect. 3.

2 Proposed Work

Generally, once authentication and authorization are done, no further control is
imposed on the data flow model in traditional data retrieval system. However this
application specific security is not enough for data security in shared environment.
There is a need to control data flow in shared environment.

We have proposed a data retrieval system for health care service which provides
data security during transmission. Patient's identity related information and diagnostic
information are all sensitive to health care service. All this while, patient information
and data must be kept private so that any unauthorized person is unable to access them.
In this context we have used XML format for patient data storage and XML based
double layered encryption scheme for securing collected data to provide end-to-end
security while retrieving health data. When the data is stored in the database it is
encrypted using one set of keys. While the request is served for retrieving the data,
another layer of encryption is imposed with random keys.

2.1 The Security Constraints

In this work we have considered data access by multiple users. Each user request needs
to be handled in logically separate fashion in case of multiple users wanting to retrieve
storage data. Therefore while executing the user requests it must be ensured that different tasks, like, user validation module for task A and the user validation module for
task B must be executed separately, so that the output of task A or task B cannot be

inferred by any other curious task. Also the set of tasks performed for one user's request should be executed separately and securely. For realization of such requirement we have used the concept of Separation of Duties (SoD) and secure information flow concept.

In our proposed model we first break up one user request (task) into small subtasks and assign each subtask with a security constraint value. The security constraint value directs the execution scheduling of the subtask. The separation of subtasks and the ordering of execution will produce a secure data retrieval system.

2.2   The Security Components

The request (say, by a doctor) will pass a unique request–id to request tracker and a random RSA public and private key will be generated temporarily. The request will be divided into subtasks like user authentication, user authorization, data access, key access. Each subtask is assigned with a time stamp value and a constraint value (const_c_value). According to our security model the constraint value will be set in such a way that the user authentication will be executed first, and then user authorization will take place. Only after successful authentication and authorization, data request and the corresponding key request from the corresponding data storage are invoked. The other subtasks that will execute in parallel in shared environment also follow the proposed strategy for secure data retrieval as shown in Fig. 1.

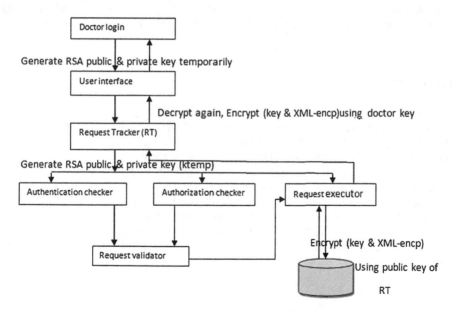

Fig. 1. Block diagram and work flow of the proposed work

For that particular request id, request executor will fetch corresponding encrypted xml file and key to decrypt that file from patient_file. It encrypts both of these information using request tracker's public key and sends to request tracker. Request tracker will decrypt that data with its private key and encrypted xml file will be encrypted by doctor's public key and sent to doctor. In doctor side, the encrypted file will be first decrypted using doctor's private key and then again decrypted using the key sent by executor to get original xml file.

3 Conclusion

In our approach a single user request is served faster than multiple requests in the proposed scenario. However, in case of a multiple user request scenario the task execution follows the constraints rules and necessary actions are taken with the user request privilege. This makes execution bit slower than that of a normal cloud environment. In case of data sharing by user, for example if a doctor needs to share a patient data with other doctors – the same patient data retrieval process by each doctor will be an unnecessary strategy. So we propose the concept of collaborative access request by the user, where the original doctor shares his data with other doctors by sharing a shared buffer. This approach dramatically reduces the data retrieval cost by 60%. Though we have not discussed the details of the collaborative access control here, we have implemented a simplified form of data share approach and measured the time taken to complete a request. However the collaborative data access has lots of security issues to be incorporated with.

Acknowledgments. This work is supported by Information Technology Research Academy (ITRA), Government of India under, ITRA-Mobile grant ITRA/15(59)/Mobile/RemoteHealth/01.

References

1. Factor, M., et al.: Secure logical isolation for multi-tenancy in cloud storage. In: IEEE 29th Symposium on Mass Storage Systems and Technologies (MSST), IEEE (2013)
2. Liu, D., et al.: Scheduling tasks with Markov-chain based constraints. In: 17th Euromicro Conference on Real-Time Systems (ECRTS 2005), IEEE (2005)
3. Singh, J., et al.: Integrating messaging middleware and information flow control. In: 2015 IEEE International Conference on Cloud Engineering (IC2E), IEEE (2015)
4. Pasquier, T., et al.: Data-centric access control for cloud computing. In: Proceedings of the 21st ACM on Symposium on Access Control Models and Technologies, ACM (2016)
5. Saha, S., Das, R., Datta, S., Neogy, S.: A cloud security framework for a data centric WSN application. In: Proceedings of the 17th International Conference on Distributed Computing and Networking, p. 39. ACM (2016)

Author Index

Printed in the United States
By Bookmasters